Trinitarian Matters

Edited by
Laceye C. Warner & Cameron Merrill

Introduction by Edgardo Colón-Emeric

Trinitarian Matters

1700 Years *of* Shaping Christian Identity and Practice

Nashville

Trinitarian Matters
1700 Years of Shaping Christian Identity & Practice

Copyright © 2025 Abingdon Press
All rights reserved.

No part of this work may be reproduced or transmitted in any form or by any means, electronic or mechanical, including photocopying and recording, or by any information storage or retrieval system, except as may be expressly permitted by the 1976 Copyright Act, the 1998 Digital Millennium Copyright Act, or in writing from the publisher. Requests for permission can be addressed to Rights and Permissions, The United Methodist Publishing House, 810 12th Avenue South, Nashville, TN 37203-4704 or emailed to permissions@abingdonpress.com.

Library of Congress Control Number: 2025945597

978-1-7910-4054-3

Scripture quotations unless noted otherwise are taken from the Common English Bible, copyright 2011. Used by permission. All rights reserved.

Scripture quotations marked AMP are taken from the Amplified® Bible (AMP), Copyright © 2015 by The Lockman Foundation. Used by permission. www.Lockman.org

Scripture quotations marked ESV are from the ESV® Bible (The Holy Bible, English Standard Version®), copyright © 2001 by Crossway, a publishing ministry of Good News Publishers. Used by permission. All rights reserved.

Scripture quotations marked KJV are from The Authorized (King James) Version. Rights in the Authorized Version in the United Kingdom are vested in the Crown. Reproduced by permission of the Crown's patentee, Cambridge University Press.

Scripture quotations marked NEB are taken from the New English Bible, copyright © Cambridge University Press and Oxford University Press 1961, 1970. All rights reserved.

Scripture quotations marked (NIV) are taken from the Holy Bible, New International Version®, NIV®. Copyright © 1973, 1978, 1984, 2011 by Biblica, Inc.™ Used by permission of Zondervan. All rights reserved worldwide. www.zondervan.com The "NIV" and "New International Version" are trademarks registered in the United States Patent and Trademark Office by Biblica, Inc.™

Scripture quotations marked (NRSV) are taken from the New Revised Standard Version Bible, copyright © 1989 National Council of the Churches of Christ in the United States of America. Used by permission. All rights reserved worldwide. http://nrsvbibles.org/

Scripture quotations marked (NRSVue) are taken from the New Revised Standard Version, Updated Edition. Copyright © 2021 National Council of Churches of Christ in the United States of America. Used by permission. All rights reserved worldwide.

Book cover with a textured white background framed by a thin gold border. The title, *Trinitarian Matters*, is centered in large gold serif font. Below it is a gold illustration of three interlocking circles. The subtitle, "1700 Years of Shaping Christian Identity and Practice," is in smaller dark blue serif font. At the top, the editors' names, "Edited by Laceye C. Warner & Cameron Merrill," appear in dark blue, with "Introduction by Edgardo Colón-Emeric" in italic gold script.

MANUFACTURED IN THE UNITED STATES OF AMERICA

Contents

Introduction vii
Edgardo Colón-Emeric

SECTION 1: Nicene Faith in Theology & Biblical Interpretation 1
The Jerusalem Council in Acts 15: 3
Strive For Unity, not Uniformity
Jung H. Choi

Nicaea, the Spirit, and Sanctification 17
Daniel Castelo

Biblical Pressure and Trinitarian Hermeneutics 31
C. Kavin Rowe

Creation and Monotheism 51
Janet Martin Soskice

The Challenge of Preaching on Trinity Sunday 59
J. Warren Smith

SECTION 2: Nicene Faith in Preaching 73
Variety Anxiety 75
Luke A. Powery

My Favorite Part of the Creed 83
Brent A. Strawn

The Miracle of Faith 93
Alma Tinoco Ruiz

A Sermon on Matthew 28:16-20 99
Bishop Connie Mitchell Shelton

The Trinity Forms Us and Sends Us 103
Bishop Kenneth H. Carter Jr.

Into the Trinity 107
Edgardo Colón-Emeric

SECTION 3: Nicene Faith in Worship & Practice 115
Chalcedonian Preaching 117
William H. Willimon

How Great Is Our God: 123
The Trinity in Contemporary Christian Worship Music
Lester Ruth

Theological Touchstone: 145
Wayfinding through Times of Uncertainty
M. Jan Holton

Ecotheology and Contemporary Christianity 161
Fred P. Edie

The Face of Christ in the Face of Conflict: 179
Preaching the Nicene Creed in a Storm-filled Season
Jerusha M. Neal

Into God's Own Life: 193
Reclaiming Nicene Faith for Church Renewal and Mission
Laceye C. Warner and Cameron Merrill

Acknowledgments 213

Contributors 215

Introduction

Edgardo Colón-Emeric

In June 2013, I had the opportunity to fulfill a long-held wish. A Methodist friend took me to visit the Tretyakov Gallery in Moscow. This museum housed, at the time, one of the most illustrious icons of the Trinity. Made for the monastery of St. Sergius, Andrei Rublev's icon represents the Old Testament story of a manifestation of God by the home of Abraham and Sarah in Mamre (cf. Genesis 18:1ff). The *Troitsa*, as this icon is known in Russian, draws viewer's attention from the hospitality of the patriarchs to the availability of the divine persons. The subtlety and sophistication of the figures and the hues of this image have long been recognized. I had read much about this image. I had regularly interpreted it in my theology courses. Seeing it in person was a satisfying and even elevating experience. At the same time, it was odd to see this piece within a museum. It is more than a masterpiece to be admired by tourists listening to a museum audio guide about its history. It is an icon to be venerated by pilgrims and worshippers singing the Trisagion: "Holy God, holy strong, holy immortal, have mercy on us." It is an open window to the maker of heaven and earth.

The *Troitsa* represents in vibrant hues what Christians believe in their hearts. From everlasting to everlasting, the one God is a Trinity of persons—Father, Son, and Holy Spirit. This affirmation of faith distinguishes Christianity from every other religion in the world. Despite the insistence of its teachers from the church's first centuries—that Christians do not worship three gods—the doctrine of the Trinity can come across as a softheaded, halfhearted adoption of monotheism by polytheists. It certainly would be

Introduction

conceptually easier to speak of one God or even of many gods. To speak of God as Triune in the ways that Christians do requires invoking the language of mystery, a mode of discourse that has faced sharp criticism since the Enlightenment. Consider, for instance, John Toland's, "Christianity not Mysterious." This 1696 treatise had sufficient notoriety that John Wesley felt obliged to engage its argument. Toland sets out to defend Christianity by stripping it of those doctrines that are against or above reason. For Toland, mystery, particularly in its sacramental mediation, hides the simplicity of the gospel and supports a priestly caste to protect them. Toland's reaction is motivated by a bundle of concerns (anticlerical sentiment, rationalist rejection of the doctrine of original sin, and more), but he is not wrong in protesting against abuses of this category. The language of mystery at times becomes a shelter for intellectual indolence and spiritual timidity. The approach to mystery as a puzzle to be solved, only to be abandoned as too hard, is not the Christian way. The mystery of the Trinity is light. It does not forbid entrance or limit access to experts; it invites all to move up and in. When John of the Cross visited Teresa of Ávila at the Monastery of the Incarnation, it is said that her religious sisters saw the two of them levitating when discussing the doctrine of the Trinity. When approached with believing intelligence and persistent humility, the inexhaustibility of the mystery of the Triune God is uplifting.

If Rublev's *Troitsa* (along with its reproductions) is perhaps the most venerated icon of the Trinity in the world, the Nicene Creed is without a doubt the most affirmed profession of Trinitarian faith throughout history. The year 2025 marks the 17th centennial of the Council of Nicaea. The council or synod convened by Emperor Constantine in the town of Nicaea in 325 undertook three main tasks: settling the doctrinal dispute raised by Arius, fixing a common date for the celebration of Easter, and developing a shared confession of faith. These tasks shared a common goal—Christian unity. Much has been written about Emperor Constantine's role in the council. Certainly, he was particularly interested in the role that Christian unity could serve in holding a diverse and disparate empire together. The bishops at the council, for their part, were particularly interested in unity not chiefly as social glue but as an expression of the Christian community's continuity

Introduction

with the apostolic witness. The presence of political forces and ecclesiastical ambitions are a matter of historical record, but these do not define or exhaust what happened in Nicaea. In making their own the Nicene profession of faith whether in substance or in spirit, Christians then and now can say with Athanasius, "The Word of the Lord which came through the Ecumenical Synod at Nicaea, abides forever."[1]

In a time of cultural polarization and homogenizing movements, the World Council of Churches along with many world communions (Roman Catholic, Orthodox, Anglican, Methodist, Lutheran, etc.) is commemorating the year 2025 as a time for Christians of all denominations to discern new ways of "living the apostolic faith together." The felicitous coincidence of the Eastern and Western dates for Easter in 2025 is being welcomed as an encouragement to work towards a common calendar that would see Orthodox, Catholics, and Protestants celebrating the resurrection of Christ on the same day. The Nicene Creed (or to be more precise the Nicene-Constantinopolitan version of 381) is being lifted up as a symbol of the one faith professed by all Christians and as a charge to overcome the divisions accrued during the creed's long reception history. The World Council of Churches' commemoration, while attentive to the patristic era and the developments that led to the formulation of the Nicene Creed, is focused on the question of how Christians understand and work for visible unity. In the words of its current president, Jerry Pillay:

> Recalling the significance of the Council of Nicaea renews our call for full visible unity, the foundation of the ecumenical movement. It reminds us that our goal is not just increasing theological agreement but a unity that is visible and tangible, reflecting the oneness of the body of Christ.[2]

The synod of Nicaea and the Nicene Creed continue to serve as beacons for Christian unity. The proceedings of Nicaea in the fourth century evoke the deliberations of the great council of Jerusalem in the first century. On that occasion, Christian leaders gathered to debate the terms on which Gentiles were to be included in the young church. The disciples listened to those who had witnessed the Spirit's work among Godfearers like Cornelius the centurion. They searched the scriptures. They walked together in thoughtful, prayerful discernment until at last they could boldly declare, "it has seemed good to the Holy Spirit and to us" (Acts 15:28 ESV). The "us" spoken of here is not an "us" defined by opposition to a "them." It is a Spirit-gathered "we." It is the "new we" of the Pentecost community that prays with Jesus to "our Father." The same "we" professed in Nicaea's words, "We believe." In a time when churches are dwindling in the West and dividing around the world, Nicaea can orient the church's announcement of the Triune God's reign in joyfully lifegiving ways. Significantly, the World Council of Churches is linking the commemoration of the 1700th anniversary of the Nicene Creed to the 40th anniversary of the Kairos document in South Africa. The Nicene Creed rejected the separation of divinity and humanity proposed by Arius. The Kairos document rejected the separation of blacks and white sanctioned by Apartheid. In linking these two events, there is an invitation for a fresh reception of these historic texts, a Nicene reading of Kairos and a "kairotic" reading of Nicaea.

The commemoration of Nicaea in 2025 offers an opportunity for theological schools to present the gifts of the academy to the church in support of its mission to the world. The Trinitarian grammar that Christians developed throughout the centuries is subtle, and students struggle to grasp it. I recall teaching on the doctrine of the Trinity to Methodists in Moscow, and the friend who took me to the Tretyakov gallery interrupted the translator to correct the word being used to translate the Trinitarian term "person." The translator apparently used a Russian term equivalent to "individual," which is precisely not what is meant by the Trinitarian term "person." The development and deployment of terms like "person" and "consubstantial" are not intended to solve the mystery but to preserve it. Facility with the technicality of Trinitarian language requires long periods of rigorous instruction. This is why schools established for the training of Christian ministers and scholars devote significant attention to the historical development and contemporary questions of Trinitarian theology. However, even as the academic study of this doctrine is invaluable for the church's mission, it is important not to lose sight of the basic fact that Trinitarian faith is the mother tongue of all Christians by virtue of their baptism in the name of the Father, Son, and Holy Spirit and their life of discipleship. The Nicene Creed offers a primer for Trinitarian

Introduction

faith. What Paul said to the Corinthians can be applied to Christians professing the Nicene Creed in any age, "just as we have the same spirit of faith that is in accordance with scripture—'I believed, and so I spoke'—we also believe, and so we speak" (2 Corinthians 4:13 NRSV).

The contributors to the collection of essays and sermons in this book are all associated with the Divinity School at Duke University. We also believe in the Nicene Creed, and so we speak. We are laypersons and clergy, ministers and academics, Protestants and Catholics. Since it opened its doors in 1926, this Divinity School has pursued theological education in the catholic spirit of the Wesleys. In other words, it is ecumenical in its reach because it is rooted in United Methodism. At the heart of the school's mission is "to serve and bear witness to the Triune God in the academy, the church, and the world." This book intends to join Christians of diverse communions in commemorating Nicaea and journeying toward visible Christian unity. Towards that end, I highlight three elements of Trinitarian doctrine in need of special remembrance, reflection, and revival.

First, as with Rublev's icon, the doctrine of the Trinity teaches the truth about God. It is well known that the scriptures do not present a fully developed doctrine of the Trinity. Indeed, the word "Trinity" itself would not be coined until the third century by the North African theologian Tertullian. For this reason, some have dismissed the teaching as a Hellenistic imposition on a simple Jewish faith. On the contrary, the confession of God as one and three has its roots in the great deeds of God narrated in the scriptures of what Christians call the Old Testament when these are read through the revelation of Christ. This truth, Christians believe, is revealed to humanity through the story of Israel, Israel's God, and the life, death, and resurrection of Jesus Christ. The oneness of God is the daily profession of every Jew (Deuteronomy 6:4). The plurality of persons in God is dimly perceived throughout the writings of the prophets who speak of the Spirit of the Lord and the writers who tell of God's wisdom (Proverbs 8). The blurred picture of this plurality comes into focus in Jesus. His Jewish followers upon hearing what he said, seeing what he did, and touching his risen body came to be believe that he was sent from God and was also God (John 20:28). It was not long before the Tetragrammaton revealed to Moses in the wilderness (Exodus 3:14) is attributed to Jesus in early Christian hymnody (Philippians 2:11). These disciples were instructed to teach and baptize in the name of the Father, Son, and Holy Spirit (Matthew 28:19). It is to this baptismal practice and the transmission of the teaching of the name into which Christians were anointed that the formulation of creeds is due. These professions of faith with their compact phrases and scriptural vocabulary served as a way for new believers to read their way into the unfolding story of the Triune God and the church's mission for the world.

Second, the doctrine of the Trinity teaches the truth about humanity. Human beings are made in God's image (Genesis 1:26). This teaching has become the basis for affirming the dignity of all human beings regardless of sex, gender, race, class, or ability. Each and every human being is a person who uniquely bears God's image. We are made, in the words of Charles Wesley, as transcripts of the Trinity.[3] Human sociability is not only an evolutionary adaptation; it images the origin and goal of humans in the God who is eternal relatedness. The image of the Trinity in human beings is not a static stamp but a dynamic performance. It is a gift and a task. It is by being known and being loved, by knowing and loving, by being and doing that humans transcribe the Trinity in history. The norm for this transcription is Jesus Christ himself. Thus, it is by imitation of Christ, by growing in the image of Christ that human beings grow in openness to the indwelling of the Trinity. This is why for John Wesley, the way of salvation is Trinitarian. As he states in his sermon, "On the Trinity," the substance of Christian faith is the Trinity of persons.

> I know not how anyone can be a Christian believer till 'he hath' (as St. John speaks) 'the witness in himself'; till 'the Spirit of God witnesses with his spirt that he is a child of God' that is, in effect, till God the Holy Ghost witnesses that God the Father has accepted him through the merits of God the Son—and having this witness honours the Son and the blessed Spirit 'even as he honours the Father.'[4]

Third, the doctrine of the Trinity teaches the truth about the world. As God's creation, everything bears traces of the Trinity. Even in a world marred by violence and injustice, the beauty of a sunset, the goodness of fruit trees, and the deep interconnectedness of ecosystems point to the Triune God as

Introduction

their source and end. In the Nicene Creed, the act of creation is explicitly attributed to the first person of the Trinity in the biblical phrase "maker of heaven and earth." At the same time, the creed goes on to speak of Jesus as the one through whom "all things were made" and of the Spirit as "the giver of life." The world as creation cannot be understood in isolation from the Trinity of persons who out of nothing (*ex nihilo*) made all that is, "seen and unseen." The Nicene commemoration expands our consideration of creation to include angels and other unseen creatures whose intelligence, antiquity, and number exceed ours by orders of magnitude untold. In his sermon "The New Creation," John Wesley speaks of the consummation of all things in the Trinity, where "there will be a deep, an intimate, an uninterrupted union with God; a constant communion with the Father and his Son Jesus Christ, through the Spirit; a continual enjoyment of the Three-One God, and of all the creatures in him!"[5]

The commemoration of Nicaea is a gift and task for all Christians. Even if this book is written by people associated with a theology school at a research university, it is far from suggesting that Trinitarian doctrine is only to be taught by or to academics. As I mentioned earlier, Trinitarian faith is the mother tongue of all Christians. The Wesley brothers understood this better than most. This was the reason why although they professed faith in the classical creeds of the church, they published "Hymns on the Trinity" in 1767, a collection of 188 poems and hymns inspired by William Jones's book *Catholic Doctrine of the Trinity*. The hymns in this collection are exemplars of sound, simple Trinitarian language.

> *Fixed on the Athanasian mound,*
> *I still require a firmer ground*
> *My sinking faith to bear:*
> *I want to feel my soul renewed*
> *In the similitude of God,*
> *Jehovah's character.*[6]

Wesley valued the Nicene Creed. He used it as an olive branch in his letter to a Roman Catholic in order to show how much Protestants and Catholics shared despite their divisions. Wesley also valued the Athanasian Creed.

Introduction

He regarded its Chalcedonian language to be the best he had ever seen, even if he disapproved of its use of anathemas. Nevertheless, Wesley knew that Trinitarian faith needs more than creeds or theological tomes for nourishment.

> *Furnished with intellectual light,*
> *In vain I speak of thee aright,*
> *While unrevealed thou art:*
> *That only can suffice for me,*
> *The whole mysterious Trinity*
> *Inhabiting my heart.*[7]

Ultimately, Trinitarian doctrine teaches us how to enlist the intellect and the will in opening the heart to the indwelling of the Trinity. I end this introduction by returning to the Tretyakov gallery. The journey of Rublev's icon of the Trinity from a monastery to a museum and back again reads to me like a parable for the future of the doctrine of the Trinity. It could be relegated to the status of a historical heirloom, something to be displayed behind glass, to be handled only by experts trained in classical languages and medieval metaphysics. It could be coopted by patrons who treasure it as a way of burnishing their Christian bona fides for cultural power. It could fall to iconoclasts who out of zeal for reductive historical narratives and Manichaean worldviews torch creeds and canons with critical theories. Yes. Trinitarian doctrine has been weaponized in the past, and this could happen again; its anathemas can be unsheathed; its "we believe" can be sharpened to a fine point. It is impossible to make theology tamperproof. The best way to avoid abuse is to practice good use. I have in mind practices like reading the creed backwards by starting with the confession of faith in the Holy Spirit (a Pentecost reception of Nicaea) and walking together with Christians from the majority world (a confession of faith from the margins).

The friend, who took me the Tretyakov gallery, told me a curious story. A previous visiting professor to their seminary also went to see the Rublev icon. When standing in front of the *Troitsa*, the professor burst into the doxology, "Praise God from whom all blessings flow! Praise him all creature here below! Praise him above ye heavenly host! Praise Father, Son, and Holy Ghost!" The sound of singing alarmed the guards who feared some kind of protest, which

Introduction

in a sense, it was. Icons and doctrines of the Trinity are doxological at heart because the end is communion.

> *This glorious Trinity*
> *We worship evermore:*
> *None less, or greater of the Three,*
> *None after or afore:*
> *The Persons Three are One;*
> *And who by faith embrace,*
> *We soon on his triumphant throne*
> *Shall see him face to face.*[8]

Notes

1. Cited in Torrance, *The Trinitarian Faith*, 15.
2. https://www.oikoumene.org/sites/default/files/2024-05/TowardSixthWorldConf_EN_web.pdf.
3. Charles Wesley, "Psalm VIII," in *Collection of Psalms and Hymns* (1743) [2nd ed. of 1741], 67; https://divinity.duke.edu/initiatives/wesleyan-methodist/cswt-jw.
4. "On the Trinity", *Wesley Works*, 2, 385.
5. John Wesley, "The New Creation (1785)," in *John Wesley's Sermons*, eds. Albert C. Outler and Richard P. Heizenrater (Nashville: Abingdon, 1991), 500.
6. Charles Wesley, "XIX," *Hymns on the Trinity* (Bristol: Pine, 1767), 102. The Center for Studies in the Wesleyan Tradition. https://divinity.duke.edu/sites/default/files/documents/67_Trinity_Hymns_%281767%29.pdf.
7. Wesley, "XIX," *Hymns on the Trinity* (Bristol: Pine, 1767), 103.
8. Wesley, "I," *Hymns on the Trinity* (Bristol: Pine, 1767), 88.

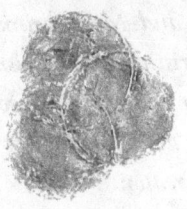

SECTION 1

Nicene Faith in Theology & Biblical Interpretation

At the heart of Christian faith lies a profound mystery: The One God revealed in Scripture is Father, Son, and Holy Spirit. The Council of Nicaea's articulation of this truth in 325 CE marked not just a historical moment but a continuing wellspring for Christian theology and practice. As we celebrate its 1700th anniversary, the essays in this section demonstrate how Nicaea's theological insights remain vital for contemporary ministry by offering fresh perspectives on how we understand God, read Scripture, and pursue holiness in today's world.

Jung Choi's "The Jerusalem Council in Acts 15" opens our collection by exploring how the first ecumenical council provides a model for unity amidst diversity. Drawing parallels between ancient and contemporary church conflicts, Choi shows how the early church's commitment to both truth and inclusion remains instructive for today.

Daniel Castelo's "Nicaea, the Spirit, and Sanctification" illuminates the vital connection between Nicene pneumatology and the Christian pursuit of holiness. Through careful examination of Wesley's pneumatological heritage and early church sources, Castelo reveals how the seemingly brief statement about the Holy Spirit in the original Nicene Creed carried remarkable theological weight.

Kavin Rowe's "Biblical Pressure and Trinitarian Hermeneutics" addresses how we read Scripture in light of Trinitarian doctrine. Through careful exegesis of key biblical texts, Rowe demonstrates that Trinitarian interpretation emerges from the Bible's own internal pressure and logic.

Janet Soskice's "Creation and Monotheism" explores how the doctrine of creation ex nihilo shaped Christian monotheism and understanding of Christ's divinity. Drawing from Jewish and Christian sources, Soskice demonstrates how the Nicene confession of Christ as "begotten, not made" emerges from deep reflection on God's identity as sole Creator.

Warren Smith's "The Challenge of Preaching on Trinity Sunday" bridges theological reflection and pastoral practice by offering insights for proclaiming Trinitarian faith in ways that both honor orthodox doctrine and speak to contemporary congregations.

Taken together, these essays demonstrate how Nicene theology continues to inform and enliven Christian faith and to form biblical imaginations by offering fresh insights for ministry while remaining grounded in the church's historic confessions. For pastors and church leaders seeking to articulate ancient truth in contemporary contexts, these pieces provide both theological depth and practical wisdom. As we face today's challenges of religious pluralism, biblical interpretation, and spiritual formation, these essays show how the Nicene heritage can help us articulate and embody the gospel with both conviction and grace.

The Jerusalem Council in Acts 15

Strive for Unity, not Uniformity

Jung H. Choi

The "Jerusalem Council" or "Council in Jerusalem" in Acts 15, where apostles and elders gathered, is considered the first ecumenical council—the first "Holy Conferencing," as Methodists would say.[1] For a long time, Christians have gathered not only to discuss various theological matters but also to worship God in different dialects and accents, inspired by God's Spirit. Christians have gathered to aspire to create a unity, which is different from uniformity. We celebrate many meaningful landmarks for ecumenical councils and conversations towards unity. The Council of Nicaea will mark its 1700th anniversary in 2025. And the 11th Assembly of World Council of Churches gathered in Karlsruhe, Germany in September 2022.[2] As the world is filled with escalated polarizations and divisions, it is all the more crucial and urgent for Christians to have profound and renewed conversations. We must follow Jesus's mandate to strive for unity and to be united in God's love.

In this paper, I would like to explore the unity, not uniformity in Acts 15, which is considered to be the first Church Council. I suggest a complex picture of the call for the unity in spite of (or because of) differences. This paper considers the references to Acts 15 in several bilateral ecumenical dialogues, and then brief exegesis of Acts 15 ensues. It will end with a reflection on the call to unity, not uniformity.

Acts 15: Ecumenical Gatherings for Unity

The Central Committee of the WCC's 10th Assembly elaborated the concept of the ecumenical pilgrimage of justice and peace with a three-dimensional approach that is organically, not sequentially, connected. The three-dimensional approach is:

- Celebrating the Gifts (*via positiva*)
- Visiting the Wounds (*via negativa*)
- Transforming the Injustices (*via transformativa*)[3]

The Jerusalem Council—with two tales that narrates the historical meeting—also reflects this intertwined approach of these three ways (*via positiva*, *via negativa*, and *via transformativa*) with its promise of unity amongst diversities, its acknowledgment of the fragile nature of unity possibly due to human nature of frailty, and yet its trust in the continued guidance of the Holy Spirit that transforms and renews all God's people.

The Jerusalem Council in Acts 15 has been referenced and discussed in several different ecumenical conversation settings. In particular, from the First Anglican/Roman Catholic International Commission (ARCIC), "Authority in the Church I (1976)" delineates the importance of the Council of Jerusalem and the Christian gatherings that ensue "either regional or world-wide" (§9). The section begins, "Ever since the Council of Jerusalem (Acts 15) the churches have realized the need to express and strengthen the *koinonia* by coming together to discuss matters of mutual concern and to meet contemporary challenges" (§9). This agreement is supposed to affect the entire Church. As the same ARCIC document continues to note, "The decisions of what has traditionally *been called an 'ecumenical council' are binding upon the whole Church; those of a regional council or synod bind only the churches it represents*. Such decrees are to be received by the local churches as expressing the mind of the Church. This exercise of authority, far from being an imposition, is *designed to strengthen the life and mission of the local churches and of their members*" (§9, emphasis added).[4] The Jerusalem Council in Acts 15 offers an important model for later ecumenical councils and ecumenical conversations, which can illumine various ways that ecumenical conversations have transpired on unity, not uniformity, amongst diversities.

The Methodist-Roman Catholic International Commission (MERCIC) statement titled "Towards a Statement on the Church (Nairobi 1986)" notes the significance of unity amongst diversities shown in Acts 15.[5] Since this passage in §5 is so crucial, I cite it in full:

> In the New Testament period, diversity of time, place and circumstances produced diversity among groups of believers—diversity of community structures, diverse formulations of the faith, diverse traditions shaped by different histories and problems, diverse house meetings places within the same city, diverse Christian centers. Nevertheless, passages in the New Testament, such as the account in *Acts* 15 of the Council of Jerusalem, attest to *koinoia* among such diversities, and to a sense of *the* Church to which all Christians belong. There are also passages, such as *1 Jn* 2:19, that suggest the breaking of the *koinoia* because certain diversities were deemed intolerable distortions of what was from the beginning.

The same statement continues to explore the theme of unity in Acts 15 in §43:

> *Acts* 15 shows Peter, Barnabas, Paul and James as all speaking to the issue of the admission of Gentile converts without circumcision, but indicates that James insisted on their observance of specific purity laws. *Gal* 2 and *Acts* 15 have led many to suspect that Peter's position in relation to Judaism stood in between that of James on the one side and of Paul on the other. Some would regard the failure to mention Peter in the second half of the book of *Acts* as a sign that his authority had declined; others would regard the fact that Luke concentrates on Peter first and then on Paul as reflecting the author's purpose to show how Christianity gradually moved from Jerusalem and the mission to the Jews, towards Rome and the Gentile Mission.

We must remember that the Jerusalem Council gathered because they had conflicting opinions about the core of faith and salvation; the meeting was called because of both dissents (*stasis*) and discussion points or inquiry (*zetesis*; Acts 15:2).[6] A profound ecumenical problem was posed: should Gentile Christians be considered as Christian and as legitimate members of the Church?[7]

Amid this tension, a beautiful story of unity is shown in Acts, when those who attended on the crucial gathering agreed on the most important part of salvation, when Peter says, "we believe that we will be saved through the grace of the Lord Jesus, just as they [the Gentiles] will" (Acts 15:11 NRSV). James then adds, "Therefore I have reached the decision that we should not trouble those Gentiles who are turning to God" (Acts 15:19 NRSV).

Acts 15:22 emphasizes the consensus nature of the agreement: "Then the apostles and the elders, with the consent of the whole church" (NRSV) or "with the whole church" (KJV, ESV, et al.). Since there was not yet a biblical canon that they drew on, they appealed to the wondrous works of the Holy Spirit that is correlated to the teachings in the Gospel. They realized that God's Spirit already incorporated Gentile Christians into the Church, as Peter stood up and said to them, "And God, who knows the human heart, testified to them [the Gentiles] by giving them the Holy Spirit, just as he did to us" (Acts 15:8 NRSV), and then Paul and Barnabas gave testimonies of "the signs and wonders that God had done through them among the Gentiles" (Acts 15:12 NRSV).[8] Indeed, Peter's speech had ended with the powerful message: "we believe that we will be saved through the grace of the Lord Jesus, just as they will" (Acts 15:11 NRSV).

Two Tales of the Apostolic Councils in Jerusalem

It is also crucial to see that, as "Towards a Statement on the Church" (Nairobi) leads us and as John Wesley's sermon on Acts 15 guides us,[9] when we read both Acts 15 and Galatians 2 side by side, we see an important and highly complex picture of unity and diversity. Both the texts (Acts 15:1-21 and Galatians 2:1-10) explore the Apostolic Meeting(s).[10] There are important figures who come to the Jerusalem Council to discuss their theological beliefs. Paul and his companions, Barnabas and Titus, join the council. From the Jerusalem Church, Peter and James (the "acknowledged pillars" in Galatians 2:9 NRSV) as well as "the apostles and the elders" (Acts 15:2 NRSV) are those who gathered for the Jerusalem Council. As we saw above, they agreed on what is essential (Acts 15:28) for salvation: they reinforced faith in Christ as the basis of salvation and accepted God's inclusion vision for both Jews and Gentiles.[11] Accordingly, they agreed that the Gentile believers need not be circumcisions, and then the Council of Jerusalem would divide mission work between Peter and Paul. As is portrayed in Galatians 2:7-10, Paul reports that the Jerusalem Council yields a good result: they reached an important agreement that Peter will bring the gospel to the circumcised (Jewish people) while Paul is sent to the Gentiles.

It is worthy to note important divergences between these two texts (Acts 15 and Galatians 2). While the precis of the theological agreement is the same in these two texts, conditions for the agreement is different. Acts 15 delineates a particular set of conditions that James narrates, "but we should write to them to abstain only from things polluted by idols and from fornication and from whatever has been strangled and from blood" (Acts 15:20).[12] On the other hand, Galatians 2 has only one condition or request: "They asked only one thing, that we remember the poor, which was actually what I [Paul] was eager to do" (Galatians 2:10 NRSV).[13]

While a harmonious picture of unity has been achieved among the early followers of Christ, divisions ensued after the Jerusalem Council. This picture should not surprise readers of Acts; after all, as Jaroslav Pelikan notes, "in virtually every chapter of the book of Acts there is evidence of ongoing theological disagreement, at the surface or hovering just beneath it."[14] In Acts 15, Paul and Barnabas—who has been an advocate for Paul when others did not trust Paul—depart from each other's company due to different opinions on John Mark. Furthermore, in Galatians 2:11-14, Paul condemns Peter for not eating with the Gentile Christians in Antioch. After the volatile encounter between Paul and Peter, it seems that Paul completely works apart from the Jerusalem Church, rather than taking collections to the Jerusalem Church from the gentile mission churches as he agreed. Is unity and harmony fragile?

These conflicting narratives (or narratives punctuated with conflicts) draw us powerfully into the layered voices and diverse cultures entangled with various social locations. The narratives warrant the readers to explore complicated relationships between diverse early Christian communities such as Jews living in the diaspora, Jews living in Palestine, and Gentiles. Peter and James are Jews who were born and raised in Roman Palestine; Paul and Barnabas were ethnically Jewish and yet were born and raised in diaspora.[15] There are also growing populations of Gentile Christians such as Titus, whose presence provoked the seminal question in the Council of Jerusalem. There different voices and cultures are worthy to be reflected on. The Seventh Assembly of the WCC (Canberra, 1991) stated in "The Unity of the Church as Koinonia: Gift and Calling," "Diversities which are rooted in theological traditions, various cultural, ethnic or historical contexts are integral to the nature of communion" (§2.2).[16] The two tales of the Jerusalem Council might come from *both* divergent socio-cultural locations *and* diverse theological traditions in nascent Christianity. But then again, theological traditions as well as cultural, ethnic, and historical contexts are inextricably intertwined.

The exploration of the (dis)agreements, unity, and conditions from the Jerusalem Council in the first century invites us to examine further our contemporary racial and ethnic relations in the landscape of Christianity in diaspora. For example, we can find a clue on this matter in various studies on diaspora Asian Christians in the United States with regard to ethnic church and cultural preservation. What do different heritage groups agree on as Christians?[17] How do we see and solve the tension between ethnic particularism and religious universalism?

We also note that in these two portrayals of the Jerusalem Council, there exists what Luis Menéndez Antuña refers to as a "textual crevice," that takes the form of absence, of a void, of a lack of presence.[18] Whose voices are clear? Whose voices are considered as silent? Whose presences are ignored? Coming back to the different conditions of the agreement, would Paul agree with the conditions that were proffered by James in Acts 15? Since Galatians 2 has a different description of the conditions, it seems that it is not how Paul understood the condition. We don't have a way of knowing, for Paul does not speak much in Acts 15, other than speaking in front of "the whole assembly . . . of all the signs and wonders that God had done through them among the Gentiles" (Acts 15:12 NRSV). As Paul penned Galatians, we do not get to hear

Peter's perspectives about his actions in Antioch (2:11-14). The Peter whom we see from Paul's presentation in Galatians 2 is vastly different from Peter in Acts 15. There, Peter is a champion who supports the Gentile mission, for he obeys the Holy Spirit who breaks the boundaries between the Jews and the Gentile especially after a mysterious eye-opening experience in Acts 10. After all, it is Peter who said this powerful message: "And God, who knows the human heart, testified to them by giving them the Holy Spirit, just as he did to us; and in cleansing their hearts by faith he has made no *distinction* between them and us" (Acts 15:8-9 NRSV; emphasis added). Acts 15 and Galatians 2 also expound the point that the whole community was there in the Jerusalem Council.[19] What stories, testimonies, and dissenting opinions did they share that we do not get to hear?

What do these stories of fragility and vulnerability among early followers of Christ teach us? These texts lay bare conflicts without hiding them. When we are gathering at the table surrounded by Christ's love, we are coming from heterogeneous environments, experiences, and communities where we belong. With people's differences, divisions and cracks are bound to happen. Yet we are called to work towards reconciliation and unity with the Holy Spirit's help. If unity is equated with uniformity, which flattens the complex voices of people who come to serve God and love Jesus Christ, it is not a unity to which we are called to. As an important ecumenical maxim goes, unity is not uniformity.[20]

Uniformity is an effort to erase people's various voices and privilege one voice of faith over others. As Harding Meyer aptly says, "'Unity in reconciled diversity' aims first and foremost to bring to expression the fact that the unity of the church which is being sought does not—or need not—mean the achievement of a single invariable entity, whether in the sense of a melding of the existing churches into one church with a new identity and a new name or in the sense of the absorption of them all into one of the existing churches."[21]

Peter's claim in Acts 15:9 that God "has made no *distinction* (*diekrinen*) between them and us" is noteworthy because this expression does not mean that "them" and "us" become the same. This verse is remarkably similar to Paul's manifesto, "There is no longer Jew or Greek, there is no longer slave or free, there is no longer male and female; for all of you are one in Christ

Jesus" (Galatians 3:28 NRSV).[22] Neither Peter nor Paul says that to be one and united in Christ means the erasure of differences of Jesus-followers. The earliest stories of serving God and spreading the good news that "Jesus is the Lord!" came from believers' love for God—whether they were from the Jerusalem communities who had gone through so many hardships, or from the diaspora who had gone through trauma and longing, or from the Gentiles who had needed to claim their space in the new faith.

Via Transformativa: Transformed by the Holy Spirit's Guidance and United By God's Love

At this juncture, I would like to remind of us the three-fold schema that this short paper starts with, posing important questions for us.

- What kinds of gifts do we have? (*Via Positiva*)
- What kinds of divisions and misgivings, trauma, and suffering do we have that divide us, the body of Christ (*Via Negativa*)?
- Assessing these illuminating and yet daunting paths, to what work is the Holy Spirit guiding us in our walk of solidarity, renewal, and unity (*Via Transformativa*)?

Just as the tales of the Jerusalem Council penned by Luke and Paul are not afraid of laying bare divisions in the earliest Christian communities, we are also not to be daunted by divisions and dissensions. Rather, we are called to see these dissentions as a crucial part of discerning how God is leading humanity.[23] We are called to face the divisions, dissensions, pains, and traumas that come from it, and we are called to walk the way of reconciliation and unity with God's Spirit. As seen in Acts 15:8-9, we are called to be united in God's love and transformed by the Holy Spirit's guidance.

We are to be reminded again of the centrality of the Holy Spirit as elucidated in §16 of the Anglican/Roman Catholic statement "Authority in the Church I (1976)":

Local councils held from the second century determined the limits of the New Testament, and, gave to the Church a canon which has remained normative. The action of a council in making such a decision on so momentous a matter implies an assurance that the Lord himself is present when his people assemble 'in his name' (Mt 18:20), and that a council may say, *'it has seemed good to the Holy Spirit and to us'* (Acts 15:28). The conciliar mode of authority exercised in the matter of the canon has also been applied to questions of discipline and of fundamental doctrine. What decisions (as at Nicaea in 325) affect the entire Church and deal with controverted matters which have been widely and seriously debated, it is important to establish criteria for the recognition and reception of conciliar definitions and disciplinary decisions. *A substantial part in the process of reception is played by the subject matter of the definitions and by the response of the perspective through the Spirit's continuing guidance of the whole Church.* (emphasis added)[24]

As we see again and again in the Acts of Apostles, which is also fittingly called as "the Acts of the Holy Spirit," the Holy Spirit moves and inspires people in such mysterious and unexpected ways. The Holy Spirit brings people into God's community/*oikonomia* where people proclaim that "Jesus is the Lord." It is not a unification unto a uniformity; rather, it is a call to unity *and* keeping our distinct voices that come to love God.

It is important to see how the Book of Acts portrays God's agency that carries the humankind. In the Jerusalem Council, Paul and Barnabas are witnesses of "the signs and wonders God has done through them among the Gentiles" (Acts 15:12 NRSV). Both Acts and Galatians agree that the mission to the Gentiles comes from God, as God's gift (Acts 15:11; Gal 2:9).[25] It is God who leads us and we are to obey the Spirit's leading, such as in Acts 2 when people are glorifying God in various languages. The Holy Spirit is driving us in mysterious ways and, many times, beyond our understanding. This could seem radical for some. We see how the Holy Spirit leads Peter into Cornelius's household in Acts 10, and we see how the Holy Spirit prods Paul for the Gentile mission that may sound a bit too radical for many in the Jerusalem Church in Acts 15. While God's agency takes the most significant role in the journey of Christian faith, our agency and cooperation with the divine agency is also essential. Neither those earliest Jesus-followers nor we are passive beings, automatons without wills and volitions. It is significant that the Jerusalem Council in Acts 15:28 says, "It has seemed good for the Holy Spirit *and* to us" (NRSV, emphasis added); there the "it" could refer to the decision itself or perhaps to the unity created among those who attended.

We are thus called to *strive for unity*. I use the expression of "strive for" here, for this verb—the translation of *zēloō*[26]—is fittingly used in a beautiful harmony and yet a mysterious co-existence of the divine and human agencies. In explicating the divine gifts from God in 1 Corinthians 12–14, Paul says:

1 Corinthians 12:31	"But *strive for* the greater gifts. And I will show you a still more excellent way." (NRSV) ζηλοῦτε δὲ τὰ χαρίσματα τὰ μείζονα. Καὶ ἔτι καθ' ὑπερβολὴν ὁδὸν ὑμῖν δείκνυμι.
1 Corinthians 14:1	"Pursue love and *strive for* the spiritual gifts, and especially that you may prophesy." (NRSV) Διώκετε τὴν ἀγάπην, ζηλοῦτε δὲ τὰ πνευματικά, μᾶλλον δὲ ἵνα προφητεύητε.
1 Corinthians 14:39	"So, my friends, *be eager to* prophesy, and do not forbid speaking in tongues." (NRSV) ὥστε, ἀδελφοί μου, ζηλοῦτε τὸ προφητεύειν, καὶ τὸ λαλεῖν μὴ κωλύετε γλώσσαις.

Gifts (*charismata*) come from God, but Paul also encourages the readers to "strive for" gifts from God. What a mystery![27] Thus our call to "strive for unity" also reflects our reality and our hope: unity can only come from the Holy Spirit and it can even be brittle, but we are invited to strive for it, trusting God's steadfast and faithful love for the humanity. Unity is a gift from God, *and* we are to work on and strive for it. This concept is tightly connected to what John Wesley said in "Scripture Way of Salvation" (III.10); there Wesley expounds on the nature of the sanctification and the necessary "works of mercy" or "practices of mercy."[28] Wesley knew so well that the routine practices of the means of grace takes a central stage in Christians' spiritual growth. It is God's Spirit who guides and sanctifies us in our Christian journey; at the same time, we are to participate in ordinary practices, trusting God's way.[29]

The Holy Spirit prompts us and guides us to cooperate in this journey towards unity. We are invited to walk this journey with obedience and boldness. We open our hearts to God and ask God: "Come Holy Spirit, fill us with your love and let us be united by your love."[30] May our hearts be strangely warmed by the Holy Spirit and by God's love.

Notes

1. Many church historians have also considered Acts 15 as a model for councils (or synods, as these two concepts were interchangeably used in the early centuries of Christianity) in the fifth and sixth centuries. See how many of our bilateral discussions look to the Jerusalem Council as a point of discussions. Everett Ferguson, "Creeds, Councils, and Canons," in *The Oxford Handbook of Early Christian Studies*, ed. Susan Ashbrook Harvey and David G. Hunter (Oxford University Press, 2008), 434. See Hermann Josef Sieben, *Die Konzilidee der alten Kirche* (Schönigh, 1979) for more discussions on ecumenical councils in general. Jaroslav Pelikan (*Acts*, Brazos Theological Commentary on the Bible [Brazos Press, 2005], 175) also succinctly said, "This entire chapter [i.e. Acts 15] has served throughout Christian history as a model for decision-making in the church and as a charter both for authority at church councils and for the authority of church councils."
2. https://www.oikoumene.org/news/wcc-11th-assembly-31-august-8-september-2022.
3. World Council of Churches, *Towards An Ecumenical Theology of Companionship: A Study Document for the Ecumenical Pilgrimage of Justice and Peace* (WCC Publications, 2022), 11–12.
4. http://www.christianunity.va/content/unitacristiani/en/dialoghi/sezione-occidentale/comunione-anglicana/dialogo/arcic-i/testo-in-inglese5.html.
5. http://www.christianunity.va/content/unitacristiani/en/dialoghi/sezione-occidentale/consiglio-metodista-mondiale/dialogo/documenti-di-dialogo/en4.html.
6. Luke Timothy Johnson, *The Acts of the Apostles*, SP 5 (Liturgical Press, 1992), 259. As a reporter in the 11th Assembly in Karlsruhe, Germany said, "We gather here because we *disagree*." (https://www.youtube.com/watch?v=8Y_WoC89Pq8&ab_channel=World CouncilofChurches).

Section 1

7. William J. Abraham, "Method in Ecumenism," in *The Oxford Handbook of Ecumenical Studies*, ed. Geoffrey Wainwright and Paul McPartlan (Oxford University Press, 2021), 639.
8. Abraham, "Method in Ecumenism," 640.
9. John Wesley's note on 1 Corinthians 15 and Galatians 2 have many overlaps. https://ccel.org/ccel/wesley/notes.i.vi.xvi.html; https://ccel.org/ccel/wesley/notes/notes.i.x.iii.html Wesley's references to Acts 15 are in the following:
   Acts 15:7, 8: Preaching text 11/05/39, Islington; source: diary (p. 20)
   Acts 15: Preaching text 10/14/40, London, Foundery; source: diary (p. 32) https://wesleyworks.files.wordpress.com/2022/07/register-04_register_of_john_wesleys_preaching_texts.pdf
10. New Testament scholars are divided on whether Acts 15 and Galatians 2 describe the same meeting in Jerusalem. What stands out is that Galatians serves as the primary source for the account of the Jerusalem Council in Acts 15 (Richard Pervo, *Acts*, Hermeneia (Fortress Press, 2009),369. Douglas Campbell (*Paul: An Apostle's Journey* [Eerdmans, 2018], 182) suggests that in Gal 2:1-10 Paul describes the events of Acts 15. While I align with Campbell's perspective, the aim of this paper is not to argue or prove one interpretation over another. Instead, I aim to explore the insights that emerge from reading Acts 15 and Galatians 2 together, which can illuminate our effort towards unity.
11. Johnson, *Acts*, 268.
12. This condition is repeated in Acts 15:29: "You abstain from what has been sacrificed to idols and from blood and from what is strangled and from fornication. If you keep yourselves from these, you will do well. Farewell."
13. Paul passionately fulfilled his agreement to remember the power by setting up a collection from his Gentile mission communities. See Rom 15:25-27; 1 Cor 16:1-4; 2 Cor 8:1–9:15. *The Harper Collins Study Bible: New Revised Standard Version*, ed. Harold W. Attridge and Society of Biblical Literature (HarperOne, 2006), 1975.
14. Pelikan, *Acts*, 170.
15. For a helpful work on Paul and his politics of identity, see Yung Suk Kim, "The Politics of Identity in Paul's Gospel: In the Case of the Antioch Incident (Gal 2:11-14)," *Encounter* 80 (2020).
16. https://www.oikoumene.org/resources/documents/the-unity-of-the-church-as-koinonia-gift-and-calling-the-canberra-statement.
17. For example, Sharon Kim, "Shifting Boundaries within Second-Generation Korean American Churches," *Sociology of Religion 71* (2010): 98–122; Helen Kim, "Reconstructing Asian America's Religious Past: A Historiography," in *Envisioning Religion, Race, and Asian Americans*, ed. David K. Yoo and Khyati Y. Joshi (University of Hawai'i Press, 2020).
18. Luis Menéndez Antuña, "Topographies of Silencing: Review of *Minoritized Women Reading Race and Ethnicity* by Jin Young Choi and Mitzi Smith," presented at the Annual Meeting of Society of Biblical Literature, November 30, 2020.
19. Johnson, *Acts*, 261.

20. Harding Meyer, "'Unity in Reconciled Diversity': A 'Confession-Related Conception of Unity," in *The Oxford Handbook of Ecumenical Studies*, ed. Geoffrey Wainwright and Paul McPartlan (Oxford University Press, 2021), 559.
21. Meyer, "Unity in Reconciled Diversity," 560.
22. Caroline Johnson Hodge says, "The unity in Christianity Paul articulates in [Gal 3:28] has often been cited in support of the view that Paul advocates an erasure of embodied identities, including ethnic and racial ones, for a non-ethnic, religious identity, Christianity. But notice that this is *not* what Paul says. The unity Paul speaks of in Christ in itself ethnically specific; it is tied to Israel. Those who are baptized into Christ become descendants of Abraham, and thus heirs of God's promise. This new identity is described in terms of ethnicity, kinship, and standing before Israel's God" ("Paul and Ethnicity," *The Oxford Handbook of Pauline Studies,* ed. Matthew V. Novenson and R. Barry Matlock [Oxford University Press, 2022], 10).
23. Johnson, *Acts*, 270.
24. https://www.christianunity.va/content/unitacristiani/en/dialoghi/sezione-occidentale/comunione-anglicana/dialogo/arcic-i/testo-in-inglese5.html.
25. Johnson, *Acts*, 269–70.
26. Most contemporary scholars have translated ζηλόω as "to strive to obtain." For the discussion of this translation, see Anthony C. Thiselton, *The First Epistle to the Corinthians: A Commentary on the Greek Text,* NIGTC (Eerdmans, 2000), 1082–87.
27. For more on this, see Jung H. Choi, *'Earn the Grace of Prophecy': Early Christian Prophecy as Practice* (Th.D. diss, Harvard University, 2016); idem, "Gender, Race, and Normalization of Prophecy in Early Christianity and Korean and Korean-American Christianity," in *Minoritized Women Reading Race-Ethnicity: Intersectional Approaches and Early Christian (Con)Texts* (Lexington Books, 2020), 89–109.
28. http://wesley.nnu.edu/john-wesley/the-sermons-of-john-wesley-1872-edition/sermon-43-the-scripture-way-of-salvation/.
29. Sangwoo Kim, "Praying Advent: Preparing the Way," in *All the Good: A Wesleyan Way of Christmas*, ed. Laceye C. Warner (Abingdon Press, 2021), 64–65.
30. *The United Methodist Hymnal*, 432, refrain: "Jesu, Jesu, fill us with your love, show us how to serve the neighbors we have from you."

Nicaea, the Spirit, and Sanctification

Daniel Castelo

In his "Letter to a Roman Catholic," John Wesley made the following remark regarding the "Third Article" of the Nicene Creed, which is devoted to the Holy Spirit:

> I believe the infinite and eternal Spirit of God, equal with the Father and the Son, to be not only perfectly holy in himself, but the immediate cause of all holiness in us; enlightening our understandings, rectifying our wills and affections, renewing our natures, uniting our persons to Christ, assuring us of the adoption of sons, leading us in our actions, purifying and sanctifying our souls and bodies to a full and eternal enjoyment of God.[1]

Drawing on John Pearson's *Exposition of the Creed*, Wesley gives in this elaboration a compelling and full account of the person and work of the Holy Spirit. Among their many qualities, the remarks have a robust trinitarian character, for they stress the Spirit to be eternal and equal with the Father and the Son, and Wesley highlights the Spirit's connection to holiness. In a succinct and poignant way, these elaborations capture features of what a Nicene account of the Spirit is and should be. They also indicate something about the character of Wesleyan theology. These remarks essentially bring these two details together so that one can make the argument that Wesleyan theology operates out of a robust Nicene pneumatological framework. Such is the case both for Wesley and the movement he and his associates helped spawn. When Wesley remarks in the "Large Minutes" that God's design in "raising up the preachers called 'Methodists'" was "to reform the nation and in particular the Church, to spread scriptural holiness over the land,"[2] he is making a claim that operates out of an account of holiness that is very much driven by a specific Nicene pneumatological accent. What "scriptural holiness" is and how it is "spread" all work out of a Spirit-logic. For this reason, Wesley's renewal movement only makes theological sense when it is cast as a kind of Spirit-movement, and the character of this Spirit-movement relies on pneumatological features of a Nicene faith. In what follows, we will explore what this Nicene account of the Spirit means as well as stress ways it can be understood in an authentically Wesleyan way.

I

Much has been made of the brevity associated with Nicaea's remarks about the Holy Spirit in its articulated form. The profession of faith on this score almost sounds like an afterthought: After remarks on "one God, the Father Almighty" and in "one Lord Jesus Christ, the Son of God" in the extensive, so-called "First" and "Second Articles," respectively, we receive the following: "And (we believe) in the Holy Spirit" (Greek original: *kai eis to hagion pneuma*; Latin translation: *et in Spiritum Sanctum*).[3] That five words are employed to demarcate an emerging understanding of one of the triune persons sounds like a paltry and inadequate effort. The focus of the Nicene Creed of 325 seems to be on opposing Arianism with its elaboration of the Second Article (the longest of the three) and the inclusion of the (in)famous "*homoousion*" term, that the Son is of "one essence" with the Father.

Additionally, after the five words on the Holy Spirit, the following denouncements of Arianism are on offer: "However, those who say: 'There was a time when he was not' and 'Before he was born he was not' and that he was made from nothing or who say that the Son of God may be a different hypostasis or essence, or may be created or subject to change and alteration, (such persons) the Catholic Church anathematizes."[4] If one steps back and does not include these remarks in a tabulation and instead focuses on the so-called Second and Third Articles of the Nicene Creed of 325, we have a Greek wordcount of 53 versus 5, respectively. It is no wonder why people with pneumatological interests often move quickly from Nicaea to the First Council of Constantinople in 381 and its associated creed—sometimes itself called "the Nicene Creed," but more accurately "the Nicene-Constantinopolitan Creed." In this latter creed, one finds a much more suitable elaboration in its Third Article after it repeats (in a slightly different grammatical structure) the words of Nicaea: "And (we believe) in the Holy Spirit, the Lord and Giver of life, who proceeds from the Father, who together with the Father and the Son is worshipped and glorified, who has spoken through the prophets."[5]

As easy as it is to move hastily from Nicaea to Constantinople and to name the latter's credal outlay as pneumatologically superior to the former because of its prolixity, the five words of Nicaea devoted to the Spirit do mark a significant achievement, one that contemporary confessors should acknowledge to the fullest degree.

Importantly, these words register the connection between "holiness" and "Spirit-language," particularly in a gesture towards personifying a divine identity. This effort should not be taken for granted, especially given biblical backgrounds and the state of pneumatology at the time. In the Old Testament, spirit-language (i.e., cases that involve the Hebrew term *ruach*) can have many referents and connotations, but when a divine spirit is spoken about (approximately one-third of such instances), any number of possibilities and readings can emerge, including that this One may be an angel or agent of God. The language of holiness, for that matter, is *not* a typical association one makes with pneumatological language in the Old Testament. Only two instances make the connection In one passage, David is seeking pardon for his actions with Bathsheba and says, "Do not cast me away from your presence, and do not take your holy spirit from me" (Psalm 51:11 NRSV). Elsewhere a prophet speaks about Israel rebelling and grieving God's spirit, and yet God had put God's spirit in the people at the time of Moses's deliverance (Isaiah 63:10-11). Clearly, two passages do not constitute a pattern. But by the time the intertestamental period emerges, the association becomes a bit more prominent, and this is indicated in such texts as Wisdom 9:17 and 2 Esdras 14:22, as well as in several places in the Dead Sea Scrolls.[6]

Section 1

When one surveys the New Testament, the connection is canonically first stressed in the fourfold gospel testimony. The Synoptic Gospels, in announcing the baptism of John the Baptist and its distinction from the baptism of the One who is to come, point to the latter's baptism as being in the *Holy* Spirit (Matthew 3:11; Mark 1:8; Luke 3:16). Matthew (1:18, 20) and Luke (1:15, 35, 41, 67; 2:25-26) go so far as to make connections between holiness and Spirit-language prior to the pericopes devoted to John the Baptist. For its part, the Gospel of John approaches Spirit-talk in rich and distinctive ways, but it also begins with reference to the Holy Spirit during its own John the Baptist pericope, depicting the Baptist as proclaiming that the One who called him told him that the One to come will baptize in the Holy Spirit (John 1:33). After other references to the Holy Spirit, John nears the end of his gospel by depicting the disciples experiencing a unique, Pentecost-like moment before the resurrected Jesus when the latter breathes on them and says, "Receive the Holy Spirit" (20:22 NRSV).

By the time the reader reaches the Acts of the Apostles, the connection between holiness and the Spirit is assumed and repeatedly stressed: The Holy Spirit is the One who prompted Jesus in his post-resurrection instructions (1:2), who will fulfill the claims associated with Jesus's baptism (1:5), who will give power to the disciples once they wait in Jerusalem (1:8), and who spoke at the time of David (1:16). As Acts progresses, the Holy Spirit goes on to fill the disciples who were waiting in the Upper Room (2:4), and Spirit-allusions feature prominently in Peter's Pentecost sermon with a final, explicit reference to this One's patterned qualifier: "This Jesus God raised up, and of that all of us are witnesses. Being therefore exalted at the right hand of God, and having received from the Father the promise of the Holy Spirit, he has poured out this that you both see and hear" (2:32-33 NRSV). These depictions are quite remarkable; they lead Frey to say, "It is striking how often the Spirit [in Acts] appears as an acting subject, so that one could even consider the Spirit the true protagonist and leader of the church whose directions and actions are followed by the human protagonists."[7] To this point, Christians often refer to the fifth book of the New Testament canon as the "Acts of the Apostles," but in accordance with Frey's observation, the book could be theologically and experimentally titled the "Acts of the Holy Spirit."

Nicaea recognizes this connection between God's Spirit and holiness, one that was only slightly present in the pre-New Testament witnesses but that blossomed exceedingly at the time of Jesus's ministry and its immediate aftermath. In fact, one can say that the sustained use of the qualifier "holy" with referents to "spirit" in the New Testament stresses an emerging scriptural presentation of what would be understood by the church as the Third Person of the Trinity, that is, a distinct entity to the person of the Son incarnate in Jesus who nevertheless works in and through him as well as on his behalf after Jesus's ascension. Put another way, the shifting patterns of Spirit-talk in the Bible point to a rising account of a distinguishable identity—not just any "spirit" per se, but the "Holy Spirit" who is signaled as working hand in hand with Jesus to accomplish the Father's will. The language of "holy" in conjunction with "spirit" demarcates a *someone*; the linguistic connection serves to name—and so personify—an identifiable agent who is described at critical junctures within Jesus's unfolding mission in the world. For its part, Nicaea signals this biblical momentum and gestures towards its significance for a Christian doctrine of God.

Now, it may be the case that we as contemporary readers see these connections and assume subsequent trinitarian logics to the point that we are distracted from recognizing how important Nicaea's pneumatological gesture is. It is a gesture that pivots on the New Testament pattern of interconnecting the Son and the Spirit. At many critical moments in Jesus's life and ministry, the Spirit is explicitly mentioned as leading, prompting, and anointing Jesus. Many examples could be lifted, but a sampling could include: Luke's speaking how the Spirit prepares the way for Jesus (chs. 1–2); Matthew's noting how Jesus is driven by the Spirit to the temptation (4:1); and Jesus claiming Isaianic antecedence by suggesting that the Spirit of the LORD (YHWH) is upon him (Luke 4:18). These and other examples show an intricate and powerful connection between Jesus, the Son incarnate, and the Spirit of God, the Holy Spirit. On one end, Jesus is the ultimate charismatic figure, the Messiah and Christ who is anointed by the Spirit and who in turn is the Spirit-baptizer. On the other end, the Spirit is the Spirit of Jesus, the One who empowered his ministry and who will support Jesus's disciples after Jesus's ascension by bringing to the disciples' remembrance all that Jesus said and taught.

Section 1

Furthermore, the Son and the Spirit are interconnected to such a degree that they share the titles of both "Lord" and "Paraclete." Given this interconnection, one can say that the fight against Arianism is not simply one tied to who the Son is in some kind of individuated way; rather, it is a fight against all those who would push against the fullness of the Son's being and revelation, matters which are at pivotal points pneumatological at their very core. Therefore, similarly to how Jesus and the Spirit worked in tandem at various points in New Testament depictions, the Second and Third Articles of the Creed work in theological coordination with one another. The logic holds that a faithful people cannot confess one without the other.

In the interconciliar period of the fourth century, the time between Nicaea in 325 and Constantinople in 381, a flurry of pneumatological activity took place. For contemporary readers, that activity can help substantiate and elaborate what may have been an important and yet rudimentary, implicit, and textually understated logic at the time of Nicaea. For instance, a relevant question at the time was, "If the Son is God and is in turn led, prompted, and supported by the Holy Spirit, should the Spirit in turn be stressed as properly God as well?" Many people were asking questions like this at the time, and some were fiercely opposed to this possibility. At one level, the scrutiny and questioning are understandable, in that people at the time were asking basic and consequential questions related to the Christian doctrine of God. On another level, one can see how these opponents showed family resemblances to the Arian cause, insofar as similar arguments against the divinity of the Son could be raised in relation to the divinity of the Spirit. If the so-called Second and Third Articles work in tandem (as I have been arguing thus far), then pressure on the latter theme (the divinity of the Spirit) would undoubtedly be a stressor on the former (the divinity of the Son). Several key figures from the early church recognized this threat and responded in kind. We will briefly mention two, Athanasius of Alexandria and Basil of Caesarea.

In the case of Athanasius, he is often remembered as a champion of Nicaea during this interconciliar period. He was present at Nicaea, but he grew in prominence and authority after the council was over. He is often remembered for his work *On the Incarnation*, which addresses Arian concerns in a myriad of ways. One way involved stressing the connection between the works of creation and salvation; at one point, he states, "the renewal of the creation has been wrought by the Self-same Word Who made it in the beginning. There is thus no inconsistency between creation and salvation; for the One Father has employed the same Agent for both works, effecting the salvation of the world through the same Word Who made it in the beginning."[8] Inherent to this reasoning is that both creation and salvation are properly the works of God. Another anti-Arian argument in this piece highlights how the Son addressed the thoroughgoing corruption of the creation by taking it on and healing it from within. This healing can be spoken of in terms of sanctification. As Athanasius notes, "He sanctified the body by being in it."[9] This incarnational logic is the grounding for the most famous phrase of the piece: "He, indeed, assumed humanity that we might become God."[10] People typically rush to stress that Athanasius means "God-like" at the end of the phrase; he certainly does mean this, but he does not outright say it, which raises the stakes about how seriously we are to think of the Incarnation's effect upon us. It certainly was a radical move on the part of God to create the possibility for a vile, sinful, and corrupt people to be holy before God. Wonderfully and mysteriously, Christ sanctified our bodies so that we could be holy before a holy God. The inherent reasoning here is that only God could make us God-like, that is, holy.

Athanasius extends a similar logic in another of his works, the so-called *Letters to Serapion*, but in this case, he sustains this reasoning along pneumatological lines to argue against opponents of the Spirit whom he identifies as reflecting features of the Arian cause. These opponents, whom he calls "Tropikoi," believe the Spirit to be a creature and to have an angelic identity based on their particular mode of exegesis (*tropos*) of certain biblical passages. Athanasius quickly points out (and in concert with our claims above) that "these people by disparaging the Holy Spirit also disparage the Son."[11] For Athanasius, "there is one holiness which comes from the Father through the Son in the Holy Spirit."[12] Athanasius proceeds by stressing the Spirit's work of sanctification through a number of references to Paul's writings. He concludes this reasoning by saying, "So, he who is not sanctified by another, nor participates in sanctification, but is himself the one who is participated in, the one in whom all creatures are sanctified: how can he be one of the 'all things' and proper to those who participate in him?"[13] In other words, the work of sanctification is properly God's work, and since the Spirit sanctifies, the Spirit must be God. The same idea applies to divinization or deification. Athanasius argues that "it is through the Spirit that all of us are said to be partakers of God," and after citing several passages, he concludes, "But if we become sharers of the divine nature by partaking of the Spirit, someone would have to be insane to say that the Spirit has a created nature and not the nature of God. For it is because of this that those in whom the Spirit dwells are divinized. And if he divinizes, there can be no doubt that his nature is of God."[14] This reasoning leads Athanasius to a highlight of the *Letters to Serapion*, for his arguments lead to an anti-Arian conclusion with regard to the Spirit: "And so, it could not be any clearer that the Spirit is neither of the many nor even an angel, but he is the only one. Or rather, he is proper to the one Word and proper to and the same as the one God in substance."[15] On that last point, Athanasius makes an explicit, extraordinary move: the term *homoousios*—so vital and consequential for anti-Arian polemic within the Nicene Creed in relation to the Son's identity—is now registered with regard to the Spirit. The Spirit, like the Son, is *homoousios*—of "one substance"—with God.

As for our other early church figure, Basil of Caesarea—one of the so-called Cappadocian Fathers—is credited with writing one of the earliest treatises on Christian pneumatology, *On the Holy Spirit*. A major focus of this volume is to tie soteriology on the whole to a trinitarian logic, which Basil affirms even at this early stage of pneumatological reflection. Against those who would deny and fight the claim that the Spirit is divine (the so-called *Pneumatomachoi*, the "Spirit-fighters"), he stresses, "It is impossible to believe in the Father and the Son without the presence of the Spirit. He who rejects the Spirit rejects the Son, and he who rejects the Son rejects the Father."[16] He strategically follows this remark with a reference to 1 Corinthians 12:3 ("no one can say 'Jesus is Lord' except by the Holy Spirit").

This claim of the unity of the godhead is simultaneously amenable to extensive elaborations on the Holy Spirit as a distinct subject. After an extensive treatment of pneumatological formulas in Scripture, Basil stresses some major pneumatological themes, one of which is sanctification:

> All things thirsting for holiness turn to [the Spirit]; everything living in virtue never turns away from [the Spirit]. [The Spirit] waters them with [the Spirit's] life-giving breath and helps them reach their proper fulfillment. [The Spirit] is the source of sanctification, spiritual light, who gives illumination to everyone using [the Spirit's] powers to search for the truth—and the illumination [the Spirit] gives is [the Spirit's self].[17]

From these claims, one can determine that Basil believes a proper work of the Spirit is sanctification, which is in itself no small matter as it constitutes a major feature of ancient soteriological concerns. The granting of holiness is properly the work of God, and per Basil, the Spirit is the sanctifying agent within the godhead. As he goes on to say, "[The Spirit] is called holy, as the Father is holy and the Son is holy. For creatures, holiness comes from without; for the Spirit, holiness fills [the Spirit's] very nature. [The Spirit] is not sanctified, but sanctifies."[18]

These remarks on the biblical and patristic witnesses resonate well with both the "Large Minutes" understanding of Methodism's purpose as well as with Wesley's expansive elaboration on the Third Article of the Creed. The emerging biblical consensus by the time we canonically reach Paul is the sense that the Spirit is an identifiable entity who works in conjunction with Jesus to accomplish the Father's will, and one way to demarcate this Spirit from other spirits is the qualifier of "holy." It is the Holy Spirit who equips and works through God's people as they "spread scriptural holiness over the land." The Spirit does this because the Spirit is holy, and in being holy, the Spirit can and does sanctify. In sanctifying creatures, the Spirit demonstrates the Spirit's self to be a person of the trinitarian godhead. These many points all work within and rely upon a Nicene structure.

II

If one can say that Wesleyan theology relies on a Nicene and trinitarian logic and that this logic establishes the theological grounding for Wesley and the Methodist movement as a whole, then how do these dynamics demonstrate themselves? In other words, where can one see evidences of this centrality? We will pursue two possibilities that have been elaborated by Methodist scholars.

The first possibility is the overall theme of grace. Students of Wesleyan theology know the importance of the theme of grace all too well for Wesley's theology. When Randy Maddox titled his monumental theological survey *Responsible Grace*, implicit in this gesture is the centrality of grace (and a particular understanding of it) within Wesley's theological account.[19] God's gracious activity is first and foremost, and we humans are in turn to respond accordingly to this grace with an awareness and capacity made possible by that very grace. God's work, then, makes us able to respond (response-able) so that through this derived momentum we move forward on the "way of salvation." For this reason, Wesley was prone to speak of grace in a myriad of ways, including that it is prevenient, justifying, and sanctifying. The idea, of course, is not that these qualifiers demarcate distinctly different "things" in character or design; rather, grace and its qualifiers represent God's availability and activity along each step of our spiritual journey. Wherever we find ourselves in our walk with God, God is already there, both able and willing to respond to us at our point of need. Again, those with a cursory understanding of Wesleyan theology are familiar with these features of the theological terrain.

What may be less obvious in Wesleyan theology is how to think of grace as a theme all its own—in other words, how to define it. Richard Heitzenrater notes that Wesley never really set about to define grace; rather, Wesley focuses more on what grace does.[20] In this, Wesley is not alone, for even his own Anglican background evinces this pattern: Not one of the Thirty-nine Articles is exclusively devoted to defining grace, although several make reference to it in their soteriological exposition. This lack of definition is tolerable to some degree, for it allows a level of flexibility that makes grace a useful theme for elaborating the complexity that is the Christian life. However, this lack of definition also has a downside, in that grace comes across repeatedly in an objectified way, particularly in close association with action verbs. As Heitzenrater notes, "Such descriptions seem to imply that grace is a 'thing' that can be distributed," yet he goes on to ask, "but what is 'it' that is being dispensed in such ways?"[21]

Defining and systematizing in theology are always dangerous activities because they have a way of over-theorizing what is ultimately a way of life; however, defining matters of faith can be an important activity if unhelpful, unravelling, and ultimately nefarious tendencies present themselves in its place. Grace should not be considered a "thing" that is simply applied, given, and effective at various points along the *via salutis*. But if it is not a "thing," how should one go about describing (and so in some sense, defining) it?

Heitzenrater does this work in his chapter along several fronts. First, he takes into account the Anglican heritage (including its reliance on Hooker) and Wesleyan themes to delineate four compatible ways of thinking of grace: "God's favorable inclination toward humankind," "God's love manifest in acts of salvific assistance for humankind," "God's continuing presence within humankind," and "the beneficial effects of God's relational activity for and with humankind."[22] Notice the centrality of "God" in the first three ways. Heitzenrater notes these characterizations speak more to the "nature" of grace, and the fourth speaks to effects or "results" of grace (although the latter also has a reference to God). These last depictions suggest broader terms by which to think of grace: its "nature," "work," and "results."[23] Since both the "work" and "results" of grace stem from its "nature," one can say a primacy exists on this last feature of grace. And of course, when one moves to speak of the nature of such theological (i.e., God-related) themes like "grace," "love," "mercy," and others, one is shifting into ontological-theological domains. Heitzenrater is aware of these theological dynamics so as to move to an overarching definition of grace that would generally fit the Wesleyan corpus: "the active presence or power of God."[24]

Now, one could easily characterize the Holy Spirit in the Christian life as "the active presence or power of God." Plenty of biblical passages would support this move. However, the warrants for such an identification run deeper than simply proof-texting. Grace as a theme in Wesley involves relationality, influence, presence, power, effects, and so on. Much of the same can be said of the Spirit as the Spirit emerges as both a triune person and a distinctive agent in the New Testament and early church tradition. Again, the resonances should not be taken for granted. For instance, these associations do not work well with depictions of the Father, and in some respects, they do not fit as neatly with those of the Son—especially if one highlights the incarnate Son in his pre-resurrection dimensions, that is, bound by space, time, embodiment, and so on. These associations, however, certainly resonate with depictions of the Spirit.

Where does this reasoning lead us? In the case of Wesley, it leads to this summarizing statement by Heitzenrater: "although the Spirit is not always named explicitly [when Wesley speaks of grace] . . . the third person of the Trinity is in many ways the most apt focus of Wesley's understanding of grace."[25] Such a claim has hermeneutical implications: When a person sees Wesley referencing grace, one is to have as a first reference the Holy Spirit, the One who is the "active presence and power of God." This interpretive strategy does not mean that we must cast the triune persons competitively, nor does it mean that we insert something theologically artificial in our reading of Wesley—not at all (or as Paul would say, *mē genoito*!). It would mean, rather, that interpreters should recognize the fullness of Wesley's Nicene, trinitarian, and pneumatological commitments at that crucial point of making sense of his theology of the Christian life, that is, our life with God. As Heitzenrater further states:

> Wesley's theology of salvation (soteriology) is trinitarian, synergistic, dynamic, and perhaps above all a thoroughgoing theology of grace . . . While his view is certainly christocentric in typically Protestant fashion, Wesley's position is also very trinitarian, as salvation is from God, in Christ, through the Holy Spirit. If anything, Wesley's theology has a stronger pneumatological emphasis than many other mainline Protestant positions.[26]

Naturally, if the Spirit is pivotal for a Wesleyan and Methodist understanding of grace, one can venture a second possibility for evidences of the centrality of a Nicene and trinitarian logic to the Wesleyan vision, this being the means of grace. Again, students of Wesleyan theology know and appreciate the theme of the means of grace. Students sometimes learn typologies Wesley himself used for the means of grace, and students also typically appreciate how this topic was at the center of Wesley's eventual break with the Moravians during the "Stillness Controversy."

Of course, the means of grace can be misconstrued along commodificationist lines when they are depicted as ways of establishing or guaranteeing the grace, presence, and favor of God. One way of resisting this tendency is to think of the means of grace as "active forms of waiting." The logic of this phrase helps legitimate and place an emphasis on the importance of human responsiveness, but this within a framework that stresses human agency only as it takes its lead from, and is directed back to, the God of Christian confession. Additionally, resistance to this tendency can take its cue from a basic question stemming from this phrase itself: In participating in the means of grace, one is waiting for what or for whom? And when this question is taken seriously, pneumatology becomes an essential way of substantiating the theme: When people participate in the means of grace, they are actively waiting on the presence and power of the Holy Spirit.

Wesley's sermon "Means of Grace" has always been an important expression of this logic, as are other places in his works overall. The Nicene Creed itself explicitly says little about the Spirit—those five Greek words we alluded to earlier. But those words, the creed itself, and its originating council all point to the active presence of the Holy Spirit to shape, edify, heal, save, and purify/sanctify the people of God. The creed hints at a Spirit-logic. The Spirit is holy because God is holy, and God's mission is to make God's people holy. But the creed also functions within a broader Spirit-logic, that the Spirit has been and continues to be active in the world to give God's people what they need to be proficient and equipped for every good work, to be renewed in the image of God, and to be saved and sanctified before God's impending reign. More pithily expressed, the Nicene Creed both expresses and is an expression of the Spirit's gracious posture to the world.

In this and in so many other ways, the Spirit proves to be our Helper, Companion, and Advocate—in other words, our divine, holy Paraclete.

Notes

1. *Works of John Wesley*, 14:169–70.
2. *Works of John Wesley*, 10:845.

Section 1

3. The Nicene Creed in its various versions and translations is here drawn from Heinrich Denzinger, *Compendium of Creeds, Definitions, and Declarations of Matters of Faith and Morals*, ed. Peter Hünermann, 43rd ed. (Ignatius Press, 2012).
4. Denzinger, *Compendium*, 51.
5. Denzinger, *Compendium*, 66.
6. For a narrative of the textual journey that constitutes the "personalization" of the Spirit, see Jörg Frey, "How did the Spirit become a Person?" in *The Holy Spirit, Inspiration, and the Cultures of Antiquity*, ed. Jörg Frey and John R. Levison (De Gruyter, 2014), 343–71.
7. Frey, "How did the Spirit become a Person?" 363.
8. Athanasius, *On the Incarnation*, trans. A Religious of C.S.M.V. (St. Vladimir's Seminary Press, 2002), 26 (§1).
9. Athanasius, *On the Incarnation*, 46 (§17).
10. Athanasius, *On the Incarnation*, 93 (§54).
11. Athanasius the Great and Didymus the Blind, *Works on the Spirit*, trans. Mark DelCogliano, Andrew Radde-Gallwitz, and Lewis Ayres (St. Vladimir's Seminar Press, 2011), 54 (1.1.3).
12. Athanasius, *Works on the Spirit*, 85 (1.20.4).
13. Athanasius, *Works on the Spirit*, 88 (1.23.1).
14. Athanasius, *Works on the Spirit*, 90 (1.24.4).
15. Athanasius, *Works on the Spirit*, 96 (1.27.3).
16. Basil the Great, *On the Holy Spirit*, trans. Stephen Hildebrand, Popular Patristics Series 42 (St. Vladimir's Seminary Press, 2001), 48 (§27).
17. Basil, *On the Holy Spirit*, 43 (§22). In this passage in particular and throughout the present chapter, gendered language for the Spirit has been avoided. Not only is this decision supported by the grammar conventions of Greek (in which *pneuma* is neuter), but it also works out of the understanding that gender constructions are not needed for believing in the Spirit's personhood.
18. Basil, *On the Holy Spirit*, 76 (§48).
19. See Randy L. Maddox, *Responsible Grace: John Wesley's Practical Theology* (Kingswood Books, 1994).
20. Richard P. Heitzenrater, "God with Us: Grace and the Spiritual Senses in John Wesley's Theology" in *Grace upon Grace: Essays in Honor of Thomas A. Langford*, ed. Robert K. Johnston, L. Gregory Jones, and Jonathan R. Wilson (Abingdon Press, 1999), 87–109, at 87.
21. Heitzenrater, "God with Us," 89.
22. Heitzenrater, "God with Us," 90.
23. Heitzenrater, "God with Us," 90.
24. Heitzenrater, "God with Us," 92.
25. Heitzenrater, "God with Us," 97.
26. Heitzenrater, "God with Us," 97.

Biblical Pressure and Trinitarian Hermeneutics

C. Kavin Rowe

> *In life and in death we belong to God... [W]e trust in one triune God, the Holy One of Israel whom alone we worship and serve.*[1]
>
> *The question of the relation of the persons of the Trinity to one another, and the question of the divinity and humanity in the person of Christ as a question of ontological relations could only arise when the Old Testament had lost its meaning for the early Christian church.*[2]
>
> *The church's struggle with the Trinity was not a battle against the Old Testament, but rather a battle for the Old Testament.*[3]

In the present day, the church would be hard pressed to find more significant questions than the question of the relation of the God of the Old Testament, the "Holy One of Israel," to the God of the New Testament and the corresponding question of the doctrine of the triune God and biblical interpretation. Put simply: Who is the God of the whole Bible? and How do we read the Bible in light of this God?

It is not my intention to relate the history of the development of the doctrine of the Trinity, nor do I intend to chart in detail the later exclusion of this doctrine from biblical exegesis with the rise of historical criticism in the modern period. Instead, this essay will seek to explore what I take to be the internal logic and connection of the two questions above and, on that basis, make a few constructive proposals about how and in what direction ecclesial biblical exegesis is to proceed in light of our present state of affairs. But first we need briefly to appreciate some dynamics of the problem that confronts us.

I

The juxtaposition of the statements the "one triune God" and "the Holy One of Israel whom alone we worship and serve" in the confession of the Presbyterian Church (USA) sets the problem in sharpest relief. The continuity posited here is that of identity between the God who revealed himself to Israel by name as YHWH and the later church doctrine of the Trinity. It is this point that is ultimately at issue in the antithetical statements of the Old Testament scholars Claus Westermann and Brevard Childs.

That Westermann does not stand alone in his denial of the necessary relation of the Old Testament to the later ecclesial formulations should be obvious to anyone familiar with the present state of critical exegesis. This view turns primarily on the understanding of history that arose underneath and alongside of the historical-critical method wherein history came to be seen as a strictly linear development. Church dogma with its watchwords (*homoousios*, *hypostaseis*, etc.) was clearly later than the biblical texts in the chronological sequence of events. Therefore to understand and interpret the Bible in light of the Trinity was of logical necessity to pervert the truth of historical development and damage beyond repair the historical sense of the text.[4] Further, the later credal formulations were deemed products of Greek philosophical thinking that lay entirely outside the biblical horizon, so that to affirm a positive connection between church dogma and the biblical testimony was to impose an alien conceptual coating on the texts and lapse into fanciful allegory under a form of thought fundamentally adverse to the living religion of the Bible. Under such assumptions, the worship and practice of the church, which confessed one God as Father, Son, and Holy Spirit, were divorced from a historical, biblical exegesis that resisted such understanding and interpretation as anachronistic distortions. When pressed, these assumptions disclose the propagation of a theology (!) that would destroy the connection between the reality to whom the Bible testifies and the reality whom the church worships. That is, at bottom, the question of trinitarian interpretation of Scripture turns out to be essentially bound up with the divine referent of Scripture.

Such a brief sketch hardly does justice to the complexity involved in the course of historical-critical interpretation, but it is needed nonetheless to feel at least somewhat the weight of the problem. The historical-critical approach is correct in a crucial and far-reaching aspect: the doctrine of the Trinity is later than the biblical texts and to suggest that the biblical writers were consciously thinking in later credal terms is in fact a major anachronistic mistake. Thus if we are to respect this basic insight into the movement of external history, we will have to pursue the relation of the triune God to the Bible in a different manner.

Within much recent Christian understanding of the doctrine of the Trinity is the important point that we know the immanent Trinity (God is triune in himself) on the basis of the economic Trinity (the activity of God in history);[5] thus it is that God's act is revelatory (and some would say constitutive) of his identity.[6] It follows that God's act and identity cannot be separated but are to be held together. The difficulty for our present topic is, of course, how to respect the economy of God in light of his immanent reality. The problem is acute in connection with trinitarian interpretation of the Old Testament. In other words, if we interpret the Old Testament in light of God as Trinity, is this not to let the immanent Trinity overrun the economic expression? Does not such a complete fusion actually dissolve any meaningful understanding of the course of biblical history and, resultantly, of God's divine economy?

Does it not matter for interpretation that God in his good pleasure and sovereign freedom did not choose to reveal himself fully as Trinity until "the fullness of time," and even then only in a latent sense in comparison with the later creedal affirmations? Thus the doctrine of the Trinity itself in seeking to preserve the economy of the Bible does justice to certain aspects of the insights of the historical critics regarding the movement of history and, hence, should caution us against an easy, immediate trinitarian interpretation of the biblical texts, or, indeed, any interpretation of the Bible that runs roughshod over the course of "external" history.

II

Keeping before us the historical and theological questions of the preceding section with respect to the divine referent of the biblical text, we can appreciate the far-reaching significance of Childs' claim with which we began this essay: "The church's struggle with the Trinity was not a battle *against* the Old Testament, but rather a battle *for* the Old Testament." Those who know well volume I/1 of Karl Barth's *Church Dogmatics* will recognize in Childs's assertion Barth's statement to the same effect: The doctrine of the Trinity (which proceeded from the reality of God in Jesus Christ and the implications thereof) was "not a battle against the Old Testament, but . . . was a battle for the Old Testament, i.e., for the one eternal covenant of God with men sealed in time, for acknowledgment of the perfect self-unveiling of God."[7] To that end, three questions will shape the remainder of this essay as one which hopes to contribute to the crucial task of theological exegesis: (1) Is there a necessary and essential connection between the Old Testament and trinitarian doctrine, or has this doctrine left the Old Testament behind? (2) What is the specific nature of the relation of the Old and New Testaments to the doctrine of the Trinity? (3) What do the answers to questions one and two mean for trinitarian interpretation of the Bible?

III

The question of the necessary connection between the Old Testament and the Trinity immediately involves the New Testament and its relation to the Old. That is to say, our question really concerns the point of connection between the Old and New Testaments. It is safe to say that the doctrine of the Trinity would never have arisen on the basis of the Old or the New Testament taken in isolation. The problematic emerges precisely because the writers of the New Testament presupposed the authority of the Old Testament and made explicit use of the theological grammar that undergirds the Old Testament's language about the one God.

Simply stated, the Lord and Redeemer of Israel was the one and only God of the world. He was not part of the world in any way but instead was totally other than the world. As its sole creator, the Lord God required absolute allegiance from his people and would not tolerate the worship of any other thing other than himself: the Lord is a jealous God. Thus there exists in the Old Testament a qualitative distinction between God the Creator and everything else, creation.[8] This distinction corresponds to the directives for Israel's worship: true worship was worship of the Creator and worship of any part of creation was idolatry (for Paul's view on this matter see especially Romans 1:18-25). Such "monotheistic" affirmations with respect to reality and to worship are seen in thetic form in the *Shema* of Deuteronomy:

> Hear O Israel: The LORD [YHWH/ *Kyrios*] our God, the LORD [YHWH/ *Kyrios*] is one [*heis*]. You shall love the LORD [YHWH/ *Kyrios*] your God with all your heart, and with all your soul, and with all your might. (Deuteronomy 6:4-5 LXX)

The negative implication of the positive command of Deuteronomy 6:5 is found a few verses later and follows from the utter singularity of the Lord God expressed in Deuteronomy 6:4:

> You shall fear the LORD your God; you shall worship/ serve *[latreuseis]* him; you shall cleave to him; and you shall swear by his name. Do not follow any other gods . . . because the LORD your God, who is present with you, is a jealous God. The anger of the LORD your God would be kindled against you and he would destroy you from the face of the earth. (Deuteronomy 6:13-15 LXX)[9]

The intertextual dependence upon the first two commandments of the Decalogue is clear:

> I am the LORD your God . . . you shall have no other gods before me. You shall not make for yourself idols in the likeness of anything, whether in the heavens above, or on the earth beneath, or in the waters under the earth. You shall not worship them or serve them

because I am the LORD your God, a jealous God who punishes the sins of the fathers upon the children to the third and fourth generation of those who hate me. (Deuteronomy 5:6-9 LXX)

A further and crucial point to be made is that the Creator of the world and Redeemer of Israel had a proper name and had revealed this name to Israel. In Hebrew the name is YHWH. How this name was conveyed in Greek is debated, but it is safe to say that the writers of the New Testament understood this name in Greek as *kyrios*. In almost every single instance where the New Testament cites the Greek Old Testament (LXX) as it corresponds to the Hebrew Old Testament YHWH, the New Testament authors wrote *kyrios* for the divine name.[10]

That the Creator of the world was the only true God, that this God demanded total and exclusive worship, and that this God's proper name YHWH was rendered in Greek in the New Testament by *kyrios* assume tremendous importance precisely at the point of the Old Testament's relation to trinitarian doctrine. Obviously in this essay there is not space for extensive commentary, but we must nevertheless note a few texts whose representative significance is of paramount importance.[11]

Exegesis

1. Joel 3:5 (English 2:32); Romans 10:13; Acts 2:21: Nearly half a century ago, C. H. Dodd argued on the basis of the use of Joel 3:1-5 in Romans 10 and Acts 2 that this Old Testament text was an important *testimonium* for the early church. There is debate about the *testimonia* hypothesis, but suffice it to say here that there is strong support for Dodd's point in that both Paul and Luke draw upon this Joel text and use it in a christologically transforming fashion. We will look briefly only at Romans 10:13.[12]

Joel 3:5 is essentially the same in the Masoretic text and the LXX, as well as in Romans 10:13. The key phrase reads: "All who call on the name of the Lord [*to onoma kyriou*] will be saved." Through the verbatim citation of Joel 3:5 in Rom 10:13, Paul's christologically explicit use of *to onoma kyriou* here issues in a dialectical identity of subject. The theological medium is that of overlap and resonance such that the conjunction of the text of Joel 3:5

with Romans 10:13 produces the conceptual space wherein the resonating identification between YHWH and Jesus occurs. The name which *is* the God of Israel alone *(kyrios)*[13] is now the name which *is* Jesus *(kyrios)*. The salvific name in its original context was YHWH; now the salvific name is Jesus. In Joel the Israelites would have called out "YHWH" to be saved, and now in Romans all would call out "Jesus." "The name of the LORD" = YHWH has become, by virtue of the intersection between Joel and Romans, "the name of the LORD" =Jesus.

2. John 20:28: Doubting Thomas's confession of Jesus as "My Lord and my God!" *(ho kyrios mou kai ho theos mou)* does not cite directly any particular Old Testament passage. This homologia, however, invokes language fundamental to Old Testament "God-talk," both in terms of identity and in terms of worship. Psalm 35:23-24 (LXX), to cite only one of many pertinent examples, reads[14]:

> Rise up, O LORD [kyrios], and give heed to my judgment!
> My God and my LORD *[ho theos mou kai ho kyrios mou]*,
> to my cause . . .
> O LORD my God *[kyrie ho theos mou]*!
> Do not let them exult over me!

Reading John 20:28 in conjunction with the divine grammar of the Old Testament brings forth a claim of ontological identity between YHWH, the God of Israel—*ho kyrios ho theos*—and the risen Jesus Christ—*ho kyrios ho theos*. Thomas's address does not, however, fuse or confuse the differentiation between Jesus and the Father. Rather, throughout the Gospel of John the evangelist maintains the differentiation of Father and Son. The logic of John 20:28 read with the *inclusio* of John 1:1 and in the context of the Gospel as a whole allows for a differentiation of YHWH into Father (the Sender, the One who is revealed, etc.) and Son (the One who was sent, the Revealer, etc.), while simultaneously maintaining that the Father and Jesus the Son are in fact "one" *(hen;* 10:30). They are together "the Lord God" *(ho kyrios ho theos)*, even as the Father is "greater" than the Son in the way that the sender is greater than the one who is sent.

Section 1

We must now pause briefly to take note of a crucial implication of Romans 10:13 and John 20:28.[15] Among both Protestant and Roman Catholic exegetes and systematic theologians[16] there is a common (and in many ways understandable) assumption that YHWH, the God of the Old Testament, is the Father *only*.[17] This assumption, however, will not stand under exegetical scrutiny. The New Testament texts never identify the Father as the Son or vice-versa, but they do give the divine name *kyrios* (= YHWH) to both the Father and the Son. The word *kyrios* (and less frequently *theos*) and the way in which it is used in the New Testament in Old Testament citations, hymns of worship, prayers, soteriological statements, etc. exerts a unitive pressure in two directions with respect to its referent, toward the Father and toward Jesus. This pressure moves us to the conclusion that YHWH is not the Father alone. There is a differentiation into Father and Son within the unity of the one Lord *(kyrios heis* in Deuteronomy 6:4).

3. *2 Corinthians 3:17a:* However isolated an occurrence it may be,[18] 2 Corinthians 3:17a is not a liability for trinitarian theology (as has often been thought) but instead is an asset. The simplest and most straightforward way to translate the Greek is as follows: "the Lord *(ho kyrios)* is the Spirit *(to pneuma)*." Contrary to first impressions, this statement is not an identification of the person of Jesus with that of the Spirit. It is, rather, a gloss on the *kyrios* of what is a fairly loose citation of Exodus 34:34 in the previous verse[19]:

And whenever Moses went in before the LORD *[kynou]* to speak to him, he removed the veil until he went out (Exodus 34:34 [LXX]).

But whenever he turns to the Lord *[kynon]*, the veil is removed (2 Corinthians 3:16).

The Lord *[ho kyrios]* is the Spirit *[to pneuma]* (2 Corinthians 3:17a).

Paul's Spirit-identifying gloss on *kyrios* subsumes the Spirit under the divine name *kyrios* which is used both of the Father and of Jesus the Son. Richard Hays rightly notes the helpful translation of the New English Bible: "However, as Scripture says of Moses, 'whenever he turns to the Lord the veil is removed.' Now the Lord of whom this passage [Exodus 34:34] speaks is the Spirit."[20] Here, then, the Spirit is not Jesus, nor is Jesus the Spirit, but both are "the Lord" *(ho kyrios)*. The very next phrase confirms such a differentiation within the identity of the Lord: "and where the Spirit of the Lord *(to pneuma kyriou*)—freedom!" (2 Corinthians 3:17b). Read canonically, then, the full unity of God as expressed through his name *kyrios* is that of Father, Son, and Spirit: the *kyrios heis* (one Lord) of Deut 6:4 is in the New Testament differentiated into *kyrios patēr* (Father), *kyrios iēsous* (Son), and *kyrios pneuma* (Spirit). Thus the oneness and unity of God is not impaired but is dynamically upheld through the use of his name *kyrios* for the Father, Son, and Spirit, the one Lord God.[21]

4. *Galatians 4:4-6:* In Galatians 4:1-7 Paul expands his earlier point with regard to Abraham (3:23-29) and assures the Galatian believers of their status as children and heirs of God. The principal appeal of the argument is to the presence of the Spirit. Within this larger unit with its emphasis upon the Spirit, vv. 4-6 display Paul's view of the economy of God *in nuce*. It should be mentioned that the divine economy, by definition, entails God's relation to his creation ("redeem those under the law," etc.), but for our present topic we need only to look at the logic and implications of Paul's language about God:

> But when the fullness of time came:
> God sent forth *(exapesteilen)*
> his Son,
> born of a woman,
> born under the law . . .
> God sent forth *(exapesteilen)*
> the Spirit of his Son . . .
> crying "Abba Father."

This expression of the divine economy reveals a fundamentally trinitarian pattern. God the Father (*theos* is always the Father in Galatians) exists in relation to his Son as well as in relation to the Spirit of his Son. The Spirit of the Father's Son, in turn, testifies (in the hearts of believers) to the Father of the Son. This relationship between the Father, his Son, and the Spirit of the Father's Son is mutually constitutive, which is to say that the economy of the one God, the creator of the world, is here spoken of in a way in which each of the three "persons" are immediately interrelated: the Father is the Father of his Son; the Son is, obviously, the Son of his Father; and the Spirit is the Spirit of the Son of the Father. This relationship has two further dimensions.

First, the relationship between the Father, Son, and Spirit is eternal.[22] Paul's emphasis in "born of a woman," following from the apocalyptic phrase "when the fullness of time came" (4:4), may rest upon the birth of Jesus or upon his entire life, death, and resurrection or upon its redeeming effects, or upon all three, inseparable as they are. Regardless, there can be no question that the "fullness of time" read in conjunction with "born of a woman" *assumes* a relationship of prior existence between the Father, Son, and Spirit and a doctrine of incarnation, however nascent. Second, the relationship implies some type of movement in the life of God himself. This movement can be characterized, at least in some sense, as outward in nature, a sending out *(ex-apostellō)*, and is in fact the inseparable events of the incarnation and giving of the Holy Spirit. Taking these two points together allows and even requires us to affirm an intrinsic incarnationality within the life of the eternal God realized, as it were, in the fullness of time. The incarnation and the gift of the Holy Spirit make a difference for our understanding of the trinity of God.

5. *Romans 8:9-11:* Though the particular points of emphasis are somewhat different, Romans 8:9-17 contains similar affirmations to those of Galatians 4:1-7 regarding the believers' status as children of God (cf. esp. 8:15-17). So, too, there is a marked focus upon the Spirit. For our purposes we will take note of the strictly theological implications of Paul's language about the Spirit. The crucial point is the interchangeability between "of Christ" and "of God" (the Father) with reference to the Spirit. Hence, "the Spirit" in verse 9a is the "Spirit of God" *(pneuma theou)* in v. 9b, and the "Spirit of Christ" *(pneuma Christou)* in v. 9c. "Christ in you" in v. 10, as Gordon Fee rightly observes, is not an identification of Christ and the Spirit but rather is "simply Pauline shorthand for 'the Spirit of Christ in you'."[23] In v. 11 Paul then switches back to speaking about "the Spirit [who] is life" (v. 10) as "the Spirit of the One who raised Jesus from the dead," that is, the Spirit of God the Father:

The Spirit (8:9a):
  Spirit of God the Father (8:9b)
    Spirit of Christ (8:9c)
      [Spirit of] Christ (8:10)
  Spirit of God the Father (8:11)

This linguistic flexibility carries tremendous significance when we remember that for Paul the Spirit of whom he speaks is none other than the Spirit of the God of Israel. That is to say, Paul's reflexive interchanges call forth an understanding of the one Spirit of the creator God that exhibits the awareness of the Spirit of this God precisely as the Spirit of Christ, experienced as the presence of God/ Christ/ God in Christ, etc. The connection, then, is of an inseparable nature such that the Spirit of the God of the Old Testament is now indissolubly bound up with the human figure of the risen Jesus Christ—the Spirit of Christ. It is such inseparability that allows for the reflexive interchange present here in Paul's pneumatological grammar.

Implications

The theological logic of the texts above forces us to reject the widespread position represented by Westermann at its general level and to conclude that there is a necessary and essential connection between the Old Testament and, at least, economic trinitarian doctrine. This connection is mediated most explicitly through the New Testament's pre-supposition and use of the Old Testament, that is, at the point of the unity of the Testaments in their testimony to the self-same God in the one divine economy.

The overlapping use of the divine name *kyrios* for the God of Israel and for the human person Jesus Christ within the citations and theological grammar of the Old Testament presses for an identity of subject matter, as does the use of *kyrios* for the Spirit in 2 Corinthians 3:17a (cf. the third article of the Creed of Constantinople). Further, the inseparability of the Spirit's identity as the Spirit "of God" (the Father) and the Spirit "of Christ" (the Son) requires an understanding of the dynamism of the one God of the Old Testament as essentially and formally related to the Spirit of God as the Spirit of the risen Jesus. Thus at the point of the unity of the Testaments there is a foundational trinitarian syntax that informs the pattern of language about the identity of the one Lord God of the Old Testament as the Father, the Son, and the Spirit revealed in the fullness of time in the single divine economy.

The New Testament and early church made claims about the human person Jesus of Nazareth and about the Spirit (see above texts) that required *specification in terms of ontology*. It would not do simply to state the claims (YHWH is somehow both Father and Jesus Christ; the Spirit is somehow inseparably the Spirit of God the Father and of the human person Jesus Christ; there is a trinitarian pattern of salvation, etc.). The relation of God the Father, Jesus Christ, and the Spirit as well as the relation of Jesus's divinity and humanity had to be specified in terms consistent with the most fundamental theological thrust of the Old Testament, that of the unity and singularity of the one Creator God and the directives for exclusive worship that were inextricably bound with this God's identity. That YHWH *(kyrios)* is both God the Father and Jesus Christ leads of necessity to the question of "essence," or "being," most acutely at the point of the Christian worship of Jesus Christ. If the Old Testament counts for anything, we cannot worship a mere human (one who is created) instead of, in conjunction with, or over against the one God of the Old Testament. Such worship would mean rank and obvious idolatry, the total denial and destruction of Old Testament monotheism. The early church had to find a way to account for its claims and practice, and such an accounting was necessary along ontological lines because of the continuing authority of the Old Testament. Athanasius saw to the heart of the matter most clearly in terms of the person of Jesus Christ, and Basil the Great in terms of the Holy Spirit—Jesus Christ and the Spirit must be of the same "essence" as God the Father—then and only then do the claims of the New Testament make any sense within the framework of an authoritative Old Testament theology.[24] Thus it can be seen that instead of breaking with the Old Testament, the questions of the relation of the persons of the Trinity to one another and of the divinity and humanity of Christ could only properly emerge by taking the Old Testament with utmost seriousness in relating the person of Christ and the role of the Spirit to its central theological thrust regarding the identity of the one God. To put it into dogmatic terms: we cannot simply confess an economic Trinity but must also move to specification with respect to the immanent Trinity if the Old Testament is to retain its authoritative witness. Conversely, the Old Testament's affirmations about God and the worship of God force us to make statements about divine ontology in light of the claims of the New Testament.

We may go one step further yet and assert that the ontological judgments of the early ecumenical Creeds were the only satisfying and indeed logical outcome of the claims of the New Testament read together with the Old. That is to say, for a Christian faith that upholds the unity of the Bible and the continuing authority of the Old Testament, the one God is Trinity in himself, affirmed on the basis of his economic expression. There is no other way to justify the claims about and worship of the fully human Jesus Christ within an Old Testament framework. It is likewise with the Spirit: given the authority of the Old Testament, to recognize the "personhood" of the Spirit in coordination with the claims of the New Testament regarding the Spirit's inseparability from Jesus Christ in worship and in presence is to affirm that the Spirit, too, is of the "same essence" as the Father and the Son. For the church to turn its back upon the Creeds is to turn its back upon the Old Testament. So, too, to turn its back upon the Old Testament is to loosen entirely the restraints that operate in the creedal formulations of the trinitarian nature of the one Lord God. To speak about the one Lord God of the Old Testament as Father, Son, and Spirit requires that this one God is in fact triune and, conversely, that the Father, the Son, and the Spirit are of one and the same essence with respect to their reality, which, in turn, is the ground of worship.

IV

A central point in the argument above has to do with the word "pressure." The pressure language itself is Childs's and, in my view, is one of the most important contributions of his *Biblical Theology* taken as a whole. The biblical text is not inert but instead exerts a pressure ("coercion") upon its interpreters and asserts itself within theological reflection and discourse such that there is (or can be) a profound continuity, grounded in the subject matter itself, between the biblical text and traditional Christian exegesis and theological formulation.[25] Thus, in terms of this essay, the two-testament canon read as one book pressures its interpreters to make ontological judgments about the trinitarian nature of the one God *ad intra* on the basis of its narration of the act and identity of the biblical God *ad extra*.[26]

While the preceding section sought to argue for a substantive and essential connection between the Old Testament and, by necessity, the whole of the Christian Bible with later trinitarian doctrine, this continuity is not sufficiently understood if we rest content with its demonstration. What exactly is continuous? That is, what specifically is the nature of the relation of the Old and New Testaments to the doctrine of the Trinity? In order to get at these questions, our discussion must assume the posture of explicit theological confession and reflection wherein the biblical text is understood as God's Word to us in which God himself is present.

Within the purview of such a posture the nature of the pressure of the biblical text can be coordinated with the divine will. As Ernst Käsemann wrote in his classic article on the righteousness of God: "God's power . . . is not silent but bound up with the Word. It speaks . . . so that we experience the pressure of its will, and, by means of the Gospel, sets us in the posture . . . 'before the face of Christ.'"[27] Thus the textual pressure we perceive can be theologically formulated in terms of the actuating influence of the divine will through the divine Word. It is in fact the divine will mediated through God's own Word that compels us to speak in trinitarian terms about God. We may even say that it is the presence of God himself in his Word that wills and moves us to speak in this way about God. "What God speaks . . . is known and true in and through the fact that He Himself says it, that He is present in person in and with what is said by Him."[28] So, finally, trinitarian language about God on the basis of the pressure of the biblical text is, perhaps mysteriously, God's own testimony to himself as Trinity.[29] Thus the continuity is rooted in God himself, which is to say that the economic expression of God's triunity proceeds from the prior reality of his immanent triunity.

V

In light of the previous two sections of the essay it may seem that the implications for trinitarian interpretation of the Bible are rather obvious. They are not. At this point I can only add my voice to the summons of Childs and others[30] and affirm that this entire area needs more and deeper reflection, especially from the biblical and exegetical wing of the church. What follows below is an attempt to draw together the implications from the above arguments and thereby indicate a particular path of fruitful theological exegesis.

Perhaps the reader will have realized by now that the central issue in the topic of the Trinity and the Bible requires us to think in two different directions. The question of whether or not there exists a necessary and essential relation between the Old and New Testaments and trinitarian doctrine focuses our attention in the direction that moves from the Bible to the later trinitarian formulations. The question of whether or not we can interpret the Bible in light of the later dogma focuses our attention in the reverse direction that moves from the trinitarian formulations to the Bible. A positive answer to the first question, such as we have given in this essay,[31] does not necessitate a sweeping and unconditional "yes" to the second question. The matter is much more complex.

How, then, can we justify trinitarian interpretation of the Bible? In my judgment, the crucial points are tied to the nature of the pressure of the biblical text and the corresponding question of the divine referent of the words of Scripture. On the basis of the exegesis of the biblical texts above, I have argued that Scripture exerts a pressure upon its interpreters to understand the God of the entire Bible as the Trinity and that this pressure is felt most acutely at the point of the intersection of the Old and New Testaments. This pressure in every instance relates to the reality of God, which is to say that the claims move from the original sense to the level of ontology. The New Testament in all its manifold diversity, while affirming its eschatological newness, so to speak, also claims that in the person of Jesus Christ there is none other than the God of the Old Testament, the Creator of the world. Such continuity can be expressed in terms of promise and fulfillment as it relates to the historical sense (cf. Childs) and movement of the testaments from Old to New, but the claims of the New Testament in light of the Old extend to that of God's reality and argue for the other side of a dialectic wherein theology discloses the nature of internal history (cf. the implications of John 1:1ff. as a commentary on Genesis 1:1ff) so that the interpreter must move also from New to Old. It is the continuity of God's reality that not only justifies but necessitates trinitarian interpretation of the Bible such that the reality to whom the words "YHWH," "Elohim," "Kyrios," "Theos," etc. point is in fact the triune God. Our question, that is, has to do with the *God outside of the text* to whom these words direct us. Thus the historical movement of the Old to New Testaments captured in the terms promise and fulfillment corresponds to the reverse movement entailed in trinitarian interpretation, both of which find their ground in the claim of the incarnation regarding the ontological reality of the self-same eternal God as he "became" flesh in the person of the first century Jew Jesus of Nazareth.

That the pressure of the Bible operates at an ontological level within history corresponds to the nature of this pressure as formulated above in terms of the pressure of the divine will through God's presence in his Word. To interpret the Bible in light of the doctrine of the Trinity does not, therefore, distort its basic content but penetrates to its core with respect to the reality of the divine identity, the living God outside of the text known truly by Israel and fully in Jesus Christ. Such interpretative liberty does not entail a dismissal of the original sense of the text but instead seeks to illuminate the full breadth of ontological reality about which the biblical text, Old and New Testament together, speaks in its entirety. In this way trinitarian interpretation of Scripture expands the original sense to include questions of ontology in view of the divine referent of the words of Scripture and addresses such questions according to Scripture's own testimonial pressure, ultimately understood as the *viva vox evangelii:* Thus, to read the Bible in light of later trinitarian dogma is to read the Bible in light of the reality of God himself as he has pressured us through his Word, that is, his speaking, to speak about him.

Notes

1. "The Brief Statement of Faith-Presbyterian Church (USA)" in *The Constitution of the Presbyterian Church (USA) Part 1: The Book of Confessions* (The Office of the General Assembly, 1994), 275.
2. Claus Westermann, "Das Alte Testament und die Theologie," in *Theologue—was ist das?* ed. Georg Picht and Enno Rudolph (Kreuz Verlag, 1977), 49–66: "Die Frage nach dem Verhältnis der Personen der Trinität zueinander und die Frage nach Gottheit und Menschheit in der Person Christi als Frage nach Seinsverhältnissen konnte erst aufkommen, als das Alte Testament seine Bedeutung für die frühchristliche Kirche verloren hatte" (p. 50).
3. Brevard Childs, *Biblical Theology of the Old and New Testaments: Theological Reflection on the Christion Bible* (Fortress, 1992), 376 (emphasis his).
4. On the matter of the "historical" and "literal" sense of Scripture, see especially Brevard Childs, "The Sensus Literalis of Scripture: An Ancient and Modern Problem," in *Beitrage zur Alttestamentlichen Theologie,* FS for Walther Zimmerli, ed. Herbert Donner et al. (Vandenhoeck & Ruprecht, 1977), 80–93, and the exchange between James Barr and

Childs on the basis of Childs's article: James Barr, "The Literal, the Allegorical, and Modern Biblical Scholarship," *JSOT* 44 (1989): 3–17; Childs, "Critical Reflections on James Barr's Understanding of the Literal and Allegorical," *JSOT* 46 (1990): 3–9; and Barr, "Wilhelm Vischer and Allegory," in *Understanding the Poets and Prophets: Essays in Honour of George Wishart Anderson*, ed. A. Graeme Auld (JSOT Press, 1993), 38–60.

5   Of course, there are those who would reject the immanent and economic distinction, but there is not room here to discuss the issue systematically. The rest of the essay will indicate some of the lines that could be taken. Colin Gunton ("The God of Jesus Christ," *Theology Today* 54 [1997]: 325–34, esp. 328–30) helpfully condenses what is at stake in the debate without lapsing into substanceless generalities. For sophisticated and nuanced arguments against our ability to speak meaningfully about God in himself apart from his creation see Friedrich Mildenberger (*Biblische Dogmatik: Eine Biblische Theologie in dogmatischer Perspektive*, 3 vols [Kohlhammer, 1991–1993], esp. §§22, 23, 24), who coordinates his dogmatic position with profound exegesis of the biblical texts.

6   See the concise survey by Christoph Schwobel, "The Renaissance of Trinitarian Theology: Reasons, Problems and Tasks," in *Trinitarian Theology Today*, ed. Christoph Schwobel (T&T Clark, 1995), 1–30.

7   Karl Barth, *Church Dogmatics* I/1 (T&T Clark, 1936), 319.

8   Such a qualitative distinction in no way implies the denial of God's immanence or relation to his creation, in particular as expressed through Wisdom, the *Shekinah*, etc. For a helpful introduction see esp. Richard Bauckham, *God Crucified: Monotheism and Christology in the New Testament* (Eerdmans, 1998).

9   In the temptation scene in Matthew and Luke, Jesus cites the form of Deut 6:13 found in MS A (codex Alexandrinus), but the order of dependence here is unclear. The Gospels read: "You shall worship *[proskynēseis]* the Lord your God and him only *[mono]* you shall serve *[latreuseis]*."

10 *Theos* is very infrequent.

11 Three points are in order: (a) I make no claim to comprehensive coverage of important texts—such texts are far too numerous (1 Cor 8:4-6; 12:4-6; Phil 2:5-11; Eph 2:18-22; John 1:1; Matt 28:19; Luke 1–2, etc.). (b) The selection of texts was made in accordance with their representative significance and, as such, is indicative of much larger patterns within the thought of the writers of the New Testament. (c) Trinitarian dogma is obviously not directly in the Bible. No one thinks that it is. The dogma rests, rather, on a reading of Scripture as a whole such that representative text selection is not at all to be identified with a "proof-texting" approach that seeks to extract phrases from their context and use them polemically to support an already existing belief.

12 For an extended exegetical treatment of Rom 10:13 and its implications for later theology, see C. Kavin Rowe, "Romans 10:13: What is the Name of the Lord?" *HBT* 22 (2000): 135–73.

13 See Gerhard von Rad for a theologically penetrating discussion of the revelation and significance of God's name in the Old Testament: *Old Testament Theology*, vol. 1 (Harper and Row, 1962), 179–87.

Section 1

14. See, e.g., Ps 29:3 [LXX]; 85:15 [LXX]; 87:2 [LXX]; 2 Kgdms 7:28; 3 Kgdms 18:39; Jer 38:18 [LXX]; Zech 13:9. So, too, in Rev 4:11 the worshipers address God as "Lord our God" *(ho kyrios kai ho theos hemōn)*.
15. Cf., e.g., Luke 3:4-6; Acts 2:25-28, etc.
16. On the Protestant side see, e.g., Paul Meyer's stimulating essay, "'The Father': The Presentation of God in the Fourth Gospel," in *Exploring the Gospel of John: In Honor of D. Moody Smith*, ed. R. Alan Culpepper and C. Clifton Black (Westminster John Knox, 1996), 255-73, esp. p. 256, and Wolfhart Pannenberg, who gives this impression in chapter five of his *Systematic Theology*, vol. 1 (Eerdmans, 1998). On the Roman Catholic side see esp. Karl Rahner 's classic, *The Trinity* (Crossroad, 1997) and Joseph Fitzmyer's technical and learned article, "The Semitic Background of the New Testament *Kyrios*-Title," in *The Semitic Background to the New Testament* (Eerdmans, 1997), 115-42, esp. p. 130 and nn. 36 and 90.
17. For still excellent theological exegesis to the contrary, see John Calvin, *Institutes of the Christian Religion* 1.13.9-20, 24-29. Contrast also Vladimir Lossky, *The Mystical Theology of the Eastern Church* (St. Vladimir's Seminary Press, 1976), 64: "If one speaks of God it is always, for the Eastern Church, in the concrete: 'The God of Abraham, of Isaac and of Jacob; the God of Jesus Christ.' It is always the Trinity: Father, Son, and Holy Ghost."
18. See, however, Richard B. Hays (*Echoes of Scripture in the Letters of Paul* ([Yale University Press, 1989], 125-53), who shows the basic importance of this entire unit (2 Cor 3:1-4:6) for Pauline hermeneutics.
19. See Hays, *Echoes*, 143ff. for an extended treatment.
20. Hays, *Echoes*, 143
21. Cf. the interesting essay of R. Kendall Soulen, "YHWH the Triune God," *Modern Theology* 15 (1999): 25-54.
22. So, rightly, Hays, *The Letter to the Galatians*, NIB 9 (Abingdon, 2000), 283 in light of Phil 2:5-11,1 Cor 8:4-6, etc. Contra James D. G. Dunn, *Christology in the Making: A New Testament Inquiry into the Origins of the Doctrine of the Incarnation*, 2nd ed. (Eerdmans, 1996), 38-44. For a succinct discussion, see Richard N. Longenecker, *Galatians*, WBC 41 (Word Books, 1990), 166-75.
23. Gordon D. Fee, *God's Empowering Presence: The Holy Spirit in the Letters of Paul* (Hendrickson, 1994), 548. See also Fee's article "Christology and Pneumatology in Romans 8:9-11—and Elsewhere: Some Reflections on Paul as a Trinitarian," in *Jesus of Nazareth: Lord and Christ: Essays on the Historical Jesus and New Testament Christology*, ed. Joel B. Green and Max Turner (Eerdmans, 1994), 312-31.
24. See, e.g., Athanasius's *Four Discourses Against the Arians*, and Basil's *On the Holy Spirit*. Geoffrey Wainwright sets forth the basic systematic issues with clarity and brevity: "The Holy Spirit," in *The Cambridge Companion to Christian Doctrine*, ed. Colin Gunton (Cambridge University Press, 1997), 273-96.
25. The pressure of the biblical text can also break apart existing systematic structures, but that is a subject for another essay. See, Childs, "Toward Recovering Theological Exegesis," PRO ECCLESIA 6 (1997): 16-26, esp. p. 17.

26 The systematic implications are evident at this point: God is as he has revealed himself to be; there is no god lying behind or beyond the God we know in Jesus Christ as attested in Scripture, etc.
27 Ernst Käsemann, "'The Righteousness of God' in Paul," in *New Testament Questions of Today* (Fortress, 1979), 168–82, esp. 176–77.
28 Barth, *Church Dogmatics III*, 137.
29 Cf. Eberhard Jüngel discussing Barth's exposition of the doctrine of the Trinity along the lines of revelation: "[t]he doctrine of the Trinity is the interpretation of God's self-interpretation;" *The Doctrine of the Trinity: God's Being Is in Becoming* (Eerdmans, 1976), 15.
30 See, e.g., the excellent article of David S. Yeago, "The New Testament and Nicene Dogma: A Contribution to the Recovery of Theological Exegesis," PRO ECCLESIA 3 (1994): 152–64.
31 I have sought to explore exegetically this positive connection in relation to Luke's Gospel in "Luke and Trinity: An Essay in Ecclesial Biblical Theology," *Scottish Journal of Theology* 56 (2003): 1–26.

Creation and Monotheism

Janet Martin Soskice

In common understanding, monotheism is the belief that there is only one God, that the ancient Israelites were monotheists, and that Christianity inherited its monotheism from its Jewish roots. However, the matter is not quite so seamless and clear. What kind of monotheism is Christian monotheism? What kind of "oneness" is at play when one speaks of belief in "one" God? In the Abrahamic faiths, monotheism is not the belief that, as it happens, there is only one god instead of six or seven, but rather that there *could be* only one god. It is here that the doctrine of creation is important. It is no slight thing that the Nicene Creed begins with the confession of belief in one God, the Father, creator of all things visible and invisible, and in one Lord Jesus Christ, begotten, not made. Creation is to the fore in this confession of Christian monotheism, and especially the teaching of *creatio ex nihilo*.

The doctrine of *creatio ex nihilo* arises from the belief in a free creator—that is, a God who creates "all that is," including space and time, from nothing (not even a vacuum) and does so freely and from no compulsion. It is the only teaching that Moses Maimonides (1138–1204 CE) thought Judaism, Christianity, and Islam shared. Within Christianity, it is an emergent teaching, rather like the doctrine of the Trinity, resulting from meditation on other core beliefs about the nature of God and God's relation to the created order. To clarify, while those who composed the book of Genesis and the Psalms did not, one assumes, have an explicit metaphysic of creation in mind, inevitably it would be asked, "If God made truly everything, would that include not only planets and angels but also space and time?" Did God, that is, create truly everything and do so without compulsion, as the book of Genesis suggests?

While having antecedents in Second Temple Judaism, *creatio ex nihilo* becomes foundational to Christian orthodoxy by the fourth century CE. It is not surprising that the teaching should become important in the years when the Christian teaching about Christ and the Trinity was being hammered out, for a key to these debates is the Christian claim to worship only one God, a point to which this chapter will return.

The term *monotheism* was first used in the seventeenth century by the Cambridge Platonist Henry Moore as part of an Enlightenment project to classify religions. Monotheism is in this way contrasted with polytheism and, less frequently, with henotheism—the allegiance to one god out of a possible range of others.[1] The Psalms, some of which are among the earliest writings of the Hebrew Bible, seem at times to attest to a henotheism where YHWH, Israel's God, is the greatest among the gods. While it is natural to read monotheistic understandings into the creation narratives of the book of Genesis, these could be read as henotheistic. Whatever terms one chooses, Jews, Christians, and Muslims reject henotheism and confess to belief in one God, the sole creator. Arabic indeed has a separate word to indicate the 'One' that is Allah from the 'one' in a cardinal series.

Various sophisticated philosophical schemes in antiquity were monotheistic. Aristotle (and arguably Plato) were both philosophical monotheists, but neither had a creator God. Plato's demiurge molds a pre-existent matter. Aristotle's God (or perhaps one should say 'god') is the cause of motion but not Being Itself. Aristotle's god is like the functioning DNA of the universe. In Aristotle's scheme, one could not have the world without god, but neither could one have god without the world. The two imply one another and are both, in his terms, eternal. Aristotle's god has no knowledge of particulars; it is not provident; it is not capable of self-disclosure—each being *sine qua non* for the Christian God. Aristotle's monotheism presumes the validity and self-positing of the existent order, with no possibility of divine in-breaking and no need to ask questions about ultimate origin. Neither Aristotle's scheme nor Plato's allowed for what one would call a personal God, which is a foundational conviction of Jews and Christians who pray the Psalms and address God in prayer.

Aristotle considered the notion of *creatio ex nihilo* to be absurd, as do many secular astrophysicists today, on the grounds that if ever there was entirely nothing, not even space and time, then there would be nothing now. Not so the religions of radical monotheism that were made possible by the revolution in classical metaphysics effected by *creatio ex nihilo*.[2] This teaching holds not only that God freely makes all things but that God is intimately present to all the created order at all times. God truly *is*. All creatures have their existence, at every moment, as gift. The God of Augustine's *Confessions*, the God who can be with him at all times and in all places, is the God who creates "all that is" and is thus intimately present to all time and all space.[3]

Turning to the emergence of the Christian doctrine of creation, it is important to see that the biblical texts to which early Christians looked were not simply the early chapters of Genesis but also the abundant mention of God as *creator* in the Psalms and the book of Isaiah. These link God's faithfulness and power to create and to save:

> By the word of the LORD the heavens were made
> > and all their host by the breath of his mouth.
> He gathered the waters of the sea as in a bottle;
> > he put the deeps in storehouses.
> Let all the earth fear the LORD;
> > let all the inhabitants of the world stand in awe of him,
> for he spoke, and it came to be;
> > he commanded, and it stood firm. (Psalm 33:6-9 NRSVue)
>
> Our help is in the name of the LORD,
> > who made heaven and earth. (Psalm 124:8 NRSVue)
>
> Listen to me, O Jacob,
> > and Israel, whom I called:
> I am he; I am the first,

> and I am the last.
> My hand laid the foundation of the earth,
> and my right hand spread out the heavens;
> when I summon them,
> they stand at attention. (Isaiah 48:12-13 NRSVue)

Second Temple Judaism, the period which saw the emergence of Christianity, was a time of foreign occupation and distress. For a people who debated the coming of the messiah and the faithfulness of God, the Psalms and Isaiah were works of solace. It is perhaps not surprising that one finds in a text of this period what seems to be an anticipation of *creatio ex nihilo*, and one which suggestively links this to the resurrection of the dead. In 2 Maccabees, a mother who has seen six of her sons martyred for refusing to eat pork encourages the youngest in this way:

> I do not know how you came into being in my womb. It was not
> I who gave you life and breath nor I who set in order the elements
> within each of you. Therefore the Creator of the world, who shaped
> the beginning of humankind and devised the origin of all things,
> in his mercy gives life and breath back to you again, since you now
> forget yourselves for the sake of his laws.
>
> (2 Maccabees 7:22-23 NRSVue)

What then of Jesus and of Christian monotheism? The recognition that Second Temple Judaism saw a flowering of intermediary figures, angels, and exalted humans has prompted considerable scholarly debate as to whether the Judaism of the period was strictly monotheistic, a debate that bleeds into that concerning the status of Jesus in the New Testament.[4] If the Judaism of the period knew various exalted figures and thus was not strictly monotheistic, then might the Jesus of the New Testament be one such exalted figure or semi-divine agent?

William Horbury suggests a contrast, in the Judaism of the Herodian age, between a "rigorous" and "exclusive" monotheism that denies other supernatural beings besides God and an "inclusive" monotheism where the supreme deity is in association with other spirits and powers.[5] But, as Richard

Creation and Monotheism

Bauckham points out, Jewish, Christian, and Islamic faiths have never had a problem with angels and such spiritual beings. What is at issue, and what affects monotheism, is whether these angels, powers, and demons were to be considered creatures and not agents of creation.[6]

Bauckham encourages a referencing of the language of "divine identity" rather than of "monotheism" when speaking of the Judaism of the Second Temple. He then identifies "key features of the one God" which distinguish this God from any angels or other exalted figures. Among those Bauckham lists are that:

- God is the sole creator, whereas all other beings are created by him.
- God is the sovereign ruler of all, subject to none, whereas all other beings are subject to his rule . . .
- Frequently God is said to be the only eternal one, "the first and the last" in the classic monotheistic assertions of Deutero–Isaiah (Isaiah 41:1; 42:8; 48:11), the one who precedes all things as their creator and will achieve his rule over all things for ever . . .
- God has a personal name, the tetragrammaton (YHWH), which names his unique identity.
- God alone may be worshipped, and God should be worshipped because worship, in the Jewish understanding, is precisely recognition of the unique divine identity.[7]

But if only the one God can be worshiped, and only God can create, then who is Christ? This question agitated the early church, with various options canvased. Adoptionists presented Christ as a normal human elevated to divinity, which would seem to exclude a role in creation. Forms of subordinationism canvassed Jesus as divine, but a lesser god. This would, of course, have compromised any claim Christianity made that Christians worshipped only one God, as would Gnostic suggestions that an additional, lesser God created the material order.

It might seem that the doctrine of creation would be a final blow to those who argue for the divinity of Christ and trinitarian monotheism, but the opposite is the case. With *creatio ex nihilo* in place, there is no room for a binary of spiritual and material, with God, the soul, and angelic beings on one side and animals, plants, and trees on the other. The only distinction is between God and creation: God the creator and everything else—earthworms, angels, meteorites, sun, and moon, all things visible and invisible. The question then becomes, and it was a pressing question in the first Christian centuries, what to do with Christ? If Christ is not to be one of the creatures, albeit an exalted one, then Christ must be one with the creator. If prayer to Jesus was not to be "idol worshipping" in a Jewish context, then Jesus must be one with God, the sole creator.[8]

The early Christian theologians readily identified Jesus with the "I AM" who spoke to Moses from the burning bush (Exodus 3:15) and with the "first and the last" (Alpha and Omega) of Deutero–Isaiah, and in doing so with the one God, the sole creator. They did so with biblical precedents. The Prologue of John's Gospel, with its strong echoes of the creation narratives of Genesis, identifies the Word Incarnate with the Word through whom all things came into being. Jesus himself makes the identification in the various "I am" sayings of John's Gospel: "before Abraham was, I am," says Jesus in John 8:58 (NRSVue), a self-identification with the one God, the creator and redeemer. On the lips of the Johannine Jesus, the "I am" takes readers back to Exodus 3, but also to the "I am" sayings of Deutero–Isaiah where, in a striking sequence of divine self-designations, YHWH declares that he *alone* is God and creator:

> For thus says the LORD,
> who created the heavens
>   (he is God!),
> who formed the earth and made it
>   (he established it;
> he did not create it a chaos;
>   he formed it to be inhabited!):
> I am the LORD, and there is no other. (Isaiah 45:18 NRSVue)

The Pauline literature frequently alludes to Christ's role in creation, identifying him with Word or Wisdom. This is famously so in 1 Corinthians:

Creation and Monotheism

for us there is one God, the Father, from whom are all things and for whom we exist, and one Lord, Jesus Christ, through whom are all things and through whom we exist. (1 Corinthians 8:6 NRSVue)

And in Colossians:

He [i.e. God's "beloved Son"] is the image of the invisible God, the firstborn of all creation, for in him all things in heaven and on earth were created, things visible and invisible, whether thrones or dominions or rulers or powers—all things have been created through him and for him. (Colossians 1:15-16 NRSVue)

Outside the Pauline writings, the author of the Epistle to the Hebrews begins by saying:

in these last days [God] has spoken to us by a Son, whom he appointed heir of all things, through whom he also created the worlds. He is the reflection of God's glory and the exact imprint of God's very being, and he sustains all things by his powerful word.
(Hebrews 1:2-3 NRSVue)

As in John's Prologue, this is all the language of creation. The book of Revelation, in its opening theophany, references back to the exclusive monotheism of Deutero–Isaiah: "'I am the Alpha and the Omega,' says the Lord God, who is and who was and who is to come, the Almighty" (Revelation 1:8). In the text that follows, *God* and *Christ* are both named as "Alpha and Omega," "First and the Last," names that themselves are glosses of YHWH—the personal name of Israel's God whose only full interpretation in the Old Testament is in Exodus 3 where a sequence of word-plays expand the name's similarity to the Hebrew verb *to be*.[9]

This is not to say that trinitarian monotheism is the only or necessarily obvious reading of the books of the New Testament. The theological controversies of the early church demonstrate this not to be the case. However, the doctrine of creation became critical in understanding Christian monotheism. With *creatio ex nihilo* in place, there is only one distinction—that to be made between God and creatures. Christ must be one with the creator, lest worship

Section 1

of Christ is idolatrous. Christ must be, as John's Gospel rather suggests, the "I am," the creator and redeemer.[10]

Notes

1   See Nathan Macdonald, "The Origin of 'Monotheism,'" in *Early Jewish and Christian Monotheism*, ed. Loren T. Stuckenbruck and Wendy E. S. North (T&T Clark, 2004), 204–15.
2   On this, see Janet Soskice, *Naming God: Addressing the Divine in Philosophy, Theology and Scripture* (Cambridge University Press, 2023).
3   For the biblical roots of *creatio ex nihilo*, see Gary A. Anderson, "Creatio ex nihilo and the Bible," in *Creation ex nihilo: Origins, Development, Contemporary Challenges*, ed. Gary A. Anderson and Markus Bockmuehl (University of Notre Dame Press, 2018), 15–36. On the significance for contemporary Christian theology, see Janet Soskice, "Why Creatio ex nihilo for Theology Today?" in *Creation ex nihilo: Origins, Development, Contemporary Challenges*, ed. Gary A. Anderson and Markus Bockmuehl (University of Notre Dame Press, 2018), 37–54; Kathyrn Tanner, *God and Creation in Christian Theology: Tyranny or Empowerment?* (Basil Blackwell, 1988).
4   On this, see Brittany E. Wilson, *The Embodied God: Seeing the Divine in Luke–Acts and the Early Church* (Oxford University Press, 2021). Wilson gives a survey of the debate but takes a different view of *creatio ex nihilo* than the one proposed in this chapter.
5   See the discussion in Wilson, *The Embodied God*, 103–4.
6   See Richard Bauckham, *Jesus and the God of Israel: God Crucified and Other Studies on the New Testament's Christology of Divine Identity* (Eerdmans, 2008), chap. 1.
7   Richard Bauckham, "Monotheism and Christology in Hebrews 1," in *Early Jewish and Christian Monotheism*, ed. Loren T. Stuckenbruck and Wendy E. S. North (T&T Clark, 2004), 167–68.
8   Khaled Anatolios sees a growing sense of the centrality of the doctrine of *creatio ex nihilo* across the two parts of Athanasius's early work, *Against the Greeks—On the Incarnation*. See Khaled Anatolios, "*Creatio ex nihilo* in Athanasius of Alexandria's *Against the Greeks—On the Incarnation*," in *Creation ex nihilo: Origins, Development, Contemporary Challenges*, ed. Gary A. Anderson and Markus Bockmuehl (University of Notre Dame Press, 2018), 119–50.
9   *Ehyeh asher ehyeh*, "I am and I will be," and "He who is."
10 See David B. Burrell, "The act of creation with its theological consequences," in *Creation and the God of Abraham*, ed. David B. Burrell et al. (Cambridge University Press, 2010), 40–52; Rowan Williams, *Christ the Heart of Creation* (Bloomsbury, 2018).

The Challenge of Preaching on Trinity Sunday

J. Warren Smith

Robert Johnson, former dean of Yale Divinity School, observed that the sermon for Easter was the hardest for which to prepare. The reason, he explained, was that Jesus's resurrection was simply the summation of the Gospel revealed in all Jesus's life and teaching, indeed in the whole of the Christian Scriptures. How could one say anything new on Easter that had not already been said in the fifty-one other Sundays of the year?

Trinity Sunday poses a similar challenge for preachers. Since the God to whom our worship is directed and whose mighty works we recall every Sunday and all the services in between is the Triune God—Father, Son, and Holy Spirit—what does a preacher say about this God that has not already been said the previous fifty-one Sundays? And even as some preachers get hung up on Easter with offering an *apologia* that explains the mystery of the Resurrection to incredulous members of the Easter congregation, so too on Trinity Sunday some pastors face a similar quandary: either attempt to explain how God is three persons in one hypostasis or throw up their hands in defeat declaring the Trinity a mystery about which no further word can be given. The former approach may stir up excruciating memories from their days in divinity school as they try to recall how they heard the doctrine described in introductory Church History and Systematic Theology classes. Or they find themselves groping for metaphors, the inadequacy of which is palpable to preacher and congregation alike. The latter is painful as the preacher fumbles around for 15–20 minutes grasping for images with which to speak about pure mystery before which all words fall impotently silent. If these are the two alternatives, no wonder pastors dislike preaching on Trinity Sunday.

Yet preaching on Trinity Sunday need not feel like a quixotic venture any more than proclaiming the wonders of the Triune God on any other occasion. Yes, our words will be woefully inadequate, but that is true every Sunday. This is nothing new. As my doctoral mentor used to say, "The Fathers of Nicaea would be the first to admit that they did not know what they were talking about." Indeed, a cry for epistemic humility was central to the defense of the Nicene formulation by the Cappadocians in their response to attacks by the so-called "Neo-Arian" Eunomius of Cyzicus. Refuting Eunomius's presumptuous claim of being able to sum up God's essence as "unbegotten," Gregory of Nyssa countered that, because God is infinite and therefore uncircumscribed, God's essence is beyond creaturely comprehension. That is, the totality of God's infinite being cannot be summed up in a single word or even in many words. Even the sum of our many words fails in an ultimate sense. In his *Commentary on the Song of Songs*, Gregory says of the Bride, a figure of the soul seeking God, that she "contrives all sorts of word-meanings but every expressive power falls short and is exposed as being less than the truth. The great David himself often does the same sort of thing: calling the divinity by a thousand names and then confessing that he has fallen short of the truth" (*Cant.* 12.377–379). If Paul declined to describe the beatific vision he beheld in his moment of mystical rapture to the third heaven (2 Cor 12:4), who was Eunomius to think himself wiser than the Apostle? Therefore, implicit in the Nicene faith understood through its late-fourth century interpreters is that all orthodox theology is at its core apophatic; that is, it is both a positive confession of God as his works have revealed him to be and at the same time a recognition that God transcends all our descriptions. This does not, however, mean that we are left able to say only what God is not (i.e., immaterial, incorporeal, invisible, incomprehensible, etc.); that is, how the Creator is ontologically different than his creatures. On the contrary, we may not be able to name God's essence but we can confess his work (*energeia*) in the world—what Ephesians (1:10; 3:2, 9) refers to as the divine economy (*oikonomia*). That is, God's salvation history from creation to the calling of Israel through the Incarnation to the mighty works of the Spirit in and through the Church.

The Church, like Moses sojourning in the dark cloud on Sinai's summit, abides in the presence of the God who is unfathomable mystery. But the Church is not dumb. It confesses and proclaims the God whom "no one has ever seen" (John 1:18 NRSVue) because his luminous incarnate Word has made him known through the light of his Holy Spirit. "In thy light shall we see light" (Psalm 36:9 KJV). Therefore, as a pastor approaches the task of preaching on Trinity Sunday, she begins remembering that the subject of Trinity Sunday is not the *doctrine* of the Trinity, but the Triune God to whom the doctrine points. For the doctrine is the grammatical rules that govern how the Church speaks about the identity and relations of the persons of the Godhead in whose name we are baptized. This is not to make light of the doctrine that was forged in the crucible of debate during the third and fourth centuries. And it is certainly not optional for United Methodists for whom the Articles of Religion are normative. Rather, the preacher should use the doctrine as it was intended: to govern how we interpret Scripture and its description of the interactions of the three persons. Therefore, the preacher's task is to deploy the Trinitarian grammar of Nicaea that her people might see the relations of the Persons implicit in the lectionary readings for that Sunday. To illustrate this point, I will spend the remainder of this essay reflecting on how the texts assigned for Years A, B, and C may be interpreted in the light of Nicaea's grammar.

Before I do that, let me say something about what I mean by "grammar." If one wants to learn a language and to speak it properly, one begins with learning the rules of syntax. A singular subject must have a singular verb. Pronouns should have clear antecedents. These rules facilitate communication and without them there can be considerable confusion. The Nicene-Constantinopolitan Creed provides rules that prevent either of three ancient and modern misinterpretations of Scripture. The first misinterpretation, adoptionism, denies the divinity of the Son insisting that Jesus was a mere mortal human being whom God adopted at his baptism even as God adopted Israel's kings at their coronation. Such a view strips Jesus of his uniqueness; he is at most merely the greatest of prophets but not God. Furthermore, it is inconsistent with Jesus's High Priestly prayer, "now, Father, glorify me in your own presence with the glory that I had in your presence before the world existed" (John 17:5 NRSVue). Thus, Nicaea teaches that we must understand Jesus to be "the only Son of the Father begotten by the Father before all ages."

The second misinterpretation, modalism, denies that a real distinction exists between the three persons and that "Father," "Son," and "Holy Spirit" are simply three names given for the different forms God assumes in history. While it affirms the divinity of the Son and Spirit, it fails to recognize Scripture's implicit distinction between the persons. For example, the prologue to John says that "the Word was *with* God" (John 1:1 NRSVue, emphasis added). Or Jesus says of his relationship with the Father and Spirit, "And I will ask the Father and he will give you *another* Advocate [aka Counselor], to be with you forever. This is the Spirit of truth . . . [who] will remind you of all that I have said to you" (John 14:16-17, 26 NRSVue, emphasis added).

The third critical misinterpretation, subordinationism, denies the divinity of the Son and the Spirit by claiming that the Son and Spirit are ontologically inferior to the Father. Although subordinationism largely rests upon Jesus's words, "the Father is greater than I" (John 14:28 NRSVue), it fails to read these words in light of Jesus's revelation, "The Father and I are one" (John 10:30 NRSVue) and "Whoever has seen me has seen the Father" (John 14:9 NRSVue). Most of all it fails to recognize the implication of the Christ hymn of Philippians, "though he [i.e., the Son] existed in the form of God, did not count equality with God as something to be grasped, but emptied himself, taking the form of a slave" (2:6-7 NRSVue), namely, that before the Son assumed the form of a servant in the Incarnation he possessed the "form" or nature that was equal to the Father's divinity. Whereas subordinationists treated the Son as a quasi-divine being—some sort of middle entity between God and creation—the Cappadocian defenders of Nicaea rightly argued that the Jewish distinction between Creator and creature is an absolute ontological difference; one is either God or a creature—there is no middle ground. Therefore, when in the words of Nicaea we confess that the Son is "begotten, not made . . . true God from true God, consubstantial with the Father," we are confessing that the Son—and the Spirit—are not creatures like us but possess the same divine nature as the Father. For only if they are truly and fully divine can we through them become partakers of the divine nature (2 Peter 1:4). Only because they are divine do Christians have the hope that, through union with Christ in the Spirit, at the resurrection we shall put off our mortal body and put on a body transformed into the likeness of his incorruptible divinity (1 Corinthians 15:51-54).

Although Scripture is the primary source of our knowledge about God, United Methodists also recognize the authority of Tradition with a capital T, meaning the wisdom of the Church passed on from the Apostles and interpreted by the great teachers or doctors of the Church. Even as scholars of the U.S. Constitution ground their interpretations, not just based on the words of the Constitution, but the writings of its authors and interpreters (e.g., Alexander Hamilton, James Madison, and John Jay in *The Federalist Papers*), so the Church draws upon the sermons and treatises of its teachers, such as Athanasius and the Cappadocians, to understand the meaning—explicit and implicit—of the Trinitarian grammar given in the Nicene-Constantinopolitan Creed.

From these teachers of the Church, we are not given definitions of God but rules for speaking of the one God in three persons. The doctrine of the Trinity, as Gregory of Nazianzus explained, gives a distinctly Christian alternative to either God as a single monad existing all alone as in Judaism or the many gods of pagan polytheism, each with competing and conflicting wills. Rather, the doctrine of the Trinity affirms that Father, Son, and Spirit are discrete persons distinguished from each other, not by different natures, but in their relations with each other expressed in biblical language: the Father is *unbegotten*, the Son is *begotten* by the Father, and the Spirit *proceeds* from the Father and the Son.

Because the Son is begotten from the Father and the Spirit proceeds from the Father and the Son, they share not only the same divine nature but also—unlike the pagan gods—one will. Thus, the biblical narrative of the divine economy reflects the essential oneness or unity of the Persons in their "unity of operations." That is, the divine plan begins in the Father who is the source of all things, is accomplished by the Son, who is the Father's agent of creation and revelation in the incarnation, and is brought to completion in the outpouring of the Holy Spirit. Thus, all three persons act together in a single creative and redemptive operation. Therefore, the Persons cannot be reduced, à la the error of modalism, to "Creator, Redeemer, and Sustainer" as if the Father alone were creator and the Son and Spirit were not. This Trinitarian grammar also gives us language to understand our ascent to, and participation in, God. Through the divine light of the Spirit, the Christian is able to behold and affirm the light of the Father manifest in the Son. In baptism, through the Spirit who bears witness with our spirits, we are united in Christ as members of his body. In this union with the only begotten Son, we are united to his Father and so are able to call his Father, "our Father." It is the Trinitarian unity of operations that governs how we understand the economy of salvation that we proclaim in our liturgy and in our preaching. The goal of the Trinity Sunday sermon is not the *deductive* presentation of these theological rules. That would require a level of familiarity with scripture and church history beyond the knowledge of most laypersons. They would most likely find such a sermon tedious and uninspiring. Rather, the sermon teaches about the Trinity *inductively* through interpreting the Scriptures according to the grammatical rules of Nicaea. Then, by the light of the Spirit, the doctrine of the Trinity will help our people both negatively by training them to think about God without falling into error and positively by showing them the marvelous, united work of God, Father, Son, and Holy Spirit. With those homiletical rules established, let us turn to the Lectionary texts for Trinity Sunday.

Year A: Genesis 1:1–2:4a; Psalm 8; 2 Corinthians 13:11-13; Matthew 28:16-20

The juxtaposition of the creation story of Genesis 1 and the great commission at the end of Matthew (Matthew 28:19-20) invites the preacher to draw together the themes of creation and new creation. But their appearance together in the readings for Trinity Sunday begs that they both be interpreted within the Nicene framework for speaking of the unity of operations between Father, Son, and Holy Spirit.

One of the early battles that catholic Christianity faced in the second century came from Marcion and the Gnostics who—because they believed that matter was inherently evil and the source of ignorance, passions, and suffering—maintained that the being who created the world and the God who would redeem human beings could not be one and the same deity. Rhetorically, they asked, "Why would an all-wise, all-powerful, and all-benevolent God create a world so full of corruption and pain?" Their answer was that he would not. Therefore, they separated the creator god of Israel from the true God revealed in Christ who came to deliver the elect from the ignorance of the material world. In the late second century, Irenaeus's account of God's economy countered these dualistic cosmologies. Because the God of Israel is the same God who revealed himself in Jesus, the Father's incarnate Word, creation and redemption are but two stages of a single unfolding plan. Redemption is not deliverance *from* the world but the healing and perfection of God's work of creation in the beginning.

Genesis 1 has traditionally been interpreted as implicitly depicting creation as the work of the Triune God. For, Genesis speaks, not only of God (i.e., the Father), but of his Spirit who moves over the waters of chaos (1:2) on which God imposes order through his spoken Word or Logos, "Let there be . . ." (1:3 NRSVue). John's prologue interprets the Genesis Creation narrative through the lens of the Christ event. The Word by which the world was made is not a mere verbal act of divine power but the *person* of the Son, and "all things came into being through him" (John 1:4 NRSVue) and who in the fullness of time assumed a human nature (John 1:14) that he might reveal the Father's grace and truth (John 1:18). Later, the third century teacher Origen explained, that the "beginning" (*arche* [Greek] or *principium* [Latin]) in which the Word was, does not denote a moment of time but the person of God the Father who is the beginning, the source of all things. Thus, the Word's creation of the world was but the accomplishment of the design of the Father in whom the Word abides and from whom he is eternally begotten. But, as John's prologue goes on to make clear, the creative work of the Word not only gave the gift of existence but life eternal through the subsequent gift of the Spirit. To those who receive him, Christ gives the power to become children of God (1:12) by being born again/from above by water and the

Spirit (3:5) whom he breathed onto the Apostles at his resurrection (20:22). Even as the possibility of creation from nothing was possible because God's Spirit—the divine Breath that possesses life in its very nature—hovered over the waters of the lifeless void, so too the presence of the Spirit—Christ's own Spirit that he breathed onto the Apostles—brings new life to those who in the waters of the baptismal font have united themselves with Christ "in a death like his" (Romans 6:5 NRSVue) that they may walk in the Spirit through whom we become members of Christ's body. And as members of his body who abide together in Christ's Spirit, we become participants in his new creation (2 Corinthians 5:17) that is the consummation of God's economy, his plan for creation from the beginning. The majesty of the name of God fills all the earth (Psalm 8:1), and to be baptized in the name of God—"Father, Son, and Holy Spirit"—is to be truly alive, to become the children of God the Word made us to be. This brings a new identity: seeing oneself within the biblical narrative of the creative and redemptive work of the Triune God.

Year B: Isaiah 6:1-8; Psalm 29; Romans 8:12-17; John 3:1-17

Year B confronts the preacher with proclaiming the paradoxical nature of the Triune God who is both fearful in his transcendence and yet immanently active in his creation ever seeking to draw his creatures into intimate fellowship with him. Isaiah's vison of the heavenly throne room is a terrifying revelation. The song of the Seraphim confesses God's holiness and glory. The three-fold doxology—often interpreted as the ascription of praise to the Father, Son, and Holy Spirit—names the ontological and moral otherness of God. Unlike creatures who do not possess life in themselves but derive it from their Creator, God the great *I am* alone is eternal Being, alone possesses life in himself. And in contrast to the humanity whose nature is corrupted by disordered loves, God is unalloyed goodness.

Therefore, Isaiah's vision of God in his transcendence is fearful and awful, in the archaic sense of the word meaning "awe inspiring." For the vision of God in his transcendent holiness confronts Isaiah with the knowledge of himself as sinful creature. When the prophet exclaims, "Woe is me . . . for

The Challenge of Preaching on Trinity Sunday

I am a man of unclean lips" (Isaiah 6:5 NRSVue), he fully apprehends his own lack of holiness. The terror Isaiah feels in the depths of his being arises from the recognition of the hubris of pride common to all who "have sinned and fall short of the glory of God" (Romans 3:23 NRSVue)—the hubris of presuming to be the lord and master of our own lives and with it the impertinence of thinking of ourselves as autonomous individuals whose minds and bodies are ours to do with as we please. Isaiah in that moment sees himself as he is, a mere creature. He is but a man and no God (cf. Psalm 9:20). His experience of the holy othernesss of God is expressed in the psalter reading (Psalm 29). God is lord over the world he created and his voice—the Father's Word through whom all things were created—that "breaks the cedars of Lebanon . . . and strips the forest bare" (Psalm 29:5, 8 NRSVue) has the right and power to do with it as he wills.

Yet, his awesome glory that fills the whole of heaven and earth (Isaiah 6:3) is but a revelation of the love out of which he willed creation's existence in the beginning. For God's transcendence stands in striking contrast with the god of Deism, so common in Wesley's day and in its various modern forms, who set the world in motion only to stand aloof from the world. Content to contemplate his own blessedness, he is indifferent to the lives of the creatures in his clockwork universe. By contrast, the Christian God is immanently involved in creation. Although God is eternal and self-sufficient in the blessed fellowship of the Trinity and therefore did not need to create, he did so out of a desire to share his goodness with creatures. As a reflection of his goodness, the universe is intended to be a sign that, like all signs, points beyond itself that we might be inspired to seek the One who is its transcendent source. This is the Father's creative intention that he accomplishes through his Son and Holy Spirit. For although the transcendent holiness is true of all three persons of the Trinity, it is the Father who remains veiled in transcendent mystery. After all, it is the Son, not the Father, who hangs upon the cross. The Father's transcendence is paradoxically represented in Greek Orthodox iconography by his absence. Except for the famous icon of Abraham's three visitors at Mamre, only the Son and Spirit are ever depicted in Greek icons; for in his transcendence, the Father is beyond representation. The Christian, like Moses to whom God reveals not his face but only his averted figure

(Exodus 23:20-23), beholds the Father indirectly through the mediation of the Son and Spirit.

Having promised in his prologue that the Father's Word would give to those who received him the ability to become children of God, John 3 identifies the power of the Holy Spirit, by which we become God's children and enter his kingdom. John draws a line between being God's beloved creatures and being a child of God. All creatures are made by God in love, but none are automatically his children at birth. A child is set apart by the intimate relationship she enjoys with her parents that is different than their relationship with any other creature. When in baptism we receive the gift of the Holy Spirit and are united to Christ, the only begotten Son, we become Jesus's adopted siblings, for we also receive the Holy Spirit, the Spirit of adoption (Romans 8:15-17). Christ is Son of God by nature; we become children of God by grace. We are given the gift of calling Jesus's Father "our Father" because the Holy Spirit, whom Paul calls "the Spirit of Christ" (Romans 8:9 NRSVue), dwells in us and unites us to him. For, where there is the Son, who is eternally united to his Father and Spirit, there we shall be also (John 14:3).

The gift of the Spirit makes us "children of God" in another sense: we are renewed in the image of our heavenly Father (Colossians 3:10). For as a child possesses the distinctive likeness to her parents by either nature or nurture, so the Christian is given the likeness of her heavenly Father through the transforming grace of the Spirit. As the Spirit placed the divine seed of the Son in Mary's womb and fashioned Jesus as the Second Adam, so in the water of the baptismal font, which in the early church was compared to a womb, the believer experiences new birth and enters into a new life in the Spirit (Romans 8:4). One who is reborn of water and the Spirit no longer walks according to the flesh—that is, the wisdom of the world—because, through the indwelling of the Spirit, she enjoys communion with Christ as a member of his body. The Word, who made us according to his image in the beginning, re-creates humanity when—in assuming our human nature—he becomes both Immanuel, God with us, and the second Adam, the father of a new human race. This new humanity, in whom we see the union of divinity and humanity modeled in the Incarnation, is possible because Christ's sanctifying Spirit dwells within the souls of the baptized that they might be partakers of God's holiness (2 Peter 1:4) and so empowered to grow up into Christ who is our head (Ephesians 4:15). Then when we are renewed in the image of the Second Adam bearing the likeness of his divine holiness through the indwelling of the Holy Spirit, we are able to ascend with our Great High Priest into the Holy of Holies not made with hands eternal in the heavens (9:24). There, like Isaiah, we shall behold the holy Trinity. But unlike terrified Isaiah, we shall not shrink back in a spirit of timidity; for our lips will have already been touched with the fiery ember of Christ's Spirit. Rather we shall be like the angels (Luke 20:36) bowing in thankful doxology, declaring the glory of God, our heavenly Father together with his Son and Holy Spirit.

Year C: Proverbs 8:1-4, 22-31; Psalm 8; Romans 5:1-5; John 16:12-15

In Proverbs, Lady Wisdom is depicted as a street preacher who, like early Methodist field preachers, goes out into the highways and byways, to the gates of the city, and the village square (1:20; 8:2-3) exhorting simpletons and fools to listen to her noble truths and righteous words (8:6-8). They should listen to this divine street preacher, because she is the Father's Wisdom who was "at the beginning of his work" and "before the beginning of the earth" (8:22-23 NRSVue). Indeed, Lady Wisdom is what C.S. Lewis refers to as the "deep magic" of creation that was before the foundation of the earth. She is the Father's divine logic (*Logos*) by which the world was ordered. Therefore, this street preacher is to be trusted to reveal how to order one's own life that it may conform to the logic of God's creation in which we dwell. Instead of suffering by swimming against the stream of nature, we, following the flow of Wisdom, find true life and discover real happiness (8:34). In the fullness of time, Wisdom "became flesh and lived among us" (John 1:14 NRSVue) by taking the form of an itinerant rabbi whom the Father sent to the highways and byways of Galilee and Samaria and to the courts of Jerusalem's Temple calling Israel to receive Wisdom's ancient message, "I came that they may have life and have it abundantly," (John 10:10 NRSVue).

The message of Wisdom incarnate turns out to be the antithesis of what the world calls wisdom (1 Corinthians 1:25-31) according to which abundant life is attained through self-exalting ambition that prioritizes personal interest with little regard for the common good. In its collective form, this ambition seeks security and peace through what St. Augustine calls *libido dominandi* or the "lust for domination" (*City of God* I, preface). Augustine goes on to identify this self-exalting ambition with the pride of Adam, who was foolishly confident in his own capacity to know the good that leads to happiness separate from following the command of God and the illumination of the Holy Spirit. For, in the hubris of trusting the autonomy of his own intellect rather than abiding in the light of Wisdom, he fell into sin, thereby bringing suffering, and death (Romans 5:12) not only upon himself but upon his whole family. Yet, out of his love for his creation, the Father sent Wisdom into the world as a member of Adam's family that the light, which Adam spurned, might reveal that righteousness necessary for life (Rom 5:18) and the holiness without which no one can enjoy fellowship with God (Hebrews 12:14-15). Jesus, incarnate Wisdom, is the Second Adam because by his righteous obedience to the Father—obedience even unto death on a cross—he becomes the father of a new humanity, a new creation (2 Corinthians 5:17), which is freed from condemnation and liberated from death, by being united to him as branches of the life-giving Vine. Christ the Vine, as in the mosaic at San Clemente in Rome, is depicted iconically as the Tree of Life in Eden and the cross of Golgotha.

Yet, if Wisdom cloaked in human flesh merely brought us an example of perfect righteousness, he would not be bringing life. For, his exemplary righteousness would only be another, more demanding form of the Law which only exposes more vividly our failure to conform to God's righteousness. Yet Jesus does not give merely a moral example, he gives us his Spirit. In his farewell lecture to the disciples on the night before his passion, incarnate Wisdom promises that he will pray to the Father to send another Counselor (*paraclete*) who will give clarity to their understanding of all that Jesus did and taught (John 16:13). Thus, the Second Adam in being anointed by the Spirit of truth at his baptism in the Jordan reveals the anointing his children will receive. For then, the light of Wisdom that the first Adam shunned is now restored to the followers of the Second Adam. In the light of the Spirit, we shall see the light of the Father manifest in the Son (Psalm 36:9) and thus be able to confess that Jesus Christ is Lord (1 Corinthians 12:3). This revelation is itself life-giving, for as Jesus disclosed to his disciples in his High Priestly intercession with the Father, "This is eternal life, that they may know you, the only true God, and Jesus Christ, whom you have sent" (John 17:3 NRSVue). The Spirit, who "proceeds from the Father and the Son, who with the Father and Son is worshipped and Glorified," shares the divine nature with the Father and Son. Therefore, the indwelling Spirit allows the life of the Son to abide in us. For this reason, the Nicene Creed calls the Spirit, "the Lord, the giver of Life" (cf. 2 Corinthians 3:3, 17)

The Spirit not only allows us to make the life-giving confession that Jesus is the incarnate Son of the only true God, but the Spirit renews the believer in the image of the Son—after whose likeness he fashioned us in the beginning—by making us partakers of his righteousness. As Paul declares in Romans, "God's love has been poured into our hearts through the Holy Spirit that has been given to us" (5:5 NRSVue). In breathing his Spirit onto us in baptism, Christ dwells in us through his Spirit and so is active in us empowering us to be righteous as he is righteous. Our works of mercy and compassion are merely the fruit of the Spirit who is at work in us. For, as Augustine observes, the Spirit is the reciprocal love of the Father for the Son and the Son for the Father (*On the Trinity* 5.12). When through the Spirit our spirit is filled with the knowledge of God's love for us and inspired to a reciprocal love of gratitude toward God, then we are finally able to fulfill the two greatest commandments, the love of God and neighbor. Thus, through our new life of holiness in the Spirit, we are able to be the "sweet fragrance of Christ" for the world (2 Corinthians 2:15-17 AMP).

SECTION 2

Nicene Faith in Preaching

Preaching the Trinity is both a profound challenge and a sacred opportunity. How does one proclaim the mystery of the Three-in-One God in ways that illuminate rather than confound, that inspire rather than perplex? The sermons in this section demonstrate how skilled preachers have risen to this challenge, showing how Nicene faith can be proclaimed with clarity, creativity, and pastoral wisdom.

Luke Powery's "Variety Anxiety" opens this collection by connecting Trinitarian theology to contemporary concerns about diversity and unity. Drawing from Paul's teaching on spiritual gifts in 1 Corinthians, Powery argues that variety is not a problem to be solved but a divine gift to be embraced, grounded in the very nature of the triune God.

Brent Strawn's "My Favorite Part of the Creed" demonstrates how creeds shape both our imagination and our proclamation. Through his exploration of Christ's descent to the dead, Strawn shows how even the most challenging aspects of credal faith can be preached in ways that illuminate God's boundless love.

Alma Tinoco Ruiz's "The Miracle of Faith" connects ancient scriptural wisdom to contemporary struggles for justice and healing. Through her meditation on Psalm 23 and stories from Colombian Christian activists, Ruiz shows how faith in God's presence sustains those who walk through dark valleys.

Bishop Connie Mitchell Shelton's sermon on Matthew 28:16-20 explores how the Great Commission reveals the Trinitarian shape of Christian mission and discipleship. Her proclamation demonstrates how baptismal identity grounds Christian life and witness in the name of Father, Son, and Holy Spirit.

Bishop Kenneth Carter Jr.'s "The Trinity Forms Us and Sends Us" shows how Trinitarian doctrine shapes both Christian formation and mission. His sermon demonstrates how the church's sending is grounded in the mutual love of Father, Son, and Holy Spirit.

Edgardo Colón-Emeric's "Into the Trinity" invites hearers to move beyond mere intellectual assent to lived experience of the Triune God. Drawing on mystical and theological traditions, he shows how Trinity Sunday offers an opportunity not just to explain doctrine but to encounter the living God.

Together, these sermons demonstrate the enduring power of Nicene faith to address contemporary challenges and inspire faithful witness. They show how the Creed's careful articulation of Trinitarian faith provides resources not just for theological reflection but for pastoral care, prophetic witness, and spiritual formation. As we celebrate the 1700th anniversary of the Council of Nicaea, these preachers remind us that confessing the Triune God is not merely an exercise in historical remembrance but an invitation to renewed faith and practice. Their work encourages today's preachers to draw deeply from the well of Nicene wisdom as they proclaim God's truth in their own contexts.

Variety Anxiety[1]
Luke Powery

On the day of Pentecost, the tongue-talking, holy-rolling, fire-breathing disciples were accused of being drunk with wine in the morning, as if it were the last day of classes at Duke. The church at Corinth was drunk in their own way too, but not with wine or even the Spirit. They were drunk on divisiveness. They were naughty and nasty and not too nice to each other. Yet they were Christians! As we might say in Dade County of South Florida, they were beat up from the feet up, tore up from the floor up. They were anxious in their own way, trying to figure out who's in charge, not sure who they belong to, learning what it means to be spiritual, how to love, what it means to be a body and what to do with your body, what to eat and how to eat and who should eat when, and when to bring a lawsuit and if to bring a lawsuit. Just anxious about everything seemingly, about being together and not knowing who to look to for leadership and guidance. They were like a spiritual ship without a sail. Read Paul's letter and you can sense the angst, the anxiety.

According to its medical definition, anxiety is a state consisting of psychological and physical symptoms that are brought about by a sense of apprehension at a perceived threat. Psychological symptoms can include feelings of fear, an exaggerated startle reflex, poor concentration, irritability, and insomnia. Physical symptoms can include tremors, sweating, muscle tension, a fast heartbeat, fast breathing, sometimes a dry mouth and the feeling of having a lump in the throat. In severe cases, hyperventilation can lead to a fall in the concentration of carbon dioxide in the blood, giving rise to an additional

Section 2

set of physical symptoms like chest discomfort, numbness or tingling in the hands and feet, dizziness, and faintness. Have you ever been anxious?

There's a whole list of things one can do to cope with anxiety according to the professionals: Make a problem list. Use relaxation techniques. Implement simple lifestyle changes. Seek help. Use sedatives, and engage in talking treatments. But what does one do when dealing with the Church and its own anxieties, such as "variety anxiety"?

"Variety anxiety" is prevalent in the church and also in the world. There aren't pills to help with this but maybe a dose of the Holy Ghost will help, help to awaken us to God's vision of variation. This variety anxiety arises when we make homogeneity holy and heterogeneity hell's angel. There's a peculiar problem in the world and church where difference of any kind is looked down upon or merely viewed strangely because sameness is believed to be the will of God and the work of the Spirit; yet anything different from what we experience or know or believe makes us uncomfortable, so we get anxious. But the Spirit of God doesn't specialize in coddling Christians. The Spirit works on making us more Christ-like and the truth is that it may be hard sometimes. Variety anxiety is not the will of God because variation is actually a part of the nature of God.

The triune God, the Trinity, is itself a variation on a theme. Three in one—Father, Son, and Holy Spirit. Three persons, yet one God. Variety is not solely the spice of life. It is the Spirit's expression at the heart of who God is in the very being of God. Even the Day of Pentecost reveals variations on a theme. All began to speak in other languages as the Spirit gave them ability. Many languages but one message: God's deeds of power. And the Apostle Paul grabs ahold of this thinking and tells the church at Corinth:

> Now there are varieties of gifts but the same Spirit, and there are varieties of services but the same Lord, and there are varieties of activities, but it is the same God who activates all of them in everyone... To one is given through the Spirit the utterance of wisdom and to another the utterance of knowledge according to the same Spirit, to another faith by the same Spirit, to another gifts of healing by the one Spirit, to another the working of powerful deeds, to another

prophecy, to another the discernment of spirits, to another various kinds of tongues, to another the interpretation of tongues . . .
(1 Corinthians 12:4-6, 8-10 NRSVue)

To another and another and another. Variety is the vision of God.

Yet those suffering from variety anxiety don't see variation and difference as a sign of unity, so they get anxious when everyone doesn't look the same or act the same or think the same. Paul's teaching on the Spirit, however, shows us that we should actually get anxious and worried when everything is the same, because the Spirit creates the diversity of gifts. But anxiety still reigns in our world.

This past week alone is evidence of the variety anxiety in society.

Two Oregon men died defending a pair of high school girls from a train passenger's religious and racial taunts. Basketball star LeBron James's home was painted with a racial slur. A noose was left hanging in the Smithsonian National Museum of African American history and culture in D.C. And there were numerous racist reactions to a Japanese driver winning the Indy 500. And yesterday in London, there was a terrorist attack. Variety anxiety still prevails in the world, and it can be very dangerous; we are not yet free because fear of the other is so rampant.

But as Christians, whether we are speaking of gifts or diversity in other ways, to be spiritual (*pneumatikos*), which is what they are debating about in Corinth, is to embrace the variations found in and through God's people. There are varieties but no spiritual soloists! There are many members, yet one body. Paul writes: "If the whole body were an eye, where would the hearing be? If the whole body were hearing, where would the sense of smell be? If all were a single member, where would the body be?" (1 Corinthians 12:17–19 NRSVue). No body part should tell another, "I have no need of you" (1 Corinthians 12:21 NRSVue), especially to the weakest and most vulnerable. Each body part, every person, every gift, matters. Since "each is given the manifestation of the Spirit" (1 Corinthians 12:7 NRSVue), everyone should be treated with dignity and respect, because the multiplicity and variety embodied in the church and world are the work of the Spirit.

Remember that "the fruit of the Spirit is love, joy, peace, patience, kindness, generosity, faithfulness, gentleness, and self-control" (Galatians 5:22-23

Section 2

NRSVue). The Spirit produces variety. There isn't just one fruit of love; all the variations of love, joy, peace, patience, kindness, generosity, faithfulness, gentleness, and self-control are aspects of the theme of fruit. Again, variations on a theme. Some consider variety or diversity as chaos and emblematic of division, but really it's a reflection of the unity of God and the context for our oneness and unity in Christ. You might not realize this when you look at examples of church behavior.

According to tradition, Jerusalem's Church of the Holy Sepulchre is built over the cave in which Christ is said to have been buried. In July 2002, the church became the scene of an Ultimate Fighting Championship (UFC) bout, as the monks who run it battled over territory. The conflict began when a Coptic monk, sitting on the rooftop, decided to move his chair into the shade. This took him into the part of the rooftop courtyard looked after by the Ethiopian monks. The Ethiopian and Coptic monks have been arguing over the rooftop of the Church for centuries. In 1752, the Ottoman Sultan issued an edict declaring which parts of the Church belong to each of six Christian groups: the Latins, Greek Orthodox, Armenian Orthodox, Syrian Orthodox, Copts, and Ethiopians.

The rooftop had been controlled by the Ethiopians, but they lost control to the Copts when hit by a disease epidemic in the 19th century. Then in 1970, the Ethiopians regained control when the Coptic monks were absent for a short period. They have been squatting there ever since, with at least one Ethiopian monk always remaining on the roof to assert their rights. In response, a Coptic monk has been living on the roof also, to maintain the claim of the Copts. So in July 2002, when the Coptic monk moved his chair into the shade, harsh words led to pushes, shoves, until a full-blown brawl broke out, including the throwing of chairs and iron bars. At the end of the fight, eleven of the monks were injured, including one monk unconscious in the hospital and another with a broken arm. This makes WWE look like "Little House on the Prairie." From this scene and other future fights in this church, you might come away with the view that diversity in the Church is a problem. But Paul doesn't believe so, and neither do I. Although there are varieties, it is the same Spirit, the same Lord, the same God who activates all of them in everyone—the one and the same Spirit who gives each gift.

Variety Anxiety

Paul's emphasis on the one body and the one Spirit implies that diversity is not a negation of unity but the essential environment for it. You can only have unity if the members of a body are varied or diverse, for the church unifies when it diversifies. Otherwise, all you have is uniformity, not unity. Uniformity means everyone looks the same, acts the same, and thinks the same. That is not unity; that is, to coin a term, *clonality*. And the Spirit doesn't make clones of Christ; instead the Spirit makes diverse followers of Christ.

Variation is the gift of the one Spirit. Diversity isn't the problem like many institutions want to claim. Uniformity is the theological problem, because it is anti-Spirit, since the Spirit is the one who plays variations on the theme of "Jesus Christ is Lord." What variations reveal is the beauty of God as multiplicity and diversity. Pentecost is a Christian feast because of the unified diversity or variety. The miracle of Pentecost is that with all the variety voiced, there was still unity and oneness. Pentecost is actually about being one, which is different from uniformity, because oneness is unity and unity implies diversity and variety. The church can't be one and be uniform. Sameness is actually more theologically—and specifically, pneumatologically—problematic than variation. Variation is a gift of the Spirit, whereas sameness suggests that we are in charge, because we like to be with those who look like us, act like us, and think like us.

But the dynamite of Pentecost blows up all of that in the power of the Spirit. There are varieties, and all these are activated by one and the same Spirit. All drink of the same Spirit; no one gift eclipses another. Until we come to this realization, there will be variety anxiety in the academy, church, and world. But I don't know about you; I don't want just red robins as the only bird species or grits as the only breakfast food or roses as the only flower or Powery as the only preacher. I want and need variety in my life as a Christian, because varieties on all levels bring me closer to the heart and creation of God, which is a beautiful, unified diversity.

When we enter the scientific realm of biodiversity, scientists identify 1.75 million different species. That includes 950,000 species of insects, 270,000 species of plants, 19,000 species of fish, 9,000 species of birds, and 4,000 species of mammals, and they are still discovering more! If you look at the species biodiversity in a pond alone, you may identify different plants, such as cattails and water lilies. Then you might see a garter snake, a bullfrog or even a red-winged blackbird. Then there may be some invertebrates and worms under leaves or on grasses. Biodiversity is not just species-related either; there's also genetic and ecological biodiversity, so there are lots of variation in the world, because there's a lot of variation in God.

But these Spirit-initiated variations are not untethered, but are moored, to a main theme in Paul's letter. His concern for oneness is obvious, but he's adamant about two other themes; one is a subtheme, while the other is the main one. The subtheme is encapsulated when he says that each person is given a manifestation of the Spirit "for the common good" (1 Corinthians 12:7 NRSVue). Throughout his letter, he urges the church at Corinth to act in ways that build up the community and not tear it down. In a seventeenth-century commentary, Presbyterian minister Matthew Henry writes that the gifts "are not given for show, but for service; not for pomp and ostentation, but for edification; not to magnify those that have them, but to edify others."[2] Our varieties of gifts are to benefit the whole community. The test of the charism, the gift, is how it benefits the whole church. The variety is not for variety's sake or some sickened political correctness. It is a revelation of who God is and an expression of the Spirit's movement toward a whole, holy, and unified church, the body of Christ. Who I am and what I do and with what I've been gifted is never for myself; it is always for the other. As Albert Einstein once said, "Only a life lived for others is a life worthwhile."

This isn't the only theme Paul plays, though it's a good one. If we were left only with that subtheme, we might as well be talking about a rotary club. But we are talking about the church, the body of Christ. Paul's primary theme is Jesus Christ because the fundamental criterion that one is possessed by the Spirit is the confession that "Jesus is Lord." The foundation of the spiritual life, with all of its varieties, is Jesus Christ. Authentic Christian spirituality is rooted in Jesus, not in the excess of spiritual gifts. Every Christian is a spiritual person whose common identity with others is found in Christ. United to Christ, diverse Christians are united to one another in the Holy Spirit.

The Spirit plays variations on this Christian theme: "On Christ the solid rock I stand, all other ground is sinking sand, all other ground is sinking sand."[3] Without this ground of our being together, we will sink into divisions over diversity. But if we remain firmly planted on the rock of Jesus Christ, we will be a spiritual people who embrace variations as the way of the triune God in the world. Then they will not only know we are Christians by our love or by our joy, but even with all of our variety they will know we are Christians by our unity. May it be so.

Today, say "bye-bye" to variety anxiety and "hello" to the vision and unity of God. In other words, "hello" to theodiversity. Amen.

Notes

1. A sermon preached in Duke University Chapel on Ascension Sunday, June 4, 2017
2. Matthew Henry, *Matthew Henry's Commentary on the Whole Bible, vol. 6* (Fleming H. Revell, 1980).
3. "My Hope Is Built," *The United Methodist Hymnal*, 368.

My Favorite Part of the Creed

Brent A. Strawn

"In which also he went and made a proclamation to the spirits in prison . . ."
"He descended to the dead . . ."

Our Favorite(s)

I imagine if we stopped and took time for responses, all of us could name our favorite song or TV show or movie. It might be hard to pick just one, of course, and so we'd have to let the more indecisive people hem and haw and in the end pick more than one. But we could definitely name our favorites if we had to.

So what about your favorite book of the Bible? Or chapter in the Bible? Or even verse in the Bible? And no, John 3:16 is not allowed. Neither is "Jesus wept." (That's John 11:35 KJV in case you are wondering.) You can't pick either of those!

I suspect this is a harder task for most of us. But why? Is it because we are torn between our love of Matthew and, oh I don't know, Leviticus? "I just can't decide!" Or between John and Philippians? Or is it because, to be completely candid for a moment, we don't know our Bibles very well, and not nearly as well as we know our TV shows, music, and movies.

Section 2

And just to continue in this mode of making-us-all-feel-guilty-this-morning, here's another question to ponder: What's your favorite part of the Apostles' Creed? Do you have one? And, if so, one final question: Why is that your favorite part?

Now it's probably not very nice for me to stand up here and lay on the guilt—not without running the gauntlet first. So, if I had to pick just one song, it'd be "How I Remember You" by the jazz singer Michael Franks, largely because I've sung it to each of my children since the day they were born. Franks is also my favorite singer, if you forced me to pick. Favorite TV show? Probably the discontinued *Friday Night Lights*. Favorite movie? Probably *The Shawshank Redemption*. Favorite book of the Bible? Wow, that's hard for a Bible professor! Give me top five! Exodus, Deuteronomy, Amos, Ecclesiastes, and the Psalms. And my favorite part of the Creed? The line that is sometimes left out of our worship services. It's the line that says, "descended to the dead." Some of you may not even know that that line is in the Creed. But it is! It comes right after Jesus "was crucified, died, and was buried" and right before "on the third day he rose again." In between those two lines is—or is *supposed* to be—this line: "He descended to the dead." That's my favorite part of the Apostles' Creed.

At this point, you might have some questions for me: "Why is *that* your favorite part, anyway? Why is it left out? And what does it mean?" Well, I'm glad you asked, because that's what the rest of this sermon is all about.

Why Is It Left Out?

So, first, let's talk about why this line is left out. *The United Methodist Hymnal* gives two versions of the Apostles' Creed, the traditional and the ecumenical. We read the traditional version just now—it's the version that omits the line about Jesus's descent. But calling this version "traditional" is odd, because the part about Jesus's descent is a very ancient part of the Creed—which means it is *completely* "traditional"![1] So why does the traditional version leave it out?

I suspect it is the same reason that people often leave out, substitute something else, or carefully define the word "catholic" in the Creed—you know, in the part where we say, "I believe in the Holy Spirit, the holy catholic church." "Catholic," in *The United Methodist Hymnal*, has two little asterisks next to it, directing you to a footnote that clarifies that the word "catholic" (with a lower-case "c") in this context means "universal," not "Catholic" (with a capital "C") as in "Roman Catholic." I mean, we are Methodists after all! And those who aren't Roman Catholic are sometimes confused or worried by the presence of the word "catholic" in the Creed.

I suspect the same holds true for the words "he descended to the dead" or, in a different, probably better translation of the original Latin of the Creed, "he descended into hell."[2] In Latin that last word is *inferna*; just hearing it, you can tell it is related to our own word "inferno." Think of Dante's book by that name in which the main character takes a guided tour of hell.[3]

Now some people—like my grandmother, for instance (may she rest in peace)—just are not going to say the word "hell" in church, or the word "catholic" for that matter, unless they can say them together![4]

I suspect, then, that my favorite part of the Creed is left out for the same reason that the word "catholic" has asterisks next to it. Because many people just don't understand what this line means, and it somehow offends their sensibilities.[5] But if we knew what this part means, then maybe we wouldn't be offended—maybe we would even be helped and encouraged.[6] Instead, in our attempts to pacify my Grandma Jensen and other well-meaning individuals, we end up censoring the Creed, striking something that it wants us to have—something that the early Church that gave us the Creed thought was crucial for us to have.

Where Does This Come From?

By why does the Creed contain this part, and why did the early Church think it was so important to include it? It wasn't just made up out of thin air, after all, and it certainly wasn't made up to offend the Grandma Jensens of the world. Where did come from? Well from several places actually,[7] one of which we heard this morning. In 1 Peter 3, we read that Christ, "by the Spirit . . . went to preach to the spirits in prison," spirits that are said to be "disobedient" and that are associated with "the time of Noah" (vv. 19-20 CEB). This is a very intriguing passage, but 1 Peter doesn't say much more about it, switching topics abruptly (or so it would seem) to baptism.

Section 2

But there are other texts besides 1 Peter 3, texts like Matthew 27, which says that when Jesus dies, "The tombs also were opened, and many bodies of the saints who had fallen asleep [i.e., died] were raised" (vv. 52-53; NRSV). Now how did that happen? Or Ephesians 4, which asks: "What does the phrase '[Christ] climbed up [i.e. ascended]' mean if it doesn't mean that he had first gone down into the lower regions of the earth? The one who went down [i.e. descended] is the same one who climbed up . . ." (vv. 9-10 CEB). Or, back to 1 Peter 4 this time, which states that "the gospel was proclaimed even to the dead" (v. 6; NRSV).

There are still other passages we might consider,[8] but the Creed itself, even without the part about Christ's descent, implies it in the very next line: "On the third day he rose *from the dead*" [emphasis added]. This is Ephesians all over again: you can't rise up if you haven't first descended. And since Jesus rose *from* the dead, that means he must have first gone *to* the dead. So, "he descended into hell" is implied in the Creed even if we leave that specific line out. Whatever the case, it's clear that this part about Christ's descent isn't made up out of thin air, but is based on these tantalizing little tidbits of Scripture scattered here and there in the New Testament. But what do they mean? How do we make sense of them?

What Does It Mean?

Well, given the long history of the Church, it should come as no surprise that there is more than one interpretation of this line of the Creed and the doctrine of Christ's descent into hell. There are a lot of interpretations, in fact, but two main ones.[9]

The first is that during the three days that Jesus lay dead, he was down there, in Hell, *taking care of business*.[10] He was fighting the devil, *mano a mano*, tête-à-tête, in hand-to-hand combat, to see who would have the keys to death. And Jesus wins! Of course! I'd like to think it was a sweet roundhouse back kick, Bruce Lee style, that knocked the last tooth out of the devil's ugly mouth. Regardless, in this interpretation of the descent, Jesus is fighting for us, snatching the keys of Death and the Grave (Rev 1:18) in order to set us all free. The idea is captured by something Jesus says early in the Gospel of John: "I assure you that the time is coming—and is here!—when the dead will hear the voice of God's Son, and those who hear it will live" (5:25 CEB). Imagine that: Jesus down there in Hell, doing work and taking names! What's not to like about that?

The second interpretation is that during the three days that Jesus lay dead, he was down there, in Hell, *holding revival*. He was preaching to all those who didn't have a chance to hear him before he came. All the great saints of the Old Testament lining up to hear the Good News of the Gospel of Jesus Christ, but so are all the others—the non-saintly, if you will, the disobedient ones who, according to 1 Peter, are in prison but who now have a chance to hear and decide to repent and believe the good news.[11] Imagine that: Jesus preaching the greatest revival the world—or *under*world—has ever seen. What's not to like about that?

Why Does It Matter?

There are other interpretations, but those are my two favorite ones for my favorite part of the Creed. Both get at why this part of the Creed is so important and why we should include it and say it every time we recite the Creed—and never, ever censor it out.

Here's why the line is so important: We all know Jesus died. The line about his descent into hell says *yet more still*—it shows us just how far he is willing to go. Christ didn't just dip his toe in the cold waters of death and say, "Oh, you're right, that *really* is unfortunate; I feel very sorry for all you human types, *really* I do." No, Jesus went the whole way: he was put to death as a criminal, buried by others in a borrowed tomb, was truly dead—for three days. There's no coming back from that. That isn't just dipping your toe in the cold waters of death to test the temperature. That's full immersion; that's drowning all the way to the bottom of the Mariana trench, into the deepest recesses of the earth (like Ephesians says) or all the way to hell (as the Creed says). Why? Why would Jesus do that?

Listen to this:

So that the work of God might be done!

So that the word of God might be heard!

Section 2

Listen to this:

There's no place God will not go to find even one lost sheep.[12]
There's no place God cannot read to reclaim God's very own.[13]

That's what "he descended into the dead" means. That's why it matters. That's why we should say it. Never censor it.

According to Dante's *Inferno*, there is an inscription over the gates of Hell. It reads: "Abandon hope, all ye who enter here." Not according to the Creed, you see. Not according to the Creed! According to the Creed, Jesus himself walked through those gates, going all the way, fighting the good fight, preaching the good news, and Jesus then walked back through those gates again, the other direction this time, with a new set of keys jingling on his belt, with the little lost sheep, one under each arm, and a whole host of others following in his train (Ephesians 4:8; Psalm 68:18). In the descent to hell, Jesus is all in. God is all in. The Spirit is all in. All in *for* us.[14]

Another author, one far more recent than Dante, has captured this beautifully. Calvin Miller, in his book *The Singer*, retells the story of Jesus as a singer who sings Earthmaker's (God's) song of love. In one passage, the Singer has an exchange with the devil, called the World Hater, about hell, the Canyon of the Damned. Here it is:

The Singer woke at midnight . . .

The air was full of moans. With groans of grief and pity, the night was crying. He had never heard the darkness cry before.

"Where are you, World Hater?" he shouted.

"Standing in the doorway of the worlds—reveling in my melodies of ugliness and death."

The Singer listened. The morbid air depressed him and he could not help but weep himself. He ached from the despair. "How long have they cried . . . ?" he asked.

The World Hater . . . shouted, "They've moaned a million years. It never stops . . . Crying is the only thing they know."

"Poor souls! Have they nothing to look back upon with joy?" the Singer asked.

"No. Nor anything to look forward to with hope."

"Could they never give up suffering for one small moment, every thousand years or so?"

"No. Never. They ache in simply knowing they will never cease to ache."

"I'm coming to the Canyon of the Damned you know."

"You dare not think that you could sing above their anguished dying that never will be dead."

"You'll see, World Hater. I will come."

"It's my domain!" the Hater protested.

"You have no domain. How dare you think that you can hold some corner of Earthmaker's universe and make it your own private horror chamber!"

"It is forever, Singer!"

"Yes, but not off-limits to the song. I'll smash the gates that hold the damned and every chain will fall away. I'll sing to every suffering cell of hate, the love song of my soul. . . ."

The troubled air grew still. The World Hater stepped outside the universe—pulled shut the doorway of the worlds.

And Crying softly slept with Joy.[15]

"I'm coming to the Canyon of the Damned you know." It is "not off-limits to the song." That, in two short sentences, is what "he descended into hell" means.

Section 2

Our Descent and New Life

One more thing. You might remember from the New Testament lesson that, right after speaking of Christ's descent to the dead, 1 Peter 3 states simply, "Baptism is like that" (v. 21 CEB). First Peter links our initiation into Christian faith—our baptism—with Christ's descent into hell.[16] Because of our baptism, because of Christ's death, we shouldn't live our lives according to our desires, "but in ways determined by God's will," the letter says (1 Peter 4:2 CEB). That's why the good news was preached to the dead, it continues, so that all might "live by the Spirit according to divine standards" (1 Peter 4:6 CEB).

The apostle Paul says the same thing in Romans: if we died with Christ, and have been buried with him (and that includes descended with him), then we are also made alive in him and can walk in newness of life (Romans 6:4). So we can, we *should*, live our lives better now, differently now—as different as life is from death. We should live our lives like people for whom God went to the greatest of lengths and to the deepest of depths, even to the darkest corner of hell.

And what's not to like about that, even if you don't like the word *hell*? It sounds like the Good News of the Gospel of Jesus Christ to me. *That's* why "he descended to the dead" is my favorite part of the creed. What's yours?

Notes

1. See "Descent of Christ into Hell, The," in *The Oxford Dictionary of the Christian Church*, ed. F. L. Cross and E. A. Livingstone, 3rd ed.) Oxford: Oxford University Press, 1997), 472: the earliest attestation is in the 4th c. (Fourth Creed of Sirmium of 359). Rufinus discusses it in his *Commentary on the Apostles' Creed* (c. AD 404).
2. *descendit ad inferna* or *ad inferos*. See James F. Kay, "He Descended into Hell," in *Exploring and Proclaiming the Apostles' Creed*, ed. Roger E. Van Ham (Eerdmans, 2004), 118–19; Kay ultimately deems them synonyms. J. N. D. Kelly thinks *inferos* is preferred as the place of the departed, not the damned: *Early Christian Creeds*, 3rd ed. (Continuum, 1972), 378 n. 3.
3. Actually English *inferno* is an Italian loanword from the Latin *infernus*.

4 Kay points out that the word *hell* is linked only to Jesus in the Creed ("He Descended into Hell," 118, see also 126 n. 19 on the sanitizing of the Creed, perhaps because of the "innumerable 'hells' of this world").

5 The issue with Wesley's censorship of the creed at this point and Article 111 of the Anglican Articles of Religion is a bit more complex, especially as he retained the descent in daily prayer and in the baptismal liturgy. See Heather Hahn, "Did Jesus descend into hell or to the dead?" (https://www.umnews.org/en/news/did-jesus-descend-into-hell-or-to-the-dead). Hahn indicates that the line was gone in American Methodism by 1792 but restored in the 20th century due to ecumenical interests. Rex Mathews has informed me via personal communication that the omission can be traced in various editions of the *Book of Common Prayer* and is no doubt bound up with anti-Catholic positions, especially regarding purgatory. See now Jerry Walls, *Purgatory: The Logic of Total Transformation* (Oxford University Press, 2011).

6 Note Calvin who called this line "the sum of our redemption" (see Kay, "He Descended into Hell," 117).

7 See, inter alia, *Catechism of the Catholic Church*, 2nd ed. (Doubleday, 1994), 179–81; Kelly, *Early Christian Creeds*, 379.

8 John 5:25 (cf. Matthew 12:39-40; Romans 10:7); Hebrews 2:14-15 (cf. Acts 3:15). See also Romans 14:9 ("Lord of both the dead and the living"); Colossians 1:18; Acts 2:27-31 (note Psalm 16:8ff.); Hebrews 11:39-40; 12:22-23; 10:20; Luke 23:43; also Ephesians 4:5; Philippians 2:10.

9 See Kelly, *Early Christian Creeds*, 380-83, on the two that follow (liberation and revival).

10 Attributed first to Melanchthon by Scott Black Johnston, "A Good Friday Sermon: Harrowing," in *Exploring and Proclaiming the Apostles' Creed*, ed. Roger E. Van Harn (Eerdmans, 2004), 130–35. Kay also finds the liberation motif in Rufinus ("He Descended into Hell," 120–21).

11 Not all in the history of interpretation would agree to the latter clause. See Kay, "He Descended into Hell," 122; Kelly, *Early Christian Creeds*, 381 and n. 7.

12 Luke 15:1-7. Cf. the Ancient Homily for Holy Saturday cited in *Catechism of the Catholic Church*, 181: "He has gone to search for Adam, our first father, as for a lost sheep . . . [H]e has gone to free from sorrow Adam in his bonds and Eve, captive with him."

13 Kelly, *Early Christian Creeds*, 382, citing Pseudo-Fulgentius: "He, so merciful and blessed, mercifully visited the region of our misery, so as to escort us to the region of His blessedness."

14 Kay, "He Descended into Hell," 121: "Rather than the final act of the passion, the descent into hell can be taken as the first act of the resurrection."

15 Calvin Miller, *The Singer Trilogy: The Mythic Retelling of the Story of the New Testament* (Intervarsity Press, 1992).

16 See further Karl Barth, *Credo* (Charles Scribner's Sons, 1962), 94: "Burial *with* Christ would then mean, we were standing under His *Name* as actually those for whom that took place, who now may *live* as those for whom it did take place."

The Miracle of Faith

Alma Tinoco Ruiz

Psalm 23 is usually read at funerals with emphasis on its last verb, "I will dwell in the house of the Lord forever" (v. 6 NIV). However, this psalm is more about journeying in life than about death. More specifically, it is about journeying with God—walking with God through life. It is also about the miracle of faith—the assurance we have of God's faithfulness even in the most challenging times.

In March this year, I took some of my students on an immersion experience to Colombia. There we met with grassroots community leaders, *campesinos* and *campesinas*, Indigenous, and Black Colombian leaders. They shared with us the struggles their communities are experiencing: displacement, persecution, oppression, the effects of climate change, violence, lack of adequate health care, lack of access to education, and many more challenges. These leaders are in a constant *lucha*/resistance, advocating for just treatment, the return of their territories, and the peace of their communities.

As I was listening to their struggles, I could not believe how they were able to continue *luchando*/resisting even when they had suffered so much and lost so many loved ones who resisted with them.

I asked one of the community leaders who has experienced much suffering how can she continue *en la lucha*, fighting for the liberation of her people, knowing the danger it represents for her and her loved ones. She answered with a peaceful voice, "*Confío que Dios está con nosotros,*" that is, "I trust God is with us."

Section 2

Many of these leaders continue resisting because they have no other option. If they do not resist oppression and injustice, they will suffer. If they resist, they will still suffer, but at least they will be at peace, knowing they are doing the right thing for their people. And all they have is their faith in God's presence among them—the miracle of faith illustrated in Psalm 23.

Some scholars believe that David wrote this prayer and song during his kingship, and some believe that it was written during David's later years. We might never know when it was written, but I imagine it was written by a mature David, a person who had tasted glory and disgrace, righteousness and immorality, and God's mercy and love in all seasons of his life.

It was written by a mature David who had learned to depend on God alone and not on his own strength or great-numbered army. It was written by a David who had encountered God's grace each time his ego and sin separated him from God. This prayer was written by a person who had learned to seek the guidance of the good shepherd and to depend on him, knowing that if he has God, he does not lack anything.

In this prayer, David opens his heart and expresses gratitude for how he has experienced God's presence in his life, even in the darkest moments.

From the deepest of his soul, David prays, "The LORD is my shepherd I lack nothing. He makes me lie down in green pastures, he leads me beside quiet waters, he refreshes my soul" (Psalm 23:1-3 NIV).

As a good shepherd who protects and guides his sheep, God tenderly cares for David. Nature partners with its creator to help David rest, satisfy his thirst, and refresh his soul, providing for his emotional, physical, and spiritual needs. Just as nature is partnering with its creator to refresh our souls today with this amazing view and tranquility.

The Psalm continues, "He guides me along the right paths for his name's sake. Even though I walk through the darkest valley, I will fear no evil, for you are with me" (vv. 3-4 NIV).

David experienced several dark valleys. Many were the consequences of being anointed by God to be king of the Israelites. For instance, he had to fight many fights to defend his people. Leadership is costly.

The Miracle of Faith

The right path is not always the easiest path. But one can experience peace in the darkest valley when we have gotten there for doing the right thing, for peace is the joy of knowing we are walking along the right path.

When we do God's will, we can experience God's peace, even while walking through the darkest valley—the peace of knowing that we are not alone and that God is with us, guiding us along the right path.

The leaders I met in Colombia had peace—the peace of knowing that even though the path they had taken was leading them to the darkest valley (dangers, exhaustion, enemies, and persecution)—they knew they had taken the right path, the path of justice, liberation, mercy, compassion, empathy, and love. Though it might not be the easiest path, it is the right one. Do they experience fear? Surely! But they gain strength knowing that God is with them.

The only thing they have when they walk through the darkest valley is their faith in the protection and comfort of their God, trusting that God is with them.

Isn't it a miracle to have faith in the protection of God even when you find yourself walking through the darkest valley? This is the miracle of faith, "the assurance of things hoped for, the conviction of things not seen" (Hebrew 11:1 NRSVue).

This is the faith the Archbishop of San Salvador, now Saint Óscar Romero, experienced. He followed God's guidance along the right path, the path for justice, liberation, compassion, love, and empathy for the people experiencing extreme poverty, persecution, and oppression in El Salvador. Romero, as the people he was defending, became the subject of threats and hatred.

Was he afraid? Yes! Especially of dying a violent death. At the same time, he was at peace, knowing that God was guiding him along this path, and he had faith that God was walking with him through this darkest valley. During this dangerous and vulnerable journey, God always refreshed his soul.

Other people walk through the darkest valleys because of loneliness, sickness, or losing loved ones. Not too long ago, I prayed Psalm 23 with two siblings in Christ receiving dialysis, and they shared with me how they find comfort in knowing that God walks with them through the darkest valley of illness.

Section 2

However, it is important to name that some of the darkest valleys David experienced were the consequences of his own actions. Like the dark valley he experienced after he violated Bathsheba's body and then killed her husband. That was probably the darkest valley David experienced, facing his evil actions, immorality, and unfaithfulness to God. However, after walking through the darkest valley of his own creation, David had the assurance that God would protect him even from his own evil.

Even at his lowest point, God was with David. How, then, would not David have the assurance of God's grace, mercy, and love?

I imagine most of you have listened to the news and have seen and maybe even experienced the effects and consequences of a rhetoric of division, hatred, and violence shared widely every day. We are creating our darkest valley. And I pray and hope that we will listen to and follow the voice of our divine Shepherd and allow him to guide us along the right path of justice, mercy, compassion, empathy, and love for each other.

David continues praying, "Your rod and your staff, they comfort me" (Psalm 23:4 NIV).

Who better than David, who was a shepherd at a young age, to understand the comfort the shepherd's tools brought to the sheep? These tools were used by shepherds to guide the sheep on the right path and to protect them. Now, David is the sheep who is grateful for that guidance and protection.

The Psalm goes on, "You prepare a table before me in the presence of my enemies. You anoint my head with oil; my cup overflows" (23:5 NIV).

David learned to depend on God, for only God can provide him with what he needs, and even more so, as God provided the Israelites with manna that fell from heaven in the desert. David shows gratitude for the many blessings he has received from God, for a grateful heart is a blessed heart.

Shepherds would use oil to help treat the sheep's wounds or injuries. As the sheep, needing the shepherd's help, David experienced God's tender care for his soul wounds.

The Psalm concludes, "Surely your goodness and love will follow me all the days of my life, and I will dwell in the house of the LORD forever" (23:6 NIV).

David doesn't say this lightly, for he experienced God's goodness and love, even when he was unfaithful and sinful. This gives him the assurance that he will dwell in God's presence forever, for nothing can separate him from God's love, grace, and mercy.

That is why I believe that Psalm 23 illustrates the miracle of faith. It illustrates the journey of life with its beauty, challenges, and pain, and the unfailing presence of God with us.

Jesus is our loving shepherd who calls us back to him when we go astray and turn our own way (Isaiah 53:6). When we walk through the darkest valley created by our own sin, our Shepperd tenderly guides us along the right path.

When we walk through the darkest valley created by violence, sickness, or the loss of loved ones, our Shepherd lovingly cares for our wounds.

Regardless of what we are experiencing now, we can all be confident that the Lord is our shepherd for all the days of our lives. We can experience the miracle of faith, the assurance that God is with us.

A Sermon on Matthew 28:16-20

Bishop Connie Mitchell Shelton

On Trinity Sunday 2023, Bishop Connie Mitchell Shelton preached the following sermon at the constitution of a new church in the North Carolina Annual Conference following a painful disaffiliation vote months prior. The new church is aptly named "Grace United Methodist Church." The assigned texts for constituting a new church are Genesis 1 and Matthew 28.

"This is a day of new beginnings, time to remember, and move on, time to believe what love is bringing, laying to rest the pain that's gone."[1] Could any of us have imagined this day, even six months ago? The heartbreak of betrayal and the pain of separation can seem so permanent and desperate and final. And yet the Holy Spirit of Pentecost still comes . . . and births the church . . . over and over again. Creator God still moves across the face of the waters and says, "Let there be light: and . . . it was good" (Genesis 1:3-4 KJV). And our risen Jesus still goes ahead of us revealing the heartbeat of God.

Today is Trinity Sunday in the liturgical life of the church. Today is the day we declare the mystery of our Triune God—three persons, of one substance, power, and eternity—the Father, the Son, and the Holy Spirit. In United Methodist congregations all over the world, we say as a gathered body that we "believe in God the Father Almighty, maker of heaven and earth; And in Jesus Christ his only Son, our Lord; who was conceived by the Holy Spirit." While explaining the Trinity remains challenging for us, the relationships among

Section 2

Father, Son, and Holy Spirit are instructive and welcoming. Trinity Sunday is celebrated on the Sunday after Pentecost, thereby reminding us that we worship God the Creator; we worship Jesus the Redeemer (fully God and fully human); and we worship the Holy Spirit (sustaining, comforting, sanctifying, and always at work within us and in the sacraments we celebrate).

This threefold nature of God isn't just theological doctrine—it's the very pattern of divine love into which we're invited. The Father's creating love, the Son's redeeming grace, and the Spirit's sustaining presence weave together in perfect unity and maintain their distinctive roles. When we say we believe in this Triune God, we're saying we believe in a God whose very nature is relationship, community, and self-giving love. This has profound implications for how we understand both God and ourselves.

The suggested Gospel text for constituting a new church is Matthew 28 known as the Great Commission. The context of this passage is essential. ("Context" simply means, what's the back story?) In Matthew's Gospel, this passage is describing the first Easter. So, if we rewind a few days, we see that the disciples were counting on Jesus to fulfill all their hopes and dreams—to break the chains of power and overthrow the oppressive regime. Instead, they witness the horror and trauma of their Jesus dying an unjust... gruesome... humiliating criminal's death. And afterwards, they are haunted by all the memories of their regret, their guilt, their shame. They slept through Jesus's request to keep watch and pray. Peter denied Jesus thrice. (I love the word "thrice" on Trinity Sunday!) They misunderstood what Jesus said and how his life, death, and resurrection would unfold. After betraying Jesus, one of their closest friends took his own life. Friends, the disciples were carrying a heavy load. It's incredibly important that we lean into their despair to fully understand our text today.

You know despair. You know disappointment, denial, betrayal, and abandonment. The heartbreak of betrayal and the pain of separation can seem so permanent and desperate and final. In our lives, in our churches, in our communities—we've all tasted that bitter cup of suffering. Sometimes suffering comes through personal betrayal, sometimes through institutional failure, sometimes through the grinding weight of systems that seem designed to crush hope. But even in these darkest valleys, we are not alone. The Spirit that hovered over the waters at creation still moves. The Son who walked the way

A Sermon on Matthew 28:16-20

of suffering still accompanies us. The Father who raised Jesus from death still brings life from places of despair. And the Holy Spirit of Pentecost still comes . . . and births the church . . . over and over again.

Back to Matthew's Gospel, so . . . a few days after Jesus's horrific death, the women bring preposterous, unthinkable, astonishing news. They said they saw Jesus and Jesus said to tell the disciples to go to Galilee and meet him at the mountain! Whiplash! Depression to exhilaration, guilt to giddiness, shame to shock, regret to restoration!

So, we pick up with Matthew 28 where our disciples head to Galilee and meet Jesus. Matthew doesn't give us any hint of a verbal exchange. The disciples don't have the opportunity to apologize or explain. Jesus doesn't offer a recap or absolve them. Jesus commissions, "*Go, make disciples!*"

Are you with me? Jesus dies a gruesome criminal's death, he lies in the tomb for three days, and God's resurrection power raises him from the dead! This is the core of our faith: *the risen Christ conquered sin and death!* And the grand finale of Matthew's Gospel is: "Go, make disciples!" This must be really important! What do we do with this?

Let me share a personal story that continues to teach me about God's surprising way of working death into new life. Years ago, my twenty-year-old niece experienced acute liver failure and was airlifted to a hospital to be placed on a transplant list. Waiting for a call for an available organ is an impossible proposition. We could not pray for an organ to be identified. For an organ to become available, someone would have to die. We instead prayed for peace and hope and life. As my beautiful, vibrant niece's life hung in the balance, we waited.

Somewhere in the deepest dark of night, the charge nurse walked into the hospital room where my sister and I were nestled on the unsleepable couch. The room illuminated a glow. The charge nurse said, "We've received word that an organ has been identified. We will prepare for a liver transplant tomorrow." My sister and I began to weep uncontrollably. We knew a family made a selfless, wrenching decision towards life, even as their loved one would not survive. I cannot adequately describe the complexity of our emotions. All we could do was receive the gift from strangers. We could not express our gratitude, nor could we run to their side and weep with them. We could not find a way to appropriate our gratitude for their selfless generosity. Or could we?

Isn't that the good news of the Gospel? God did for us what we could not do for ourselves. Jesus demonstrated God's love, even laying down his own life. We spend the rest of our lives discerning how and where to *go* to join God's mission so that we appropriate our gratitude for God's selfless generosity and Jesus's extravagant love for us! And our response is to *go* and love extravagantly as disciples of Jesus! *Go* where we aren't comfortable. *Go* be the church in the world, not in a building.

We might feel like we've been through the unthinkable and crushed by those closest to us, and yet the risen Christ speaks to us now, "Go, make disciples!" Baptize in the name of the Trinity—the Father, Son, and the Holy Spirit. Teach joyful obedience to the inclusive way of Jesus.

Pay attention to the way God's DNA is replicated in us through our spiritual and communal practices, empowered by the Holy Spirit. When we gather for worship, we're drawn into the eternal song of praise that flows between Father, Son, and Spirit. When we serve our neighbors, we participate in the self-giving love that characterizes the Trinity. When we study scripture together, we're guided by the Spirit into the truth of Christ who reveals the Father's heart. When we share Communion, we're invited into the divine fellowship that is God's very nature.

Our mission is clear—*to make disciples of Jesus Christ for the transformation of the world!* Our mission invites others into the divine dance of love and the transforming fellowship with the Triune God. Our mission bears witness to a different way of being human—one shaped by the perfect unity and self-giving love of Father, Son, and Spirit.

Hear the good news and remember with joy Jesus's final words that he is with us always—all the way to the end. We are made new because of what Jesus has done for us, through us, and in us! Jesus is with us!

"Christ is alive, and goes before us to show and share what love can do. This is a day of new beginnings; our God is making all things new!"[2] *Go!*

Notes

1 "This Is a Day of New Beginnings," Brian Wren, *The United Methodist Hymnal*, 383, stanza 1.
2 *The United Methodist Hymnal*, 383, stanza 4.

The Trinity Forms Us and Sends Us

Bishop Kenneth H. Carter Jr.

Ellen Charry, one of our more profound theologians, writes,

> That we know Father, Son and Holy Spirit as creator, redeemer and sanctifier suggests that God knows and understands that we need more help than simply to be created and set going. To this end, God's own being is structured around our needs. That the Son and Spirit are indeed God and sent into the world to repair us, brings us face to face with our need for precisely the work that God does. [1]

This comment, which rewards the reader who contemplates its meaning, connects doctrine with life, belief with practice, liturgy with daily life.

The triune God, in whose image we are created, is not absent from human failure and fragmentation: In Christ, we are offered forgiveness, and through the Holy Spirit we have the promise of the comforter. The Trinity confounds our simplistic views about God, in whom, we are told, most persons believe in some vague sense. A robust vision of the Christian God stands over and against the reduced deity who is found wanting in the midst of life's complexities.

And so, the Trinity is God's gift to us, forming us in the mysterious nature of an Unseen Power who is named in scripture, experienced in a rich and multifaceted tradition, comprehended (through a glass darkly) in tradition and bound together with our human experience. From baptismal formulas to words prayed at the Eucharist, from the strains or our doxologies to the chimes that announce the conclusion of our assemblies, this peculiar and complicated God is with us, in ways that are often beyond our grasp, and yet, surely for purposes that contribute to our identity and well-being.

And as disciples of Jesus, we are formed for a purpose. Years ago I was in conversation with Church of England Bishop Graham Cray, one of the pioneers of the Fresh Expressions movement. He was in the midst of describing existing church structures and cultural shifts in which present-day Christianity exists in England. At times these must have seemed insurmountable: clergy and laity, many of them leaders, who had settled into predictable rituals, a growing sector beyond them—a sector that seemed either bored with or cynical about the faith. And then he paused and there was a twinkle in his eye: "*But, you know, the missionary Holy Spirit is always going ahead of us!*"

The simple call to "proclaim the gospel afresh" assumes that the Triune God indeed goes ahead of us. In the Wesleyan tradition we describe this as prevenient grace. Our *missionary strategy* does not presume to take God to people. We trust that God is already moving in the hearts of men and women, constantly engaging their minds with questions. At times the movement of the Holy Spirit is disruptive and public, like a Pentecostal storm; at other times, there is a still, small voice, an awakening.

Our formation in the Trinity calls us to a *holy risk* and a *profound trust*. The risk mirrors God's creation of the world, God's love for the world. The trust is God's reminder of our eternal home, our refuge and strength. The instrument through which this work occurs is an orthodox, evangelical, inclusive, and missional church. And yet the church is an earthen vessel (2 Corinthians 4), at times revealing and extending the love of God for the world, at times hiding or constricting that same blessing.

To be re-created in God's image is to be crucified with Christ (Galatians 2), it is to receive the fruit of the Spirit (Galatians 5). This is our formation, and yes at times our reformation. To be sent forth into the world is to hear the commandments and commission of Jesus (Matthew 22; 28), and to bear witness to the Spirit that is poured out on all flesh (Acts 2)

God not only understands our needs as individuals. God knows just as deeply our needs as a church. And to know this Triune God is to come to know who we are and why we exist.

Prayer: May the Creating God baptize our imaginations, connecting our doctrine with our daily lives. May the Saving Lord Jesus meet us wherever we break bread, and may our hearts once again burn within us. May the missionary Holy Spirit be poured out on all flesh, empowering us to proclaim the gospel afresh to all generations.

Notes

1   Ellen Charry, "Spiritual Formation by the Doctrine of the Trinity", *Theology Today*, October, 1997

Into the Trinity

Edgardo Colón-Emeric

*G*racia y paz de Dios nuestro Padre y el Señor Jesucristo. I am very happy to be here as a weak instrument of God's mighty work.

Are you into the Trinity? I hope so because today is Trinity Sunday. Trinity Sunday is an odd Sunday. Most feast days of the Christian year celebrate a significant event in the life of Jesus—his birth, his baptism, his transfiguration, his passion, his resurrection. Even last Sunday, the day of Pentecost is strongly tied to the story of Jesus, because the Spirit came down in fulfillment of his promises and prayers. Today we do not celebrate an event. Today we celebrate a doctrine: the doctrine of the Trinity. The origin of this celebration goes back to the Middle Ages. The day was instituted to cap the celebration of the great fifty days of Easter with an affirmation of the God who was fully revealed through Jesus by the power of the Spirit. Trinity Sunday is the postlude to Pentecost. Today is a day for doctrine, a day not for worshipping doctrine (we only worship God), but a day for delighting in a doctrine. Are you into the Trinity?

The simple truth of the matter is that many Christians are not into the Trinity. It has been said that if the doctrine of the Trinity were to disappear from the Church, then some would barely notice the difference. This might seem hard to believe given the richly Trinitarian music resounding in this space today. And yet a recent study of contemporary church music (Vineyard) showed that most songs are either addressed to the Son (32%) or to an unspecified "You Lord" (51%). Only a small percentage are addressed to the Father (6%), the Spirit (1.4%) or all three (1.4%). The doctrine of the

Section 2

Trinity appears to be this ancient heirloom that we have inherited from our grandparents and we are not sure where to put it. Except that today is the day for dusting it off and displaying it.

There are two reasons why this neglect of the Trinity is tragic. First, there are alternative teachings out there. The largest Pentecostal church in Durham is a oneness congregation that unabashedly and explicitly rejects the doctrine of the Trinity. According to the teaching of this congregation, the doctrine of the Trinity is an innovation. Baptism is done in the name of Jesus only. In Latin America, some Methodist churches worry about singing the doxology because it sounds Catholic. In Central America, I once saw a sign along the main road leading from the airport to San Salvador which read, "They are not three. And it is not one. There are two. The Father and the Mother." It sounds like a kind of celestial, double-income, no-children family. Second, without the doctrine of the Trinity, many things that we do as Christians cease to make sense.

The word *doctrine* raises negative associations for some. I remember a person I worked with complaining about a clergy friend of mine; the chief basis of that complaint was that when he thought of this clergy person, two words came to mind: doctrine and truth. Doctrine is dismissed in many places as closed-minded, backwards looking. Today we celebrate doctrine as good news, because the word *doctrine* means nothing more than truthful teaching, and today we celebrate the chief Christian teaching that our God is a Triune God. Or to put it in the words of Gregory of Nazianzus, that when I say God, I mean Father, Son, and Holy Spirit.

I am into the doctrine of the Trinity. The intellectual challenges of this doctrine put quantum mechanics to shame. And the history of its development is nothing short of dramatic. It has a long cast of characters, heroes like Athanasius and villains like Arius, heroines like Macrina and scoundrels like Nestorius, saints and sinners. It is full of drama, political intrigue. Like a Bond movie the drama of this doctrine unfolds in exotic locales: Nicaea, Constantinople, Ephesus, Chalcedon. It even has a Q branch ready to supply its protagonists with special conceptual tools, words like *homoousios, prosopon, perichoresis* have been used to disarm opponents and save the day for Christian doctrine.

Into the Trinity

Most attempts at explaining the doctrine turn to metaphors and images. Richard of St. Victor spoke of the social trinity of the lover, the beloved, and the co-beloved. Augustine spoke of the intellectual trinity of mind, memory, and will. St. Patrick is credited with the botanical trinity of the shamrock, three petals, one leaf. There is the musical triad of *Do, Mi, So*—three notes, one major chord. There is the elemental trinity of H_2O which at the triple point of 0.01 degrees Celsius and 0.006 atmospheres coexists in thermodynamic equilibrium as ice, water, and vapor. You have probably confessed Nicene-Constantinopolitan Creed (We believe in God, the Father, the almighty), and you have probably eaten Neapolitan ice cream: three flavors, one substance.

Other attempts at teaching the doctrine turn to symbols like the circle, or three partially overlapping circles, the shield of the Trinity, the Celtic triquetra, and of course triangles of all kinds: triangles inscribed with Greek letters (*ho ōn*), triangles inscribed with the Hebrew letters (*yod, he, vav, he*), triangles inscribed with Latin words (*sanctus, sanctus, sanctus*), triangles intersected by a cross, triangles crisscrossed by three circles, triangles made up of three equilateral fish, triangles made of three identical rabbits.

The doctrine of the Trinity does not belong to experts, to professors of history or theology. The doctrine of the Trinity is your doctrine. It is a Christian doctrine. It is a mystical doctrine. The word *mystic* no doubt brings up all sorts of strange associations: the occult, the uncanny, palm-reading, voodoo, Harry Potter, and the like. In the Christian perspective, properly speaking, mystical is simply another way of saying Christian. It is mystical in that its purpose is not simply to show us the truth but to lead us into the truth.

If you are into the Trinity, you are into doctrine. The author of Proverbs hears Wisdom's call resounding not only in the academy but in the city streets. In the verses that the lectionary skipped, Wisdom extols the virtues of its teaching, "for wisdom is better than jewels . . . better than gold, even fine gold" (Proverbs 8:11, 19 NRSV). Wisdom's teaching, wisdom's doctrine makes wise the simple but confounds the proud. In the eyes of this philosopher, Lady Wisdom and Lady Poverty are friends.

But who is this Wisdom? Is this personification of wisdom a literary device or something more? It seems to be something more, because Wisdom describes herself as a partner to God. She is a partner of the Lord who is also the first of his acts. When there were no depths, she was there. Before the hills in order stood or earth received her frame, she was there in the beginning. The language here echoes that of Genesis 1 and stretches beyond it to a beginning before the beginning. Where this sage stopped, John the evangelist picked up, for "In the beginning was the Word, and the Word was with God, and the Word was God" (John 1:1 NRSV). It is this word that we hear speaking in the Gospel reading.

The disciples are gathered on the eve of Jesus's passion, not in an upper room as in Luke, but in an undisclosed location. In that space, Jesus washes his disciples' feet and teaches about how true lordship is lived out in service. After Judas leaves the room, Jesus introduces his disciples to an intensive course on Trinitarian theology.

One of the earliest Trinitarian formulas that Christians learn is the *Gloria Patri*. Glory be to the Father and to the Son and to the Holy Spirit, as it was in the beginning, is now and ever shall be, world without end. In this section of John's Gospel, a section often called by scholars "The Book of Glory," Jesus teaches the disciples about the glory of the Triune God.

Keep in mind that in the book of Isaiah we read that the Lord does not share his glory with anyone: "I am the LORD, that is my name; / my glory I give to no other, / nor my praise to idols" (42:8 NRSV). Glory belongs to God alone. And yet in the Gospels, the glory of God is given to the Son and to the Spirit. The word *glory* recurs so often in these chapters of the Gospel of John that many scholars refer to this section as the Book of Glory. Jesus does not seek his own glory. The Father glorifies the Son. The Son glorifies the Father. The Father is glorified in the Son when the disciples pray in the name of Jesus. The Son is glorified in his disciples, and when his disciples bear fruit, the Father is glorified. All that the Father has belongs to Jesus. His teaching is not his own, his words, his works, his knowing, his willing, his friends, his very identity are all linked to the one who sent him. The Spirit glorifies the Son by sharing what is Jesus's with his disciples.

It is not simply what he teaches but how he teaches that makes Jesus's teaching Trinitarian doctrine. Jesus does not teach doctrine from the outside, from an exclusively historical perspective, or from a merely philosophical perspective. Jesus teaches Trinitarian doctrine from the inside, from a mystical perspective. The Spirit is needed to lead students of the Trinity into all the truth of God. Without the Spirit the things that Jesus says about God are unbearable because they are too high. The teaching is too luminous. The doctrine is not hard to bear because it is irrational, but because it is suprarational. The Spirit completes the teaching of Jesus not by adding to it, but by leading us into it. For example, in the Father's house are many mansions, and Jesus the Son is the way to these many dwelling places. The Spirit is the one that leads the disciples by the hand along the way of Jesus. As another example, the Father is in the Son, and the Son is in the Father, so that if anyone sees the Son, he or she has seen the Father. The Spirit is the one that shows us the Son by reminding us of what Jesus has said and leading us into a deeper understanding of what he said.

You cannot be into the Father, unless you are into Jesus. You cannot be into Jesus, unless you are into the Spirit. The Spirit is our entry point into the doctrine of the Trinity, a doctrine whose sole purpose is to lead us into the Trinity itself. This is the reason why the chief Trinitarian theologians are mystical theologians.

I remember visiting the Convent of the Incarnation in Ávila, Spain, where St. Teresa de Jesús (Teresa of Ávila) lived as a nun for many years. One of the Carmelite sisters showed me around the place. She took me to St. Teresa's bedroom where I saw that she used a log for a pillow which helped me understand one of her sayings that "prayer and comfortable living are incompatible." The sister also showed me the area where St. Teresa entertained visitors. It looked like the kind of visiting area that you might expect at a prison where people face each other across bars and can speak to each other, but no physical contact is allowed. One of St. Teresa's frequent visitors was St. John of the Cross. Sister told me that during one of his visits, both saints began to talk about the Trinity; as their conversation went deeper into the truth of the Trinity, both saints began to float.

Now, I do not know if this really happened or not, but it is the kind of thing that should not surprise us if Trinitarian theology leads us into the Triune God. If you are really into the Trinity all kinds of strange things can happen.

Section 2

Look at St. Patrick, he was so into the Trinity that he began to see traces of the Trinity everywhere he looked, even in those little three green clovers known as shamrocks.

Look at Mother Teresa; she was so into the Trinity that she saw the image of the Triune God shining on the faces of the weak, the sick, and the abandoned.

But let me warn you. If you are into the Trinity, then you are into the cross. The Spirit leads disciples into the Trinity by way of suffering. The proclamation of the gospel engenders opposition and resistance. On the one hand, the opposition of those for whom the doctrine of the Trinity threatens the basic confession of Israel: the Lord your God is one. According to John, Jesus was put to death for two reasons: for breaking the Sabbath and for calling God his own Father, "thereby making himself equal to God" (5:18 NRSV). On the other hand, the gospel of the Triune God, gives rise to the puzzled opposition of the Romans who wonder: "Why, if there is room for three in one, is there no room for Caesar?" Suffering has often accompanied Christian witness to the Triune God. In Church history a confessor is someone who suffers torture for his or her profession of faith. It is no accident that the word that John uses for bearing the truth (*bastazein*) is the same word he uses to speak of Jesus bearing the cross. The way into the Trinity is the way of the cross. But there is a deeper level of suffering that is part and parcel of the way into the Trinity. When Christian art, particularly of the Western variety have attempted to depict the Trinity, they have depicted the cross. It is called the *Gnadenstuhl*, or the seat of mercy. For it is at the cross that we see the mercy of God towards the world. At the cross, the Son surrenders the Spirit into the Father's hands. At the cross, the Father, in love for the Son, bears him up and sustains him, even when the Son feels abandoned. At the cross, the Spirit is breathed out so that the witness of the water and the blood, the witness of the sacraments, may be true. The Father is silent at the cross, not because he is angry: How could he? This is his beloved Son. Nor because he is indifferent: How could he? For so he loved the world. No, the Father is silent because he is speechless. He has said it all in this one Word. And with the death of Jesus, the Father, in a sense, has been rendered mute. The final word from the cross is silence—the meaningful, merciful silence of the Father before the alleluias of Easter. The events surrounding the cross, the passion, the death, the burial, the resurrection, these things mark the highest point of divine disclosure. The Sign of the Cross is in the name of the Father, Son, and Holy Spirit.

The way into the Truth of the Trinity is the way of the cross. The Spirit leads us into communion with the Son by the path of suffering. Paul knew this well. In writing to the Christians at Rome, Paul boasts regarding the benefits of justification. He boasts about the hope of glory. And he even boasts about his sufferings, "knowing that suffering produces endurance, and endurance produces character, and character produces hope, and hope does not disappoint us, because God's love has been poured into our hearts through the Holy Spirit that has been given to us" (Romans 5:3-5 NRSV). A strange boast. How can it be that suffering produces anything good? Is not suffering destructive of character? What Paul knows—something that many of us have forgotten—is that Christian life is cruciform. Our baptism into the Father, Son, and Holy Spirit requires dying with Christ.

You cannot be into the Trinity if the Trinity is not into you. The firmness of our hope in the face of trial is that the love of God has been poured into our hearts by the Holy Spirit.

If you have been baptized in the name of the Father, Son, and Holy Spirit, and if you live in newness of life, then the Trinity is into you. If you have renounced the spiritual forces of wickedness in the high places, then the Trinity is into you. If you love your neighbor, if you forgive, if you give freely, then the Trinity is into you. If you eat his flesh and drink his blood, then the Trinity is in you.

If you are into the Trinity, you are into the deep things of God. How deep? John of the Cross cannot express this union except in verse: "How gently and lovingly//you wake in my heart,//where in secret you dwell alone;// and in your sweet breathing,//filled with good and glory,//how tenderly you swell my heart with love" ("The Living Flame of Love"). Beautiful, but what does it mean? It means that the Spirit awakens the soul to a new way of seeing things. Instead of seeing God through the world (the cause from the effects), the soul starts to see the world through God (effects from the cause). This vision is called mystical wisdom. It means that the soul is now capable of breathing with God the Father, through the Son, the Holy Spirit. It means that the soul has become by grace what God is by nature. This is where Jesus

Section 2

promises the Spirit will lead his disciples. This is the hope of glory in which Paul boasts. This is the wisdom whose call so inflamed the heart of the writer of Proverbs.

If the Trinity is into you, then you will—like Patrick of Ireland—bind yourself to the strong name of the Trinity. The doctrine of the Trinity becomes a shield, not to protect you *from* the world, but to protect you *in* the world so that you can be of service to the world—a shield against the idols.

If the Trinity is into you, then you can look at creation and see in it a theater of God's glory, a divine drama whose author is the Father, whose director is the Spirit, whose protagonist is the Son, and whose co-stars are each and every human being.

Are you into the Trinity? Is the Trinity into you?

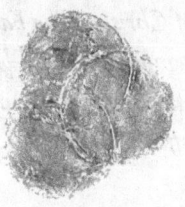

SECTION 3

Nicene Faith in Worship & Practice

The Nicene faith is not merely a matter of theological reflection or proclamation. Nicene faith shapes the daily practices and worship life of Christian communities. The essays in this section explore how Trinitarian faith is embodied in worship, music, spiritual formation, and the church's engagement with contemporary challenges.

William H. Willimon's "Chalcedonian Preaching" explores how the church's classic doctrinal formulations about Christ's divine and human natures inform faithful proclamation. His work demonstrates how ancient credal wisdom continues to shape effective preaching for today's church.

Lester Ruth's "How Great Is Our God" examines how contemporary Christian worship music expresses—or fails to express—Trinitarian faith. Through careful analysis of popular worship songs, Ruth reveals both the challenges and opportunities for fostering robust Trinitarian worship in today's church.

Jan Holton's "Theological Touchstone" offers wisdom for navigating uncertain times through spiritual "wayfinding." Drawing on pastoral experience and theological reflection, Holton shows how Trinitarian faith provides resilient hope in the face of contemporary crises.

Fred Edie's "Ecotheology and Contemporary Christianity" connects Trinitarian theology to urgent environmental concerns. His work demonstrates how understanding God as Creator, Redeemer, and Sustainer shapes Christian environmental practice and stewardship.

Jerusha Neal's "The Face of Christ in the Face of Conflict" brings the Nicene Creed into dialogue with contemporary social challenges. Through careful theological reflection on climate change, Christian nationalism, and church division, Neal shows how the Creed's affirmations offer resources for faithful witness in troubled times.

These essays demonstrate how Nicene faith moves beyond theoretical concerns to shape Christian practice and public witness. They reveal how the church's ancient confessions provide wisdom for engaging contemporary challenges from environmental crisis to political conflict. For church leaders seeking to foster faithful practice in uncertain times, these pieces offer both theological depth and practical guidance. They remind us that the Nicene heritage is not a dusty relic but a living tradition that continues to form communities of faith for mission and witness in the world.

Chalcedonian Proclamation

Will Willimon

In preaching, God solicits our participation in communication by using preachers to draw the world into conversation. No sermon is immaculately conceived; it's words of a thoroughly human preacher delivered in the name of the same relentlessly redemptive God who took interest in Samuel, Eli and sons, Jonah, Peter, and Mary. At the same time, no sermon is merely human public address; God produces more in a sermon than we can tell.

John Calvin marveled at the interaction of the divine and human that is Christian preaching: "When a person goes up into the pulpit . . . it is in order that God may speak to us through the mouth of a human being, and may be so gracious as to present himself here among us, having willed an ordinary human to be his messenger."[1]

That "the preached word is God's word" is best understood by what George Hunsinger calls the "Chalcedonian imagination."[2] From the beginning of *Church Dogmatics*, where Karl Barth tackles "The Word of God, and Experience,"[3] to the end where Barth says that God-human synergy occurs "without any confusion or mixture of the divine and human, or transformation of one into the other,"[4] the Definition of Chalcedon accounts for Barth's view of revelation.

Amid theological dispute among the followers of Apollinarius (overstressing the incommensurability of the two natures of Christ) and Nestorius (accentuating the distinctiveness and differentiation of Christ's two natures), the Definition of Chalcedon delineated the orthodoxy of Nicaea. Paradoxical clarification, not simplification, was its aim. Chalcedon celebrates the wonder of the consubstantial God/human Jesus:

> our Lord Jesus Christ, the same perfect in Godhead and also perfect in manhood; truly God and truly man . . . in all things like unto us, without sin; begotten before all ages of the Father . . . for us and for our salvation, born of the Virgin Mary, the Mother of God . . . one and the same Christ, Son, Lord, Only-begotten, to be acknowledged in two natures, *inconfusedly, unchangeably, indivisibly, inseparably*; the distinction of natures being by no means taken away by the union, but rather the property of each nature being preserved, and concurring in one Person and one Subsistence, not parted or divided into two persons, but one and the same Son . . . as the prophets from the beginning [have declared] concerning Him, and the Lord Jesus Christ imself has taught us, and the Creed of the holy Fathers has handed down to us.[5]

Christ's two natures, unified in one person (*hypostasis*) yet neither confused, mixed, nor separated and detached. Christ really is entirely, unreservedly divine *and*, in the same person, became fully, completely human.

Barth's reading of Chalcedonian logic enables him to assert a strong claim for divine sovereignty *along with* an affirmation of human freedom without divine determinism. Human agency in preaching is connected to divine agency in a Chalcedonian pattern of *asymmetry, intimacy,* and *integrity*.

> God . . . absolutely precedes and humanity . . . can only follow. Even as sovereign acts and words of God, as [God's] free acts of rule, judgment, salvation and revelation, these events are also human actions and passions, works and experiences, and *vice versa*.

Asymmetry: God's speaking precedes speech of humanity, which can only follow as response to God's initiative.[6] Intimacy: God's words can coincide with human words (and vice versa) in unity rather than separation. Integrity: God's words and human words can coexist and inhere in fellowship without merging or mixture of either the divine or the human element.[7]

Patristic formulations like the Definition of Chalcedon keep notions of Christ as complex and dynamic as the Scriptures present Christ to be. Chalcedon rebukes preachers who think our task is to simplify and reduce the gospel by adjusting to the limits of human comprehension unaided by the Holy Spirit. Chalcedon encourages our thought about God to be as imaginative as it must be to talk accurately about its divine/human subject. Furthermore, the Chalcedonian imagination protects our congregations from preacherly attempts to abridge the Trinity to the point where we are not talking about the fully human/fully divine Christ but rather an idol cut down to our size.

Revelation is the action of God in history, that is, the story of the God/human Jesus Christ.[8] We wouldn't need to be so imaginative and dialectical in our talk of God if God had not come to us as the eternal Logos, Son of God *and* human being, in our space and time. The Incarnation tests our claims about God by the person and work of Jesus, the God/human. A sermon's lack of ethical substance is exposed by how often the preacher refers generically to "God" and how seldom the preacher names "Christ." At the same time, a sermon's want of theological substance is unmasked by its depictions of Jesus as human exemplar rather than Christ, Judge of and Atonement for humanity.[9] Rigorous adherence to Christology preserves our preaching from rendering God as a merely spiritual something or as the ideal human somebody—God delivered into our hands to use as we please.

When human speaking in preaching becomes God's speaking, it's the God of Abraham, Isaac, Jacob, and Mary being most godly—that is, God refusing to be God without initiating and sustaining divine/human conversation. God speaks in human speech in order to instigate meeting, to call humanity into fellowship, subsuming us into Christ's history. Christ is not God's Plan B after Plan A fails. Christ is God's eternal self-determination not to be God without us. Humanity's interactions with God are determined by the mystery of the Incarnation, God's binding of God's self to humanity in a way that, though asymmetrical, is thoroughly intimate, without any diminution of God or any merging with humanity.

A nameless serving maid exposes the divinely designated, premier disciple, "The Rock," as a prominent Christ-denier. Peter preaches to the scoffing mob, showing thereby not only human chutzpa but also divine prodding, without ceasing to be the one who had denied his Lord. Chalcedonian dialectic permeates Scripture.

Preaching participates in the Chalcedonian wonder, human speech as God's speech, Bethlehem all over again, miraculous and mysterious, God tangibly enfleshed as a baby born to a thoroughly flawed, utterly human family, infinity dwindled to infancy, without diminution of divinity, God redefining God as God with us, a Jew.[10] Thus, Barth speaks unashamedly of the divine and human bound, by divine election, as "double agency" in which divine/human words coincide, coexist in undifferentiated, consubstantiated unity because God elects us for fellowship.

Odd that in his early days Barth was known (probably due to our first meeting him in *Romans*) as a theologian of transcendence, of divine and human oppositional distance. The "Chalcedonian pattern," as the recurring center of his theology, leads Barth to say that we "must actually put our hand in the fire"[11] and think the unthinkable—divine/human speaking that, while asymmetrical is also unreservedly intimate, sacrificing neither the integrity of divine sovereignty nor true human freedom.[12]

In *Dogmatics in Outline*, Barth defines faith as the event whereby God makes us "free to hear the word of grace."[13] Faith must be described dialectically as, "Altogether the work of God, and . . . altogether, human work . . . complete enslavement, and . . . complete liberation." Whence does faith come? "[Faith] is raised up, and lives as it is awakened by the word of God."[14] Though divinely initiated, our human faith (our responsive hearing) completes the circle of God's speaking. An unheard address, unreceived, is hardly an address. Our "yes" to revelation is only responsive, reflexive, but it is a significant confirmation of the "Yes" of God's revelation. Even in God's salvific work in Jesus Christ, there is still something for humans to do—listen, hear, respond. Our "yes" may be subsequent to God's world-changing "Yes" to us in Christ (2 Corinthians 1:20), yet it is a necessary confirmation that God's saving work is not in vain. Chalcedonian faith accounts for preaching being a two-sided exchange. "The one great Yes of God spoken in Jesus Christ includes both the turning of God to [humanity] and that of [humanity] to God."[15] God has spoken; we have heard; and thus we believe.

[Whenever God's word is received as such] as in creation and the incarnation, so here, too, we have a miracle, an event which has its only ontic and noetic basis in the freedom and majesty of God.[16]

Preachers take especial delight when a parishioner says, "Your sermon really spoke to me today," or, "Now I understand in a way I didn't before." Through us, God has succeeded not only in speaking to God's people but also in eliciting their response, the Chalcedonian imagination in motion.[17]

[Faith] cannot be merely a matter of being justified and believing. With . . . faith there arises the need for repentance, for obedience, for the Christian life. We cannot accept God's answer without placing ourselves under the question that is put to us. We cannot recognize God without accepting [God's] authority. We cannot have knowledge in relation to God without action.[18]

There is no independent, autonomous human believing (Pelagianism), not only because we are sinful, finite, and weak (though we certainly are) but also because we are created for more than belief; we are made for fellowship and conversation with God. We have no innate human capacity for this conversation. "The word of God does not rest at all on a possibility imparted to human existence," is not "integral to it or imminent in it, but in God's word itself, which human existence and its possibilities can in no sense proceed, but only follow."[19] Preaching lives by the Chalcedonian reassurance that God fully human, fully divine is God determined genuinely to be in conversation with us.

Notes

1. Quoted by Philip W. Butin, "Preaching as a Trinitarian Event," in *Trinitarian Theology for the Church: Scripture, Community, Worship*, ed. Daniel J. Treier and David Lauber (InterVarsity, 2009), 205.
2. George Hunsinger, *How to Read Karl Barth: The Shape of His Theology* (Oxford University Press, 1991), 234–80.
3. Karl Barth, *Church Dogmatics*, I/1, 198–227.

Section 3

4. Barth, *CD*, IV/1/3, 63. Barth makes no explicit references to Chalcedon in *GD*, but the "Chalcedonian Pattern" permeates the Barthian corpus, including *GD*, coming to its explicit fruition in *CD*, IV/3.
5. Philip Schaff, *The Creeds of Christendom, vol. 2*, Bibliotheca Symbolica Ecclesiae Universalis (Harper and Brothers, 1878), 62–63 (Schaff's italics and brackets). *Old Testament Theology, vol. 1* [Harper and Row, 1962], 179–87
6. As the eternal, divine Son of God who became human, Augustine and Cyril (I think) would say that Christ's divinity is his truest identity; his humanity is the instrument of his revelation and connection to us. In other words, Christ's two natures are not symmetrical.
7. Hunsinger, *How to Read Karl Barth*, 86–87.
8. Nicholas Wolterstorff complains that Barth is too Christocentric, restricting divine revelation to Jesus Christ, citing, "God's Revelation is Jesus Christ, the son of God." *CD*, I/1, 137. Wolterstorff fails to appreciate the danger of disconnecting "revelation" from this Jew from Nazareth. Nicholas Wolterstorff, *Divine Discourse: Philosophical Reflections on the Claim That God Speaks* (Cambridge University Press, 2000), 68.
9. Barth, *CD*, IV/3, 520.
10. Edward T. Oakes, S. J., *Infinity Dwindled to Infancy: A Catholic and Evangelical Christology* (Grand Rapids: Eerdmans, 1999); the title is taken from Gerhard Manley Hopkins's, "The Blessed Virgin Compared to the Air We Breathe," which speaks of "infinity dwindled to infancy . . . grace that does now reach our race."
11. Barth, *CD*, IV/3, 160.
12. Nicholas Lash notes that during the seventeenth and eighteenth centuries, in English and German culture, the word "God" came to name the ultimate explanatory principle. God as master lawyer, a mechanic, or technician rather than the One with whom we are in a speaking/hearing relationship. This "god" is the antithesis of the God/human, Jesus, and a "god" more easily defeated by modern philosophy. Nicholas Lash, *Holiness, Speech and Silence: Reflections on the Question of God* (Ashgate, 2004), 13.
13. Karl Barth, *Dogmatics in Outline*, trans. G. T. Thomson (Harper & Row, 1959), 15.
14. Barth, *CD*, III/3, 247.
15. Barth, *CD*, IV/3, 1, 5.
16. Barth, *GD*, 176.
17. Evans Crawford praises the "hum" of the African American church's call-and-response tradition as a "responsive chord" when pastor and congregation "affirm and celebrate the gospel together," reminding preachers "that they are not gods, but persons who themselves need to be spoken to as hearers." Evans Crawford, *The Hum: Call and Response in African American Preaching* (Abingdon Press, 1995), 60.
18. Barth, *CD*, 87.
19. Barth, *CD*, I/1, 223.

How Great Is Our God

The Trinity in Contemporary Christian Worship Music

Lester Ruth

Introduction

According to the Bible, every good and perfect gift is a heavenly one, coming from the Father of lights (James 1:17). Such gifts must include the fullness of the revelation of God unless we want to say that humans have their own power to conjure up a true vision of God. The witness of the apostles, recorded in their writings and crafted by subsequent Christians into a statement of faith, is that God exists and acts as three Persons (Father, Son, and Holy Spirit) in one Godhead. This is the classic Christian faith.

If this is scriptural Christianity, then why should Christians settle for anything less in the content of worship than the fullness of this revelation of God, particularly when the revelation itself is a gift from God? Why should churches be happy with worship that is less than true to God?

Perhaps churches are satisfied with worship that does not reach for a full vision because a consumerist culture leads us to believe that the most critical thing is that worship be true to us. Perhaps some are scared that our worship will become cold if it becomes "theological."

Section 3

But could not a fuller, richer vision of God actually stimulate love, not quench it? Could not a more complete vision of God lead to a deeper love, rather than away from it? Theology can give us more motives to love God, not fewer. And there is every reason why such theology could take lyrical form in songs. Christian history is full of outstanding examples of songwriters who offered up such lyrics for the church to adore the Triune God. It is not just the latest generation who knows passion for the God revealed in Jesus Christ by the power of the Holy Spirit.

The Trinity is not just an abstract concept, some theological idea that Christians are supposed to take a test on or write a paper about. It is not some detached doctrine that we know we are supposed to agree with, checking it off a list of right beliefs like items on a packing list for vacation. "Okay, kids, let's make sure we have the first aid kit and the doctrine of the Trinity just in case something happens."

The doctrine of the Trinity is a vision not only of God but also of our greatest longings for salvation and our deepest hopes in worship. It liberates by affirming the blessed thought that salvation and worship do not depend upon me. Both are gifts of participating through the Holy Spirit in the incarnate Son's communion with God the Father. People as diverse as theologian James Torrance and songwriter Matt Redman delight in this truth.[1] Thus, Trinitarian belief reminds us that God is not some passive bystander in worship or salvation, desperately hoping that we will work ourselves up before being happy with us.[2]

And this doctrine is important to help us avoid pitfalls, perhaps even idolatry. As one person put it, "Believing right things about God is an essential component in honoring God appropriately."[3] Worshiping the Trinity is a large part of what makes worship orthodox. (*Orthodox* comes from Greek words that mean "right glory.") Because how we relate to God is shaped by our worship experience of God, Trinitarian content in worship is very important. Long after the music has faded, worship songs have created in us a sense of how all this God and salvation stuff fits together. If we lose the Trinity, if we have worship that is less than true to God, we end up with a very different faith, a very different hope of salvation, and, ultimately, a very different God than the one revealed in Scripture.

In light of the foregoing, this chapter focuses on Trinitarian theological content by asking five questions about how the most-used contemporary worship songs lead Christian congregations to pray to and worship the Triune God.[4] I conclude this chapter by discussing some possible reasons the core repertoire is minimally Trinitarian and whether future worship songs will become more adoring of the Trinity.

Throughout this chapter, I will argue that the theological content of the lyrics of the top seventy-seven songs that constitute the heart of Christ in Contemporary Worship Music (CWM) between 1989 and 2005 reveals that this core repertoire has few explicit Trinitarian aspects. The Christians who write and use these songs expect them to express a relationship with God that must be rooted primarily in the heart, not in a common faith. This emphasis provides the focus of this chapter: *lex amandi, lex orandi,* that is, the rule of loving establishes the rule of praying. The classic maxim from the ancient church was *lex orandi, lex credendi,* that is, the rule of praying establishes the rule of believing.

Method of Analysis

There are five questions that govern the qualitative analysis presented in this chapter:

1. Do the songs name the Trinity or all three Persons of the Trinity?
2. Do the songs direct our worship toward the Trinity as a whole or toward one of the Persons of the Trinity?
3. Do the songs remember the activity of the Divine Persons among Themselves?
4. Do the songs see Christian wrship as participation of believers in inter-Trinitarian dynamics or activity?
5. Do the songs use the character of inter-Trinitarian relationships to explore a desired character for relationship among Christians, for example, unity, love, sacrifice, or humility?

These questions build upon each other. What they get at is an upward spiral of understanding how our salvation is communion with the Triune God.

Section 3

They try to point at dimensions of what theologians might call a Trinitarian economy of salvation, that is, how God has been revealed and acted on our behalf to bring us into fellowship with the Trinity. It assumes that redemption is a cooperative venture by the Father, the Son, and the Holy Spirit and that salvation involves being brought into the fellowship these Three have with each other. In some real way, we can experience this communion within the church, particularly as it worships.

Results

Do the Songs Name the Trinity or All Three Persons of the Trinity?

None of the seventy-seven songs explicitly uses the word "Trinity" or "Triune," and only four songs explicitly refer to or name all three Persons of the Trinity: (1) *Glorify Thy Name*; (2) *Father, I Adore You*; (3) *Shine, Jesus, Shine*; and (4) *How Great Is Our God*. The first two songs are praise songs with three verses structured on the Trinity. The description of the Trinity in *Shine, Jesus, Shine* comes as the standard feature of the recurring chorus: "Shine, Jesus, shine, fill this land with the Father's glory/ Blaze, Spirit, blaze, set our hearts on fire."[5] *How Great Is Our God* is the truly exceptional song, both in this list of four and in the entire corpus of seventy-seven songs. It alone worships the Triune nature of God ("Godhead Three in One/ Father, Spirit, Son"). Only one song in addition to these four (*How Can We Name a Love*) speaks of God as "Father." In the handful of songs that refer to the Holy Spirit, seven refer to the "Spirit," but none explicitly uses the name "Holy Spirit."

Beyond an explicit reference to the Father in the five songs above, seven more of the seventy-seven songs make clear reference to the First Person of the Trinity, using terms other than "Father." Some of these songs use other names like "Holy One" (*Give Thanks*) or "Most High" (*Our God Reigns*). Some speak of "God," but the composer clearly refers to the First Person as in "God sent His Son/They called Him Jesus" (*Because He Lives*).

Thirty-seven of the songs, however, make explicit reference to the Son, or Jesus Christ, the Second Person of the Trinity. Twenty-seven of these songs specifically speak of Jesus, Christ, or Jesus Christ. The other ten speak of Christ more generally as "Lord," "God," or "King," but Christ is clearly meant, for example, *Lord, I Lift Your Name on High* recalls Christ's coming, cross, and resurrection.

However, it is not always clear to which person of the Trinity the lyrics are referring. The most frequently used titles for the divine object of worship are "Lord" (forty-seven occurrences), "God" (twenty-eight occurrences), and "King" (eighteen occurrences). In twenty-nine of the forty-seven occurrences of "Lord," it is difficult to determine exactly who this "Lord" is, as seen in the most frequently appearing song among the seventy-seven, *I Love You, Lord*. In fourteen of the twenty-eight occurrences of the title "God," the lack of additional context or names likewise obscures the specific identity of "God." For the third most used title, "King," the level of clarity is much higher. Except in a few cases, the songs make clear that the "King" is Jesus Christ. But there is even less clarity in the five songs that do not explicitly use any common, divine title or name: *I Could Sing of Your Love Forever, Breathe, Above All, Draw Me Close,* and *When I Look into Your Holiness. As the Deer* and *You're Worthy of My Praise*, were not included because they speak of the recipient as King.

The same pattern of Christ-centeredness is seen in those songs whose purpose is to contemplate the divine name. Only one (*Glorify Thy Name*) shows an explicit intention to worship the entire Trinity, while six songs focus on Jesus Christ and three are generic contemplations of the divine name (*How Majestic Is Your Name, Bless His Holy Name,* and *Blessed Be Your Name*).

Do the Songs Direct Our Worship toward the Trinity as a Whole or Toward One of the Persons of the Trinity?

As noted above, only one song explicitly worships God for being Triune, and only two lead to direct worship of the Trinity. Directly addressing worship to the Trinity as a whole or to the Holy Spirit is the most minimal aspect of this body of seventy-seven songs. Similarly, very few songs explicitly address the Holy Spirit in worship. Of the seven that name the Spirit, only four direct worship to the Spirit—the same four that name all three Persons of the Trinity (*Glorify Thy Name; Father, I Adore You; Shine, Jesus, Shine;* and *How Great*

Section 3

Is Our God). The other three songs that mention the Holy Spirit simply make reference to the worshiper's enjoyment of the Spirit.

Directly addressing worship to the First Person of the Trinity fares no better. Of the twelve songs that make clear reference to the First Person of the Trinity (God the Father), only four explicitly worship the Father in direct address: the two songs internally structured by Trinitarian naming (*Glorify Thy Name* and *Father, I Adore You*) and two others (*Give Thanks* and *How Great Is Our* God). One other song that distinguishes the First Person of the Trinity (*Bind Us Together*) possibly addresses God the Father in petition, depending upon whether its prayer to the "Lord" has God the Father in mind. (*Open Our Eyes, Lord* is another possibility.) Perhaps some of the composers had God the Father in mind in the songs that speak of the "Lord" or "God" generically, but the lack of context or content makes it difficult to tell. However, given the stronger tendency to name the Second Person of the Trinity throughout the entire body of seventy-seven songs, it is more likely that most of these generic references are to Jesus Christ.

Directing worship toward Jesus Christ is a much stronger phenomenon. As noted above, thirty-seven of the seventy-seven songs make distinct reference to Jesus Christ. Thirty-two of these directly address Jesus Christ as the recipient of worship.

However, the basis for worshiping Christ varies in these thirty-two songs. Twelve acknowledge Jesus Christ's divine nature, either explicitly or implicitly. Several root worship of Christ in remembrance of His activity, usually referencing His death and resurrection. Others speak of Christ's exalted status, most clearly seen in those songs that are essentially strings of Christ's titles. Songs that speak of Christ's exalted status frequently connect it to His Kingship and occasionally to sheer contemplation of the name "Jesus" itself. Clearly, worship of Christ is more fully developed in the seventy-seven songs than worship of God the Father or the Holy Spirit. Of course, this assessment omits whatever conclusions might be drawn from songs that speak of "Lord" or "God" in a generic manner.

Do the Songs Remember the Activity of the Divine Persons among Themselves?

It is not surprising that the answer is "no" or "very minimally." Without naming—and thus not distinguishing between—the Persons of the Trinity, it is difficult to discuss how these Persons have acted among themselves or in concert.

As a whole, this body of seventy-seven songs is what some might call "functionally unitarian."[6] In *Glorify Thy Name* and *Father, I Adore You* the composers symmetrically make each Person of the Trinity the object of worship but do not explore how they interact. The structure of the songs, with equal statements of adoration and petition, implies equality between the Father, Jesus, and the Spirit. The third, *Shine, Jesus, Shine*, has more nuance because the recurring chorus makes Jesus the mediator of the Father's glory and the Spirit the enabler of our participation in this glory. *Shine, Jesus, Shine* is exceptional in that it implies our reliance upon Jesus Christ or the Holy Spirit to experience God the Father. *How Great Is Our God* is exceptional, too, in being the only song that makes God's Triune nature the explicit basis for adoration.

Eleven songs among the seventy-seven make clear reference to two distinct Persons of the Trinity: Eight discuss the Father and the Son, and two discuss the Son and the Spirit. Another song (*Better Is One Day*) distinguishes between the "living God" and the Spirit of this God, but it is unclear who is meant by "living God." If the Father is in view, then this is the only song that speaks of the Father and the Holy Spirit, without reference to the Son. (*Open Our Eyes, Lord* is also another two-Person song if the unspecified "Lord" is God the Father or the Holy Spirit.)

Of the eight songs that discuss the Father and the Son, six focus on the theme that the Father has given the Son to save us. Four of them have brief references: the "Holy One" has given Jesus Christ His Son (*Give Thanks*); God sent His Son for healing, forgiveness, and pardon (*Because He Lives*); we are "purchased" by God's Son (*Bind Us Together*); and Jesus is the Lamb of God (*You Are My All in All*). The two that explore this theme in greater depth are both derived from the "Suffering Servant" prophecy found in Isaiah 53. In *I Stand in Awe*, for example, God brings about the suffering of the Lamb of

Section 3

God for the singer's sin. The song *Our God Reigns* shares a similar perspective, although the emphasis on God bringing the suffering is muted.

The two remaining Father/Son songs have very undeveloped associations between the two Persons. In *Jesus, Name above All Names,* the composer speaks of Jesus as Son of God, Emmanuel, and God with us as part of stringing together names and titles for Christ without explanation. The connection between Father and Son in *How Can We Name a Love* is even more tenuous.

Similarly, the two songs that clearly speak of Jesus Christ and the Holy Spirit make only passing references to their relationship. In *You Are My King*, the singer has the Spirit of Jesus as a result of Christ's crucifixion and resurrection. In *Surely the Presence of the Lord*, the singer feels the "sweet Spirit" as a result of the Lord Jesus fulfilling the promise of His presence according to Matthew 18:20.

Apart from the lack of naming the Father and the Holy Spirit, three other factors contribute to the lack of emphasis on the activity of the Trinity.

The first is the tendency within many songs to emphasize character traits or the status of God/Jesus Christ/the Lord/the King singularly without contemplating the dynamics of the Trinity itself. The song *Forever* affirms that God is faithful, strong, and with us. *Shout to the Lord* proclaims that no one compares to Jesus as the singer's comfort, shelter, and tower of refuge and strength. *More Precious Than Silver* speaks of the Lord being of more worth than silver, gold, or diamonds. *He Is Exalted* rejoices that the King is forever exalted on high, while heaven and earth rejoice in his holy name. And *As the Deer*, a very popular song, speaks of the song's recipient being the singer's strength, shield, heart's desire, friend, brother, sole satisfaction, real joy giver, and apple of her or his eye without specifically naming the recipient as God. In these songs the nature of the Trinity and its activity are rarely put forth as the basis for the worship.

The second factor that contributes to the lack of emphasis on the activity of the Trinity is the relative de-emphasis on commemorating God's saving activity. The songs pay little attention to placing salvation within a broader metanarrative—that is, any grand, all-encompassing master story—and thus providing opportunity to recite the specific activities or internal dynamics of the Father, Son, and Holy Spirit. Usually the saving work is attributed to a single entity, whether God, the Lord (unspecified), or the Lord Jesus Christ.

In the nineteen songs that commemorate God's saving activity, almost all place the focus on the crucifixion and resurrection of Christ. For example, *Give Thanks* speaks of the Holy One having given Jesus Christ, His Son. Another, *Celebrate Jesus,* remembers only the resurrection. While it is acceptable for a single worship piece to remember only one redemptive act, one still wonders whether the overall effect in using these songs would be to create the impression that God's saving activities are isolated events—rather than part of a whole plan of salvation—and that these events are solely the work of one Divine Person—rather than being a cooperative work by God the Father through Jesus Christ in the power of the Spirit.

Only a few of the songs that recall the crucifixion place it in a wider context of saving activity: *Lord, I Lift Your Name on High* associates it with the *kenosis* (or the relinquishment of the form of God by Jesus in becoming man and suffering death), cross, burial, and exaltation; *Here I Am to Worship* associates creation, *kenosis,* crucifixion, and exaltation; and *Awesome God* makes the crucifixion the activity of the same God (Christ) who judged Adam and Eve in the Garden, brought judgment on Sodom, and is about to return. Two of the nineteen songs remember creation.

Therefore, few of the songs, unlike the New Testament, explore the internal dynamics of the Father, Son, and Holy Spirit in this wider range of saving activity. Whereas the New Testament continually explores how the Father, Son, and Holy Spirit have acted in concert on our behalf (consider how God the Father promises the birth of His Son when the Holy Spirit overshadows Mary [Luke 1] or how the Father raises Jesus from the dead through the Spirit showing Him to be the Son of God [Romans 1]), these songs tend to see the great events of salvation as isolated works.[7] With respect to the Father and the Son, there is only occasional reference to Christ's saving activity being of the Father. The Holy Spirit as an active agent in our salvation is almost nowhere to be found. This leaves even the doctrine of the atonement underdeveloped in its Trinitarian aspects in this body of songs. The two possible exceptions are derived from Isaiah 53: *I Stand in Awe* and *Our God Reigns.*

Such omissions mean that possibilities for exploring the Trinitarian aspect of salvation are missed. For example, because this music's view of salvation emphasizes it as personal experience, the songs do not explore possible Trinitarian aspects in more cosmic or church-related understandings of salvation. There is also little emphasis on present aspects of God's work. There is no emphasis on ongoing mediation, whether it be on the heavenly ministry of Christ or the saving role of the Holy Spirit. God's saving activity seems to be something done in the past that is presently enjoyed. There is also little sense of God's ongoing mission in the world—and little eschatology, or end-times thinking, in the songs.

The third factor that contributes to the lack of focus on the activity of the Trinity is a possible confusion of Persons, that is, "Lord" is often used in an ill-defined, generic way. Although the term is sometimes clearly used to refer to Jesus Christ, that is not always the case. *Open Our Eyes, Lord*, for instance, is a case where the Lord appears to be a very different Person than Jesus. *Awesome God* complicates the matter by tossing "God" into the mix: in this song "God" and "Lord" appear to be interchangeable names for whoever expelled Adam from Eden, experienced the crucifixion, and poured judgment on Sodom.

Do the Songs See Christian Worship as Participation of Believers in Inter-Trinitarian Dynamics or Activity?

There is little, if any, sense of worshipers being in Christ or Christ being in worshipers, particularly as a church-related reality during corporate worship. Because so few of the ones commemorate the internal dynamics or activity of the Trinity, little space exists for worship participation in the Trinitarian activity.

On the whole the songs tend to objectify God as the recipient of worship to emphasize a distinction between the One worshiped and the worshiper. God/Christ/the Lord/the King is someone *out there* who is to be worshiped and adored. The One worshiped is someone whom we love and enjoy and who is with us, but there is little sense of Christians being brought into the activity of this God, particularly if this God whom we worship is conceived of as a Triune community. Almost all the songs describe the dynamic between worshipers and the Divine recipient of worship, not the relationship and activity—past, present, and future—among the Persons of the Trinity. A more classic approach is to make God's activity on our behalf—from the Father through the Son in the Spirit—mirrored in the response of worship—in the Spirit through the Son to the Father. Thus the classic approach, in contrast to the tendency of these songs, puts the emphasis on God's graciousness from first to last. The classic approach keeps Jesus as the "lead worshiper" within the internal love of the Trinity.

Neither do these songs consider worship as participation in Christ's activity *through* us with reference to either the Father or the Holy Spirit. The forty-three songs that are some sort of prayer (identified by the worshiper addressing a divine "You") have virtually no sense of being addressed to the Father through the Son in the power of the Holy Spirit. The songs mainly address Christ—and occasionally the Father—in prayer, but none speak of us addressing the Father through Christ or the church's prayer being Christ praying through us. The songs also do not speak of Christ's intercessory ministry.

These omissions are partly a result of the absence of a strong emphasis on the Trinity's current activity and partly to the overwhelming character of the songs as expressing only our own human love to the divine Object of worship (in contrast to our sharing in the love which the Father, Son, and Spirit share among themselves). *I Love You, Lord* is perhaps the most representative song of the whole group. Not surprisingly, CCLI's database reveals over 400 songs with the phrase "I love you" in the title. Songs that would be truer to the Trinity would delight in how the Spirit brings us into the love the Father and Son share as described in the Gospel of John.

Do the Songs Use the Character of Inter-Trinitarian Relationships to Explore a Desired Character for Relationship among Christians, for Example, Unity, Love, Sacrifice, or Humility?

The answer is a strong "no."

These seventy-seven songs have a very low explicit consciousness of the church. Only one (*Lord, Be Glorified*) uses the word "church," and only one

(*We Have Come into His House*) has a church theme. There are a handful with an explicit sense of God's people as community, but only two are about fellowship: *We Have Come into His House* and *Bind Us Together*.

Moreover, only *Bind Us Together* derives a vision for the church from contemplating the nature and activity of the Triune God (although the song does not speak of the Holy Spirit). The song petitions the Lord for a greater measure of a unity of love, basing the request in the essential unity of God and in the activity of the Father and the Son.

Discussion

Acts of omission, not commission, cause the lack of a Trinitarian dimension in most CWM: Songwriters, marketers of the songs, and churches do not seem to value explicit Trinitarian content or even miss it if it is not included. Robin Parry's description of the British situation seems applicable to America: "If there is a problem with Christian worship songs, it is more a failure to bring out the Trinitarian dimensions of the God we worship than a problem of violating Trinitarian faith."[8]

To a significant degree, the root for this omission is the lack of theological expectations for the songs. Even when theological review does come into play, the goals are often limited to either making sure the song avoids obvious error or making sure the song expresses a scriptural idea or sentiment. In general, few composers intentionally seek to include a wider breadth of theological contemplation of the Triune God and Trinitarian activity.

If explicit witness to the Trinity is not the high priority, then what is? The songs demonstrate a common concern: *the priority of a shared affective experience in the worship of God.* Worship is seen as the expression of our hearts and ministry to God's heart. It is this law of love, *lex amandi,* that determines the rule of praying, *lex orandi.*

This concern with affections is evident in writings from and about the composers of the seventy-seven songs in this study.[9] One influential composer puts it this way: "As songwriters, our job is to hook people's hearts and emotions for the Lord . . . So a worship song . . . needs to express a universal sentiment, something we can all agree on as our own expression of love to

Him."[10] That "something" seems rarely derived from God's own Trinitarian nature and work.

This affective sentiment is frequent among the composers who describe worship as singing authentically from one's heart to express true affection to God. It is also reflected in how the composers describe the origins of their songs and contrasts with the composer's rejection of worship that is mainly singing about God. Occasionally, the composers speak of God's reception of these authentic worship songs in affective terms, too, as they speak of touching the heart of God. For these composers, then, worship is foremost about God's Presence affectively discerned and experienced. In this respect, they share a similar worship piety with many churches that use their music. Few of the composers seem to have a piety shaped by Trinitarian contemplation, so they are unaware of the omission of the Trinity.

The desire for the heart's authentic expression to God also shapes the nature of the language in the songs, which seldom leads to speaking of the Trinity. Following the lead of much recent popular music generally, CWM lyrics lean toward an oral, conversational style. Composers avoid complex sentences; attention to strict rhyming and metrical schemes is rare. Most seem to follow Paul Baloche's suggestion that "it's best to make your lyrics move straight ahead, as they would in conversation."[11] Consequently, the absence of Trinitarian content in many of the songs may be because it is not "conversational" to speak to and about the Trinity. Composer Graham Kendrick makes the same point in connecting CWM lyrics to their pop music counterparts: "It has to be said that the rock-pop genre, into which category many worship choruses fit, is not always ideal for carrying extensive, deep, or content-rich lyrics."[12]

The dynamic of composing also contributes to a lack of Trinitarian emphasis. Of the forty-four songs for which I found background information, twenty-nine were spontaneous creations. Some came about during private devotions, and a few were written while the composer was actually leading corporate worship. Four composers even wrote theirs while driving. This kind of composition allows no time for deeper theological reflection or revision.

In addition, some composers speak of their songs being God-given, since many had no intention of writing a song when they "received" a song from

God. *I Love You, Lord* is one example. The composer, a young, financially strapped housewife with no home church or friends, first prayed to God to give her a song that "He would be in the mood to hear." The resulting song, Laurie Klein reports, was "like an early Valentine" or what her editor called "a gift from God that emerged spontaneously from her lips."[13] So strong is this sense in a few composers that they speak of taking "dictation" from God, and, in such cases, there seems to be no need for further theological reflection or revision.

Another important compositional dynamic is that many of these songs were written at a low point in the composers' lives, expressing their encounter with God at that time. The economy of salvation in these songs is an intensely personal story of salvation, which would call for little theological reflection or revision.

A final compositional dynamic that tends to marginalize explicit Trinitarian content involves the sources for the songs. The most critical source for many of the songs is Scripture. The Psalms, in particular, are the scriptural material most mentioned in the accounts of composition. While the use of Psalms is commendable and has an extensive historical pedigree in Christian worship, in the case of CWM it contributes to the lack of explicit Trinitarian content. Since the Trinity is not obvious in the Psalms, the composers are not likely to tease out their Trinitarian dimensions as have some past Christian who used the Psalms as Christ's prayer to the Father or the Father's address to the Son. The same is likely true for other biblical sources, even New Testament ones. The scriptural backdrop to the songs, then, preclude asking further theological question about the songs. If a song is "scriptural," the biblical connection seems self-validating, and it does not occur to the composers to make Trinitarian concern a factor.

Some potential sources that are not in play should likewise be noted. Few songs are shaped by formal theological reflection, since few composers have theological training at the college or seminary level.[14] Few of the composers are from churches with written denominational liturgies, which are likely to have explicit Trinitarian content. Few speak of using written liturgical texts, either current or historical, as a source for inspiration. It is much more likely that over time extemporaneous praying shapes the composers' pieties from which they draw their songs, although this is far harder to document.

Although the seventy-seven songs considered here generally lack a Trinitarian dimension, this is not the case for all CWM, even from the same composers. Thus, this omission is also a result of the system that produces and markets these songs to churches. The standard commercial sources through which CWM is made available to churches[15] seem to help marginalize Trinitarian concerns not only because they reinforce the piety that creates these songs but also because they do not introduce more formal theological scrutiny of the music.

Simply stated, Christians within this production and marketing system have not noticed the omission because they have valued the songs on other grounds. They also appear to use the same criteria and vocabulary in assessing the songs: Does it carry an "anointing" from God or usher people into the presence of God? Whether or not a song is explicitly Trinitarian is irrelevant because that dimension is not necessary for a positive worship experience. Many do not care about a song's theological content. As one CWM industry executive explains, "When listening to songs for the first time I try to turn off my brain and turn on my heart. A song can break all the normal rules of songwriting but bear such a touch of God that you cannot ignore it."[16] For CWM distributors, too, *lex amandi* establishes *lex orandi*.

Because the sale of CWM is business as well as ministry, business concerns provide little motivation to address the omission of theological dimensions in these songs. Robb Redman, a former vice president at Maranatha! Music, acknowledges that decisions about repertoire and presentations often have been defined

> by the needs of the recording and marketing process (projected revenue and expenses, available musical talent, advertising, and so on) instead of the need of the congregation for worship music people can sing with theological integrity. Most producers and executives would admit they have sometimes thought more about the bottom line of a CD than its potential impact on a congregation or the individual.[17]

As business, CWM promotion shapes a culture of trendiness among church musicians. As noted by another former publisher, the emphasis typically is on singing a *new* song to the Lord, meaning the system makes keeping up with the latest song a high priority for church musicians.[18] CWM catalogs, magazines, and other promotional material often emphasize what is new or "hot," shifting their effective role from mere recording usage to promoting usage and thereby displacing more careful reflection on a song's lyrical content.

Finally, another reason these seventy-seven songs have become the most used CWM songs for the last fifteen years resides with the churches. The range and number of churches represented in the CCLI data do not allow absolute statements, but it seems that the basis for choosing CWM for worship services is not tied to explicit Trinitarian content within the songs because it is not needed to accomplish the songs' liturgical purpose.

The Major Factor Causing Churches to Overlook the Missing Trinitarian Dimension

Several possible factors have caused churches to overlook a lack of Trinitarian dimension in the song chosen for worship. For my analysis here, I refer to the widespread worship performance practice of using an extensive musical "set" (to use a common term), which consists of multiple consecutive songs, with internal repetition of each song, for the beginning of the corporate worship service.

A major factor is the churches' expectation for an experience of God's presence in and through worship music. Oftentimes, particularly when the theology of the Vineyard movement has been influential, worshipers express this expectation in terms of intimacy. This musical worship allows a deep, affective connection between the worshiper and God. The criteria for discerning achievement of this goal are primarily affective, not doctrinal.

In these "sets," a strong emphasis is placed on the music and the worship leader(s) to create an experience of divine presence. According to the typology found in certain Pentecostal and Charismatic writings, the various areas of the temple in the Old Testament provide the framework for the musical journey to a deep experience of God's presence[19] through entrance into the "Holy of Holies." Using certain key biblical proof texts and supplemental types, proponents often use Psalm 100 to provide a biblical rationale for using this temple/tabernacle model as a way to sequence worship music. Second Chronicles provides a supplemental type to demonstrate God's honoring of this musical movement by manifesting His presence. Psalm 22:3 (Israel's praise is what enthrones God) serves as a central text to establish the basic expectation that God is inhabiting praise.

Even if churches do not use this precise typology to explain the musical order, these churches often replicate a similar order for the set. The movement, generally, tends to be from "praise" or "high praise" to "worship," understood as intimate communion with God. There is also an increasing focus on the divine "You" directly addressed by the song lyric.

To achieve entering into God's presence, musical worship leaders often learn to structure the musical set by "flow," which does not take into account broader theological concern. They generally focus on key, tempo, and theme. Key allows easy and effective transition between songs. Tempo allows the movement from faster to slower as the set develops. Theme allows songs to focus on a central topic, perhaps to anticipate the main idea of the sermon. This theme-based approach tends to emphasize nouns (names for God) and adjectives (attributes for God). What these songs lack is a corresponding emphasis on verbs, understood as the activity of God within the economy of salvation and inter-Trinitarian dynamics.

A good "flow" within the musical set, which allows worshipers to see themselves on a journey into the presence of God, has several characteristics, but none is necessarily related to the Trinity. One is the expressiveness of the songs and their authenticity, honesty, and passion. Another is the repetitiveness of the songs because, as C. Michael Hawn points out, such cyclical, repetitive worship music has the ability to strike the worshiper at a deeper, different level than more sequential, storytelling musical forms. It creates an experience beyond the words to "encourage a physical response, either toward the ecstatic or toward the meditative."[20] The music's percussive nature, too, as sociologist Tex Sample suggests, allows worshipers to hear the songs as true.[21]

Section 3

This emphasis on musical sets to facilitate an experience with God potentially erodes a classic understanding of Jesus Christ as the unique mediator between humans and God the Father. Perhaps displacing Christ as mediator goes hand-in-hand with the central focus on an exalted, divine CWM. If worship's primary end is communion with the Son, not necessarily with God the Father (a communion understood as personal intimacy), then the need for Christ as mediator is itself lessened. Mediation is shifted to the music, it appears. Thus prayer in CWM is not primarily to the Father through the Son but to the Son through the music.

Conclusion

These conclusions about the seventy-seven songs considered do not apply to all contemporary songs. Indeed, some songs from the same group of composers who wrote the seventy-seven show a greater capacity for naming the Persons of the Godhead, which is the starting point for greater Trinitarian reflection in the lyrics. Some of these songs have great potential for Trinitarian worship.[22]

In addition to these songs from the same composers, there are other songs within the broader CWM corpus that are more explicitly Trinitarian. CCLI's song labels in its database, for example, point to eighty-five songs with the Trinity as a theme. (This number is actually low since not all songs with explicit Trinitarian connections have been so labeled.) Several traits connect these eighty-five songs. Just under fifty percent have a copyright date since about 2000, and almost eighty percent have copyright dates from about 1990—a promising sign. The songs much more clearly and consistently name the three Persons of the Trinity. Clear reference to the Holy Spirit is most numerous, perhaps because alternative names/titles for the Spirit are not as easily found as for the Father and the Son. These new songs are stronger in remembering God's activity, in having an ecclesial consciousness, and in having a tendency to be more dependent upon antecedent Trinitarian material. The well-known hymn *Holy, Holy, Holy* is the basis for many of the new songs.

What will the next fifteen years of CCLI data indicate if this same kind of study is conducted? Several signs indicate a possible shift. One, noted above, is the increased number of recently written songs about the Trinity, including the exceptional *How Great Is Our God*. Another is the growing awareness by CWM composers of the power of songs to shape the faith of Christian peoples. Consequently, many new composers speak of the need for submitting songs for theological review. This increased dialogue with theologians is a sign of potential change, but whether or not it will result in a theological enrichment of CWM lyrics—and overcome the Trinitarian omission—will likely depend on composers. Greater theological breadth in CWM lyrics will occur as composers get beyond threshold questions like, "Can the song's theme be found in the Bible?" or "Does it contradict good theology or the Bible?" Such questions set a minimal agenda rather than aspire to the full scriptural revelation of God.

Even now, a few composers address issues of theological fullness and breadth and include greater Trinitarian content as a goal for CWM. Notable examples include Graham Kendrick and Matt Redman.[23] Indeed, Redman now articulates an explicit Trinitarian understanding of worship:

> We praise Jesus the Son with everything within us—but we also join with Jesus in worship as He glorifies His Father. As the Holy Spirit reveals the Lordship of Jesus to the depth of our heart, He also takes us into the Son's relationship with the Father . . . Worship is *to* Jesus, yes—absolutely. We glorify the Son and magnify His name. But worship is also *in* Jesus and *through* Jesus and *with* Jesus . . . When our heavenly Father receives our worship, He receives it in the person of His Son and in the power of His Holy Spirit.[24]

A growing number of theologians and pastors within the CWM world—including Robert Webber, Brian McLaren, and Bert Waggoner, national director of the Vineyard Churches USA—supplement these composers' call for theologically enriched lyrics.[25] The emergence of Chris Tomlin's song *How Great Is Our God*, the only song among the seventy-seven that intentionally worships because of God's Triune nature, is another promising sign of a Trinitarian piety.

While these signs indicate a potential shift for the next fifteen years, widespread change will depend primarily upon developing a more Trinitarian piety. Christians will write and choose more Trinitarian songs only if love for the Trinity resides deeply in their hearts. The dynamics of *lex amandi, lex*

Section 3

orandi will not go away. As composer Brian Doerksen explains, the aim of a song is "to unlock the language of a people's hearts and for them to say, 'This is exactly what I wanted to say to God.'"[26] If Doerksen accurately assesses the way CWM is valued (and he does), then the implication is clear: A shift in the next fifteen years will mean getting adoration of the Trinity to reside deeply within people's hearts. Songs will shift as Christians learn to love the Triune God for being Triune.

Notes

1. James B. Torrance, *Worship, Community and the Triune God of Grace* (InterVarsity, 1996), 9; see also Matt Redman, *Facedown* (Regal, 2004), 52.
2. John D. Witvliet, "The Opening of Worship—Trinity," in *A More Profound Alleluia: Theology and Worship in Harmony*, ed. Leanne Van Dyk (Eerdmans, 2005), 3.
3. Robin Parry, *Worshipping Trinity: Coming Back to the Heart of Worship* (Milton Keynes, 2005), 8.
4. CCLI neither endorses nor denies any conclusions I have drawn from the use of CCLI-obtained information.
5. SHINE JESUS SHINE © 1987 Make Way Music (admin. by Music Services in the Western Hemisphere). All Rights Reserved. ASCAP Used by permission.
6. To be fair to CWM, those who use this phrase are speaking of a wider phenomenon. See note above, Torrance, *Worship, Community and the Triune God of Grace*, 20. Susan White speaks of the danger of "Jesus-centered Unitarianism" in worship today: Susan White, "What Ever Happened to the Father? The Jesus Heresy in Modern Worship," *Worship Today*: https://www.sacramental.org.uk/uploads/5/0/0/9/50096105/whatever_happened_to_the_father_-_susan_white.pdf.
7. See note above, Parry, *Worshipping Trinity*, 17–66. See how Parry explores the Trinitarian "geography" of the biblical story and Christian life; and (see note above) Witvliet, "The Opening of Worship—Trinity," in *A More Profound Alleluia: Theology and Worship in Harmony*, 3–20 for the Trinitarian "grammar" of biblical remembrance in worship.
8. See note 3 above, Parry, *Worshipping Trinity*, 133, 141.
9. I found background data on 44 songs. Three books provided information on 35 of the 77 songs: Terry Lindsay, *The Sacrifice of Praise: Stories Behind the Greatest Praise and Worship Songs of All Time* (Integrity, 2002); see also Phil Christensen and Shari MacDonald, *Our God Reigns: The Stories Behind Your Favorite Praise and Worship Songs* (Kregel, 2000) and their *Celebrate Jesus: The Stories Behind Your Favorite Praise and Worship Songs* (Kregel, 2003). Issues of the magazine *Worship Leader* provided background information on 9 more songs.

10 Paul Baloche, Jimmy Owens, and Carol Owens, *God Songs: How to Write and Select Songs for Worship* (Lindale: leadworship.com, 2004), 48, 60.
11 Baloche, Owens, and Owens, *God Songs*, 80.
12 Graham Kendrick, "Worship in Spirit and in Truth," in *Composing Music for Worship*, ed. Stephen Darlington and Alan Kreider (Canterbury, 2003), 97, 88.
13 See note above, Christensen and MacDonald, *Our God Reigns*, 68.
14 Exceptions include Henry Smith (*Give Thanks*), Leonard Smith (*Our God Reigns*), David Ruis (*You're Worthy of My Praise*), Billy Foote (*You Are My King*), and pastor Jack Hayford (*Majesty*).
15 Robb Redman, *The Great Worship Awakening: Singing a New Song in the Postmodern Church* (Jossey-Bass, 2002), 55–67. The foremost companies include Integrity Music, WorshipTogether, the Vineyard Music Group, and Maranatha! Music.
16 Craig Dunnagan (Vice President, Music Publishing and Church Resources, Integrity Music), quoted in Baloche, Owens, and Owens, *God Songs*, 204.
17 See note above, Redman, *Facedown*. He offers a caveat that these concerns do not apply equally to all CWM promoters, but even a little of this perspective is enough to marginalize Trinitarian concerns.
18 Darrell A. Harris (former owner of Star Song Records), in discussion with the author, July 2004.
19 Judson Cornwall, *Let Us Worship* (Bridge, 1983), 153–58, and see also David K. Blomgren et al., eds., *Restoring Praise and Worship to the Church* (Revival, 1999).
20 C. Michael Hawn, *Gather into One: Praying and Singing Globally* (Eerdmans, 2003), 233.
21 Tex Sample, *The Spectacle of Worship in a Wired World: Electronic Culture and the Gathered People of God* (Abingdon, 1998), 35. While no detailed study on this point has been undertaken to my knowledge, the emphasis on tempo (beat) in CWM selection hints at the accuracy of his suggestion.
22 Paul Baloche, for example, has songs based on 1 Peter 1:3-4 (*Praise Be to the God and Father*) and John 14:1-3 (*Let Not Your Heart Be Troubled*). Twila Paris has an adaptation of Charles Wesley's hymn contemplating Christ's ongoing priestly ministry before the Father, *Arise, My Soul, Arise*.
23 See note 11 above, Graham Kendrick, "Worship in Spirit and in Truth," 92, 10; David DiSabatino, "Table Talk: An Interview with Graham Kendrick," *Worship Leader* 10.7 (Nov/Dec 2001): 30. For Redman, see note above, *Facedown*; see note above, Parry, *Worshipping Trinity*, xi; and see note above, Baloche et al., *God Songs*, 215–16.
24 See note above, Redman, *Facedown*, 52.
25 Robert E. Webber, "Is Our Worship Adequately Triune?" *Reformation and Revival Journal* 9 (Summer 2000): 121–32; see also Brian McLaren, "An Open Letter to Songwriters," *Worship Leader* 10 (Jan/Feb 2001): 44–45; see also Bert Waggoner, "Leading Trinitarian Worship," *Inside Worship* 52 (Feb 2004): 5–6.
26 Brian Doerksen, "Song Writing," in *Songwriting for Worship: Study Tools for the DVD* [CD], *Equip Resources for Worship* series (Vineyard Music Global, 2004).

Theological Touchstone
Wayfinding through Times of Uncertainty

M. Jan Holton

Hic sunt dracones: Here be dragons. This mysterious phrase is etched into the edges of the Hunt-Lenox globe, one of the earliest to depict the "New World."[1] Like ancient maps before it, the globe uses depictions of monsters of various types to convey a sense of danger for areas of the unknown.[2] Though there are few, if any, remaining uncharted lands today, geographically speaking. The foreboding sense of uncertainty that comes with traversing the unknown remains intimately connected to the "uncharted" territories of our lives.

The past nineteen months of increasing uncertainty caused by a pandemic, political turmoil, wildfires, floods, hurricanes, and the long overdue reckoning over police violence and systemic inequality have challenged me to adjust my perspective on just what *crisis* means in our current context. The days when we could anticipate life returning to "normal" long enough for us to at least catch our breath are gone. We have passed the threshold of mere crisis and finally tipped into that of accelerating and compounding crises.[3] The difference is not a subtle one. Global climate changes are responsible for the increased frequency and intensity of potentially catastrophic events, thereby creating a cascade of political, economic, and humanitarian consequences. Yet the results of these changes are by no means limited to large-scale events.

Section 3

Research suggests that rising temperatures are responsible for an increase in individual illness and, perhaps more surprisingly, deaths by injury—both intentional and unintentional.[4] As with every other aspect of life, persons of color, the elderly, and those living in poverty are and will continue to be disproportionately affected by these negative events.

Here be our dragons in what for many of us feels like a new world of constant unrest. How do we navigate a way through this uncharted global space swimming with uncertainty? Does the way forward entail avoiding our dragons or facing them? How do we care for ourselves and others in the process? And how do we reckon with the reality that, for many of our neighbors, "constant unrest" has, in fact, long been the norm?

Uncertainty, especially in the context of loss and suffering, can create a high level of anxiety around what will happen to us and those we love. And, like any form of stress, anxiety can take a toll on us physically, emotionally, and spiritually. More specifically, spiritual anxiety arises around who we are in general and who we are in relation to God in particular—around how we are connected to God. This existential anxiety can evoke in persons of faith what pastoral theologian Allan Hugh Cole Jr. calls the disquieted soul, for whom, he says, "of central importance are one's assumptions about God, perceptions of oneself standing before God, and the difference those make in how one's personal life story takes shape and is lived."[5]

Ever since March 2020, when the world as many knew it suddenly had to make room for a deadly new virus, I have returned again and again to Mark 16:8. Here, having just been told that Jesus is no longer in the tomb but has been raised, Mary, Mary, and Salome are, Mark says, terrified and amazed. Terror and amazement are two sides of the same coin, and fear and uncertainty can invoke both in us. Uncertainty is the very reason we have a fear reflex. At its most helpful, fear can alert our attention to the real dangers in the unknown. Fear is also the feeling we are likely to have when God beckons us toward something new and life-giving. Most of us, like the women standing at the empty tomb, tremble in the face of what we don't know.

Journeys that we make into the unknown, whether brought about by the illness of COVID-19, unemployment, activism, or caring for others during the pandemic, can also be where we encounter the mysteries of God, the convictions of our moral center, and our deepest longings and love for God, self, and others. Unfolding moments of challenge and opportunity such as these require that we (re)form pastors and other spiritual care providers with an emotional and spiritual flexibility for navigating the urgent uncertainties of our time in ways that will cultivate long-term resilience. As people of faith, we believe in a redeeming God of love and justice whom we trust will always be at work in the world and upon whom we can rely to help us navigate whatever is in front of us. Yet personal and collective crises can test precisely this belief, introduce doubt and anxiety into the life of faith, and leave us at a spiritual crossroads.

One of the strongest and most difficult impulses my students learning pastoral care struggle to rein in is that of *fixing*. Like sailors on European ships sent to conquer foreign lands, students attempt to conquer the crisis unfolding for the one to whom they offer care. For students, this impulse typically takes form in an effort to chart a path to *doing* something by which they can measure their efficacy as pastor or chaplain. It is a reflex in response to the anxiety that emerges when faced with suffering and the uncertainty it brings—and one that threatens to diminish the agency of those to whom we offer care. The fact that uncertainty, especially in the context of loss and suffering, can create a high level of anxiety should not come as a surprise—especially to those of us who have been through tragedy, grief, illness, or other events that have opened a chasm into the unknown of our own lives. Anxiety by its very nature can be an egocentric perspective, a self-focused concern for survival. And this inward turn, in the moment, can hinder our ability to engage empathetically with others. For pastoral caregivers, losing our ability to empathize because we have slipped into an anxiety-driven fix-it mode reduces our ability to provide good care. In the extreme, it can jeopardize healthy boundaries by creating a space fraught with danger. This is no less true for anyone else.

We have long clung to a Western colonialist framework—absorbed into our public, professional, and personal lexicon—of charting courses, setting trajectories, and mapping the way forward. Yet moving forward in this historical moment as individuals and caregivers requires a new way of choosing each new step, which will only then inform us about the next. The strategy of imposing order onto chaos by mapping or charting our way through it is of little use here. Here, I invite us to shift the metaphors we use for how we go about navigating challenge. I suggest that instead of relying on any notion we might have of finding a clear and direct path through difficulty, we lean into a model of *spiritual and emotional wayfinding* that relies more on community and on reading our environment and the unfolding realities as we encounter them.

Wayfinding

In her engaging book *Wayfinding: The Science and Mystery of How Humans Navigate the World*, M. R. O'Connor takes a closer look at the science of human spatial navigation.[6] She reminds us that even before the onset of digital maps and directional devices, the idea of overlaying a map to chart a territory had a deep history in colonialism. Uncharted landscapes were long considered "undiscovered" by colonial powers and thus free for the conquering, at the expense, of course, of indigenous peoples. Not surprisingly, as suggested above, this cultural philosophy of conquering the landscape has been easily transferred to other nongeographical notions of navigating—with much the same expectation of control and expediency. We speak of "charting a path" to success or "mapping our trajectory" toward achieving a larger personal or professional goal. This preference for expediency and control reflects a deeply ingrained culture of economy in which efficiency of time is the greatest value and the only goal is to reach the final destination. However, to focus only on the destination diminishes our practice of paying attention to our place along the journey and the ways the journey can bring meaning to our lives.

This leads us to the second notion of navigation, which is quite different—that of *wayfinding*. Wayfinding is the complex process of spatial navigation using memory and natural signs in the surrounding environment to "read" an area in order to orient oneself in a given direction. Indigenous persons around the globe are perhaps the most adept at practicing wayfinding. But anyone who has grown up in the back woods, in the mountains, or perhaps on a ranch or farm may have some sense of what I mean here. The essence of wayfinding includes deep knowing, belonging, community, and embracing the story of oneself in the world around one—on the land's terms, not one's own.

Chad Kālepa Baybayan was a Pwo navigator who lead a project to circumnavigate the Pacific Ocean in five years using a traditional Hawaiian voyaging canoe and wayfinding as his sole means of navigation.[7] For him, wayfinding was not only about using the natural environment for clues rather than navigating with instruments. Baybayan described wayfinding holistically as a way of organizing the world.[8] I find this concept of wayfinding to be fundamental for understanding how to move spiritually and emotionally through an ocean of uncertainty such as surrounds us now. Jesus used his life and ministry to prepare the disciples and other followers, including us, to see that the life of the Spirit moves more fluidly than the world. Theologian Brian Brock reminds us that our task as people of faith is to "learn to recognize the voice and claim of the living God in our daily lives."[9] Brock says, "[I]f faith is a wayfinding—a necessarily sequential discovery of life with God—there is no map that can tell us where our life is going."[10]

Touchstones

Navigating through the uncertain "territories" of life is, of course, an ongoing challenge for all of us. The last two decades of my work with refugees, though, has instilled in me a particular respect for how resilient some people can be in the face of crisis and challenge. Whether making their way through dangerous territory while fleeing from violence or negotiating for food and shelter in a refugee camp or traversing the complex process of resettlement and acculturation in a new country, refugees must be flexible and always ready to respond to challenges as they unfold in front of them. Their resilience has shown me that not having a map or chart to define one's path through difficulty does not mean that one is left to flail about in despair. Indeed, the lessons I have learned from refugees have shaped the core spiritual values I find now to be essential, values that can serve as touchstones to guide us as we recalibrate to the shifting realities that challenge our way forward.

Instead of marking a predetermined linear course, we lean toward these touchstones time and again to reassess and realign. Strengthening our connection to these spiritual values can build in us emotional and spiritual flexibility in the face of increasingly perilous times. These spiritual values are deeply Christian though not exclusively so. They are not passive. They require ongoing practice and build one upon the other in ways that make them so closely intertwined at times as to render them inseparable. Though there certainly are others that we could add, the spiritual values I suggest here are hope, joy, and meaning. I choose these three with an eye toward the ways that hope opens the future to possibility, joy can reflect a heart surrendered to God, and meaning making can open the way to finding the place of our own journey within God's larger narrative of love in the world, especially through the life, death, and resurrection of Jesus.

Love, rather than standing as a single spiritual value, is the foundation from which the others flow. These values are the expression of the love ethic that is the gospel message itself. In the paradoxical way that is the gospel's, love is both starting point and ultimate end from which and to which God calls us. This love resists becoming trite and thin when we are honest about the messy reality of what it means to live in a world shaped by power, inequality, violence, and despair—and yet not only still believe in a love ethic but demand that we hold to its presence and truth.

Hope

The idea that hope emerges only amid positive experiences is a faulty one, though it is true that hope is perhaps easier to envision in times of pleasure and joy or the promise thereof. We hope for a new job, for a pay raise, for the wedding to go off without a hitch, or for any other more tangible outcome. Anyone who has ever faced suffering, illness, or their own death or that of a loved one understands that there are hopes yet more dear to us. Yet even here we should not limit our vision of what hope can be. Spiritual hope requires that we recalibrate how we understand both hope itself and meaning making and how we come to shape them and be shaped by them.

I have recently been reacquainted with the term "radical hope" and find myself wondering, Is not all hope radical to some degree? If we take into account the true finite nature of what it is to be human, is it not radical just to presume to look toward any future horizon with a posture of confidence and expectation? It was, of course, Easter 2020 when the Mark 16 passage took on a new significance for me, at the very time when Christians revisit the empty tomb. So many of us were trying to remain hopeful in the face of what was quite literally unthinkable. The smell of death and gut-wrenching grief were shockingly real for far too many on this particular Eastertide. Yes, Jesus has risen. I imagined Mary, Mary, and Salome hearing this news and standing at a threshold that they cannot yet define. On one side is the familiar though devastating grief wrapped around the death of their beloved Jesus. On the other side lies a horizon of hope that they cannot yet fully understand and that leaves them both amazed and terrified. This is a radical hope because it embraces, rather than denies or stifles, the terror of the moment. It is no less so every time each one of us looks toward our own future hopes through the shadow of the cross and its promise for us.

The idea that hope is, by inclination, future-oriented is nothing new. I will tell anyone who will sit long enough to listen of my appreciation for pastoral theologian Andrew Lester's work on hope. He helps us think about "future stories" that point toward both finite hopes (tangible needs, health, etc.) and transfinite hopes, those transcendent hopes upon which our faith depends as ways to understand the narratives of hope that sustain us.[11] Lester acknowledges that while hope is psychologically an individual disposition, it is difficult to sustain outside of community. Drawing on Erik Erikson, Lester links the capacity to hope to one's belief in the world's trustworthiness as an outgrowth of the basic trust developed in the infant in the context of a dependable and loving caregiver. Such a basic trust, Lester says, "provides a head start on believing in a God who is present, cares for them, and is concerned about what happens to them."[12] However, for people of color, refugees, immigrants, and those living in poverty, all the parental love or self-confidence one might develop does not necessarily equate to belief in the trustworthiness of the world.

In white, and particularly affluent, communities, hope is often an embodied expectation of the well-lived life. Even for those living in the face of hopelessness, it is against a backdrop that says we should expect to be hopeful. For persons of color, however, hope may come in spite of all expectations. Black and brown communities the world over have known a great deal more about the actual distance between hope and its realization when one lives in a world of violence and oppression. From these voices there is undoubtedly much to learn about hope in a world of uncertainty.

In their work on the psychopolitical well-being of marginalized communities, counseling psychologist and Black Lives Matter activist Della V. Mosley and coauthors suggest that *radical hope* includes being attuned, in each moment, to the past *and* the future—particularly as these relate to histories of oppression and resistance for persons of color.[13] Every act of hope brings forward the wisdom of our ancestors who even today in this present moment bind us to their courage in order to create meaning and hope for change in the future. It is this sense of simultaneity—being able to orient oneself in multiple directions at the same time—and, even more so, the connection to how our ancestors navigated through difficulty that can inform our own wayfinding through challenging times and that is of particular interest to us here and bears relevance to theological ideas of hope. The idea that as believers we hold a common community of ancestors in faith, as seen in the sacred texts and movements for social justice upon which we must depend as readily as we do the God who beckons us forward, is fundamental to hope as the theological touchstone that will help us recalibrate our wayfinding through crisis.

Bryana H. French and coauthors connect the idea of radical hope to radical healing in racialized communities. "Hope," they suggest, "allows for a sense of agency to change things for the greater good—a belief that one can fight for justice and that the fight will not be futile."[14] Mosley and her colleagues similarly suggest that it is agency *and* faith that "help to maintain a belief that change is not only possible but that individuals can enact [that] change."[15] When pastoral caregivers who surrender to the fixing impulse either consciously or unconsciously believe it is their job to make or provide hope for someone, they foreclose the sense of the other's agency—which, in turn, ultimately forecloses hope.[16] Caregivers can, however, model hope and accompany others on a sacred journey of wayfinding.

We can and should remind others and ourselves that we are not helpless in our efforts to shape hope no matter the circumstance. Theologian Susan Nelson suggests hope is found in the "eschatological imagination" that gives rise to those acts, large and small, that open the future.[17] Hope and certainty are not precursors to action.[18] Even in the face of great despair, each act of kindness, love, care, generosity, defiance, or resistance that refuses to let suffering and evil have the last word is the very essence of hope. For Mosley, this looks like resistance that brings faith and agency together through acts of activism that break open the possibility of change.[19]

Standing at the empty tomb, the women are watching the future break open through Jesus's act of love in the face of suffering and violence. As a touchstone, hope enhances spiritual wayfinding by grounding us in the communities of our sacred texts and movements while also reminding us that uncertainty is the place where the mystery of the sacred guides us toward a horizon of possibility.

Joy

It's entirely possible that I include joy here as a spiritual value simply because I think we need more joy in a world so full today of vitriol and hate-mongering. I suppose I should also admit to being shortsighted on the necessity of cultivating joy as an end goal of pastoral caregiving. I have often viewed joy as more akin to happiness, that is, as a fleeting emotion dependent to a large degree upon external circumstances. As such, joy seemed antithetical to suffering, the place where ministry expends so much of its care practice. But the relationship between joy and suffering is much more complex.

I am grateful to Mary Clark Moschella for inspiring in me the notion that joy is an essential touchstone for caregiving, especially when navigating times of crisis and uncertainty. Moschella points to the sustained quality of joy and shows that joy and suffering are not antithetical at all. She describes (rather than defines) joy as

> [a]n embodied awareness of holy presence and extravagant love, an awareness that dawns upon us like grace. It carries a sense of the unexpected, of surprise. The experience of joy is something intensely felt, perceived as an ancient memory bubbling up from deep inside even while it also feels given, from some great beyond, an experience so unexpected and profound that one can only try to take it in. At the same time, joy leaves a lasting impression, one that comes to the surface just as grief does, in the most ordinary of days. The

experience of joy is not fleeting or shallow, but deep and striking. It is linked to some object of goodness or wonder.[20]

Another helpful voice in uncovering the deeper meanings of joy is pastoral theologian Greg Ellison. In a conversation with colleague Georgette Ledgister, Ellison describes joy as an inbreaking force with a disruptive character—it "disrupts" our lives and forever changes how we see the world in ways that dislodge despair and that make room for the sacred.[21] It is this disruptive character of joy that allows us to lean into joy even in the midst of great suffering and turbulence, such as the times in which we are living. What better time than during the grief and fear of a pandemic, the despair and anxiety of financial loss, or the violent and traumatic encounters with oppression for persons of color for all of us to realize the invigorating and disrupting power of joy? Instead of asking how one can talk about joy at a time like this, we might better ask how a joy-filled soul can energize all of us toward recovery, care, and justice.

Cultivating a Disposition of Joy and Gratitude

Joy once nurtured can become a spiritual disposition in the lives of the faithful. How do we cultivate this spiritual disposition of joy? To cultivate, from the Latin *colere*, means to live in or to inhabit, to promote growth. Any of these, but particularly the idea of inhabiting, is what I imagine most in connection to joy. Can we cultivate joy in such a way that we *inhabit* the spiritual discipline? Ellison and Moschella both highlight that the inbreaking of God is a central characteristic found in moments of joy. We can attribute this divine inbreaking to the ways joy can reorient our perspective, especially over the long term, *reinvigorate* our convictions, and redefine how we see the world and how joy reclaims us.[22] As a spiritual disposition, it is joy that brings vitality and vibrancy—life force and energy—to our encounters in the world, especially in the face of hardship, tragedy, and struggle and the uncertainty they bring.

Joy can and should be cultivated. Moschella says,

Experiences of joy, when explored more fully, offer avenues for a deeper understanding of God's goodness and love. When we are attentive and aware of God's presence in us and all creation, when we feel the joy of this firsthand, we are freed from the paralysis of fear or despair, if only temporarily. Moments like this, when they accumulate over time, strengthen and steady us, and teach us what is good, help us know what well-being looks and feels like.[23]

The practice of cultivating joy has as its goal both depth and endurance, both of which can deepen our own spiritual resources with which we navigate life in difficult times and shape the care practices with which we accompany others through the same.

When joy becomes a spiritual disposition, a touchstone, it spurs us closer to the transcendent view of any circumstance without undermining the severity or seriousness therein. It undergirds a particular perspective that allows room for possibility and helps us lean more readily toward hope. Joy is a deeply felt inner condition that need not be outwardly expressed to fulfill its purpose; but how much more, indeed, does it flourish when shared? How do pastoral caregivers and others find the way to the spiritual value of joy? The simplest and sometimes most difficult path is gratitude. Like practices of meditation, small movements toward thankfulness can crack open the possibility of remarkable change even if it falls shy of joy in the beginning. A practice of reorienting toward the good opens the heart and mind to thankfulness. Gratitude even in small doses can help us recalibrate our responses to everyday challenges and frustrations or even deep despair. The women in the Gospel of Mark are only able to feel grief and fear—they do not yet understand that the empty tomb is the very place of joy and gratitude. But we do.

Meaning Making

Meaning making is fundamental to an individual's ability to square the sometimes tragic events of this world with a sovereign and personal God who wishes for us every good and peaceable thing. What is meaning making and how do we engage it? Crystal Park, whose research focuses on psychology and spirituality, conducted an extensive literature review of research on meaning making. She describes a surprisingly consistent set of tenets that define the process of meaning making, including the following: (a) people possess orienting systems that provide cognitive frameworks for interpreting their experiences (global meaning); (b) when experiences conflict with these orienting systems, people "appraise the situation and assign meaning to them;" (c) the degree to which the appraised and global meanings differ determines the level of distress experienced; (d) this distress initiates a process of meaning making, which is the individual's attempt to reduce this discrepancy and "restore a sense of the world as meaningful and their own lives as worthwhile." When successful, this process leads to better overall adjustment to the stressful event that was experienced.[24]

It is not enough to simply have a framework for interpreting our experience. Colonialist history and ongoing oppressive systemic practices show us how fixed meaning frameworks often serve to sustain the privileging of some at the expense of others. As noted previously, these types of frameworks require a high degree of control, such as charting and mapping, as a way to contain the unknown. To navigate even the everyday uncertainties of life, let alone those of deep crisis, meaning making requires a flexible framework for understanding experiences that allow us to adapt and integrate new experiences as they unfold. This is meaning making that leads to growth and even wisdom.

While describing a step-by-step process helps our overall understanding of meaning making, the lived experience of facing a crisis and trying to make sense of it does not lend itself to a neatly prescribed process. It's messy. A bird's-eye view of an individual's experience over a lifetime would likely reveal multiple and repeated opportunities to engage in the meaning-making process. Opportunity is a key word here. As anyone in ministry can attest, individuals do not always choose or have the skills to navigate their way out of despair even when it is possible to do so. Jesus understood this. We won't stumble upon meaning, nor can it be given to us. Meaning must be made.

Making meaning as a theological touchstone invites us to interpret our experience through a spiritual frame while not ignoring science and logic. By doing so, we are able to see beyond our particular circumstances while not ignoring the reality of them. This meaning making not only asks of us that we seek to understand how God is present in our unfolding story but also asks us to find where our story fits into the larger narrative of God's redeeming love and justice. Do we find our own story in that of the women staring in fear at the empty tomb and wondering what it might mean? This shift of perspective often makes us keenly aware that, whatever our experience or however great the uncertainty, it is not a new story. Our sacred texts are overflowing with others who have faced the same. Two things are sure: Our stories are just as important as those which have come before, and God is still bigger than them all.

The soul-aching questions of *Why me?* or *What kind of God would do or allow this?* may well be reasonable queries to make when sitting in the aftermath of grief, loss, or other crises. These are certainly questions we see over and again in the biblical narrative. These questions are sure clues that the meaning-making process is underway. We should not, though, confuse the importance of the meaning-making process with the need to find sure answers. Pastors and chaplains must remember that even as we go about the imperfect process of trying to answer the difficult questions around suffering and loss, it is even more important that we learn to live with unanswered questions. Pastoral theologian John Swinton in his discussion about pastoral responses to evil reminds us, "What we need is not an answer to the question of why God allows evil, but rather an ability to live with unanswered questions and still retain faith in the goodness of God and the hope of God's providential promises."[25] Finding one's way to a lived theology that allows this level of ambiguity requires that we seek meaning outside of certitude.

Though we have come last to meaning as a touchstone, we have in a sense been working on it from the beginning. The theological touchstones as a whole are a part of the frame by which we as people of faith make sense of our experience—joy and hope are essential to this frame. Spiritual wayfinding requires that we see that each is deeply interconnected with the other.

Finding the Way

Those in ministries of all sorts, but especially pastors and chaplains, have the honor of standing with the women in Mark—with those at the threshold where the empty tomb opens into possibility. Likewise, we accompany individuals and communities as we find our way through these times of uncertainty. We move toward the possibility promised by the empty tomb, returning again and again to the spiritual touchstones to recalibrate and reinvigorate us on the journey. With each return to the touchstones, we ground ourselves in hopeful futures with embodied joy as meaning-making people of faith claiming our place in the ongoing story of God's love in the world. It is our sacred task.

The scandal of the gospel, as I am surely not the first to note, is that through the love of Christ, we see the world differently. We can believe in love even when all evidence is to the contrary. We hope even when it seems hopeless. Hope is when love gives us the vision to imagine what is possible despite circumstances. It becomes the horizon toward which to move. We find joy even in the face of suffering. Joy is rooted in the practiced remembering of God's love for "me," even if it is experienced as the outward expression of gratitude through acts of altruism or giving to others. Further, we can make meaning even in the face of the senseless. Meaning-making occurs when love of God is the lens through which we seek to make sense of our experience in the world. We dare to engage justice even in the face of powers and principalities actively and sometimes violently resisting us. Justice is love of other, love in action on behalf of the oppressed. We can find resilience even as the pain continues, not only in its absence. Resilience is God's persistent love that becomes the strongest resource in our ability to struggle well in the face of ambiguity. When we are certain of God's love, the uncertainty around us becomes more tolerable.

To those who would say such notions of hope, joy, and meaning (and love) are thin and trite, I invite them to show me any other way, not only when the world seems sure but even when it is turned upside down.

Notes

1   Gregory Heyworth, director of the Lazarus Project at the University of Rochester, has created a 3D model of the original globe, which is on display at the New York Public Library. Kathleen McGarvey, "One of the World's Oldest Globes Is Ready for Its

Close-Up," University of Rochester Newscenter, Feb. 26, 2020, https://www.rochester.edu/newscenter/worlds-oldest-globe-hunt-lenox-lazarus-project-417532/.

2   Shirin Elahi, "Here Be Dragons . . . Exploring the 'Unknown Unknowns,'" *Futures* 43 (March 2011): 196–201.

3   The Intergovernmental Panel on Climate Change (IPCC) recently issued its *Sixth Assessment Report*. The evidence is clear: The planet is warming more quickly than anticipated. Even with an immediate reduction in emissions, the impact of climate warming will continue to accelerate for decades to come. Intergovernmental Panel on Climate Change, *AR6 Synthesis Report: Climate Change 2022*, https://www.ipcc.ch/assessment-report/ar6/.

4   Deaths caused by injury include death by drowning, transport accidents (especially alcohol-related driving accidents), falls, assaults, and suicide. Bobbie M. Parks et al., "Anomalously Warm Temperatures Are Associated with Increased Injury Deaths," *Nature Medicine* 26 (January 2020): 65–70, www.nature.com/naturemedicine.

5   Allan Hugh Cole Jr., *Be Not Anxious: Pastoral Care of Disquieted Souls* (Eerdmans, 2008), 25.

6   M. R. O'Connor, *Wayfinding: The Science and Mystery of How Humans Navigate the World* (St. Martin's Press, 2019).

7   See Polynesian Voyaging Society: Moananuiaka—A Voyage for the Pacific, www.hokulea.com/moananuiakea/.

8   "Hokule'a: The Art of Wayfinding (Interview with a Master Navigator)," National Geographic blog, March 3, 2014.

9   Brian Brock, "Discipleship as Living with God, or Wayfinding and Scripture," *Journal of Spiritual Formation & Soul Care*, 7 (2014): 22–34.

10 Brock, "Discipleship as Living with God."

11 Andrew Lester, *Hope in Pastoral Care and Counseling* (Westminster John Knox Press, 1995), 64.

12 Lester, *Hope in Pastoral Care and Counseling*, 96.

13 Della V. Mosley et al., "Radical hope in Revolting Times: Proposing a Culturally Relevant Psychological Framework," *Social and Personality Psychology Compass* 14 (January 2020), e12512, https://doi.org/10.1111/spc3.12512.

14 Bryana H. French et al., "Toward a Psychological Framework of Radical Healing in Communities of Color," *The Counseling Psychologist* 48 (2020): 14-46, at 26, https://doi.org/10.1177/0011000019843506.

15 Mosley et al., "Radical Hope," 5.

16 While we can offer visions of hope, particularly in relation to God's persistent presence, grace, and love, we cannot make others hope. They must claim hope for themselves.

17 Susan L. Nelson, "Facing Evil: Evil's Many Faces, Five Paradigms for Understanding Evil," *Interpretation* 57 (2003), 398–413. https://doi.org/10.1177%2F002096430005700405.

18 Pastoral theologian Ryan LaMothe notes numerous everyday acts of passionate and courageous caring that accompany life situations that, indeed, seem quite hopeless. Writing in the context of the reality of the climate peril we face, LaMothe suggests that feelings of hopelessness are no excuse for inaction. Ryan LaMothe, *A Radical Political Theology for the Anthropocene Age: Thinking and Being Otherwise* (Cascade, 2021), 283.

Section 3

19 Mosley et al., "Radical Hope," 6.
20 Mary Clark Moschella, "Calling and Compassion: Elements of Joy in Lived Practices of Care," in *Joy and Human Flourishing: Essays on Theology, Culture, and the Good Life*, ed. Miroslav Volf and Justin E. Crisp (Fortress Press, 2015), 99. See also Mary Clark Moschella, *Caring for Joy: Narrative, Theology, and Practice* (Brill, 2016).
21 Yale Youth Ministry Institute, "Rev. Dr. Greg Ellison and Georgette Ledgister on Joy," YouTube video, 12:17, https://www.youtube.com/watch?v=znpPjk5nVww&t=79s.
22 Yale Youth Ministry Institute, "Rev. Dr. Greg Ellison."
23 Moschella, "Calling and Compassion," 107.
24 Crystal L. Park, "Making Sense of the Meaning Literature: An Integrative Review of Meaning Making and Its Effects on Adjustment to Stressful Life Events," *Psychological Bulletin* 136 (2010): 257–301.
25 John Swinton, *Raging with Compassion: Pastoral Responses to the Problem of Evil* (Eerdmans, 2007), 47.

Ecotheology and Contemporary Christianity

Fred P. Edie

There is a building boom afoot in the community where I grew up. Word has gotten out: this small island along the southeast coast of the United States, bounded by rivers and tidal marshes, is a place where rich diversity of living things and hospitable relations between people have nurtured a flourishing community. On my half-hour daily walk I regularly spot dolphins, deer, and even bald eagles perched in Spanish moss-draped live oak trees. Strolling a block farther down the lane that winds along the river, I often run into my childhood baseball coach walking his dog. Who wouldn't want to live here?

But newcomers face a trade-off. Aside from the historic riverfront dwellings owned by the fabulously well-to-do, most homes on the island are basic ranch houses built between the 1940s and the 1980s. Thirteen-hundred square feet leaves precious little room for designer kitchens or home offices, let alone a second toilet. Some buyers are content to add a coat of paint and count themselves blessed to live in paradise. Lately, however, others are opting to demo those old ranchers all the way to the ground and then raise something twice the size (plus a three-car garage) in their place. The growing human footprint on the island covers over soil that once absorbed frequent deluges, it channels more freshwater runoff into salt-marsh estuaries, and it leaves fewer trees for shade or birds.

While this story obviously emerges out of a context of considerable economic privilege, it is representative of a growing global concern. Everywhere we look, trees disappear, fields and meadows are paved over, wild animals recede from view, a pall of smog drapes the shoulders of our cities, and poor communities, downstream of all this "development," struggle against ever-greater odds. And these are merely the visible symptoms of deeper threats to the habitability of the entire Earth household.

It is no overstatement to suggest that these are issues of life and death, that they address *ultimate concerns*, which means that, for Christians, they are theological issues. Unlike philosophers who attempt to discern life's meanings on its own terms, theologians pose ultimate questions in light of their profession of faith in the triune God. Indeed, this God is always Christians' first answer to questions of life and death: God, the creator, authors all life; Christ, the redeemer, renews all life; Holy Spirit, the sustainer, directs and preserves all life.

Even with those strong answers to ultimate questions, there remains plenty to wonder about. While scripture and theological tradition witness to bedrock convictions of God's triune identity and mission, Christian communities daily confront new obstacles and opportunities to live faithfully before God. That is why the extended theological conversation—initiated with the people called Israel, crystallized in scripture with Jesus at its center, and creatively interpreted through two millennia of church tradition—continues with passion and vitality down to the present.

One case in point is the emergence over the past half century of *ecotheology*. While mostly accepting traditional answers to theological questions of ultimate concern, ecotheology seeks to focus the continuing conversation on a growing concern not yet fully addressed: God's intent for the flourishing of the whole of creation—flora and fauna (biosystems), land, sea, and sky (earth systems), as well as human beings. The emergence of ecotheology has been prompted not only by growing evidence of ecocrisis—human-induced climate change, water-quality degradation, deforestation and land degradation, and loss of biodiversity—but also through growing esteem for simpler, more Earth-friendly ways of life practiced by many Christians, especially in less developed regions of the planet.

Ecotheology asks its own list of big questions:

1. Can a Christian faith that for millennia has prioritized human beings and their affairs as God's primary or exclusive interest be reinterpreted, reformed, or reconstructed to include God's care for the well-being of "other-than-human" creatures? On what grounds would such a move be justified?
2. To what extent, if at all, can theology converse with science as a means to reevaluate its theological understandings of cosmic/Earth systems or as the basis for constructing ecological theology?
3. Should the interpretive task of ecotheology begin with nibbling at the edges of long-presumed biblical or doctrinal orthodoxies or with the groanings of the planet and its most vulnerable creatures, including humans living in poverty?
4. Does the church bear unique gifts for bearing witness to or healing a diseased planet?
5. If the future belongs to God, what vision of it should Christians imagine and pursue?

In this chapter, I seek to help readers expand their grasp of the many possible permutations of responses to these questions of ultimate concern. In ways both predictable and surprising, scholars' fields of expertise, their locations across the theological spectrum from conservative to liberal, and their social locations (on a landscaped campus utopia or struggling alongside the people of an impoverished barrio) influence their accounts. All agree on one point, however: the threats to our Earth household are real.

I begin with ecological considerations of scripture and then move to soundings of the theological tradition in response to urgent ecological challenges. Later, I turn to theologies of liberation whose starting point is not the theological tradition but the theologically fraught sufferings and hopes of the world's most vulnerable creatures. Finally, as I am a Christian educator and practical theologian, I conclude with proposals for lived Christian faith on a fragile planet.

Section 3

Greening the Bible

Old Testament scholar Ellen Davis is among the first to interpret the Bible for an ecological age. Her strategy is informed by agrarianism, an agricultural way of thinking, practicing, and ordering life in community that prioritizes the health of land and living creatures. According to Davis, that biblical writers and communities were "people of the land," for whom the need for daily bread was never far from mind, often fails to register with many twenty-first-century readers. Presently, those of us who live far from the land, who wouldn't know alfalfa from arugula when streaking past farmers' fields at seventy-five miles per hour, are also prone to glossing over frequent biblical references to famine and abundant harvest, to sheep and goats, or to a covenant promise of land. We dismiss these features as anachronisms in the presumption that the Bible is exclusively about "spiritual" affairs. Land and water, flora and fauna serve only to decorate the margins of the biblical pages.

In contrast, Davis advocates reading scripture through an agrarian lens informed by this central question: "How do these texts view the relationship between humans . . . and the material sources of life as an essential aspect of living in the presence of God."[1]

Davis shines light on the primacy of the land as integral to Israel's interpretation of the significance of God's acts of creation as well as its fundamental importance to the community's understanding of covenant blessing and obligation. Davis reminds us that much of the Old Testament was written down amid the experience of exile to Babylon away from the Promised Land. Davis creatively translates the ambiguous Hebrew verbs in the Genesis story, and she and reinterprets a story where human beings are regarded as the crowning achievement of creation:

> "And YHWH God took the human and set him in the garden of Eden *to work and serve it, to preserve and observe it*." Even in this . . . moment . . . the human does not take priority over the land. Adam comes to Eden as a protector, answerable for the well-being of the precious thing that he did not make; he is to be an observer, mindful of the limits that are built into the created order as both inescapable and fitting. The biblical writer does not subscribe to the fantasy that our society has embraced as an ideal—that human ingenuity runs

up against physical limits only in order to overcome them. Rather, the ambiguous verbs suggest a different orientation to reality. The land instantiates limits that God has set; we encounter it as a fellow creature to be respected and even revered.[2]

Finally, according to Davis, Israel's experience of exile, as implied by Adam's banishment from the Garden of Eden, serves as a reminder of the judgment that befalls a people when it ceases to receive the land as gift and fellow creature. To misuse it, literally, is to lose it—a judgment no less harrowing for the present ecological age than for Israel.

Biblical theologian William Brown brings to reading the Bible in an ecological age openness to listening to science. This is not to say he uses science to "prove" scripture or vice versa; rather, he proposes that science and scripture are "tangentially overlapping magisteria," ways of thinking and imagining capable of evoking wonder and awe in their adherents.[3] By listening to science as he reads scripture, Brown intends to demonstrate both deeper harmonies between these worldviews and also starker separations.

As one case in point, Brown considers God's answer to Job's complaint of injustice in chapters 38 to 41. Traditionally, these chapters have been read in terms of theodicy (the problem of evil) or theophany (instances of dramatic encounter with God). Brown points out how these passages also offer a description of creation as dramatic as is found in Genesis 1–2, but with a different configuration of relationships. There is, for example, "no mention of . . . humanity's creation, let alone dominion. This is no anthropocentric world that God so loves. The world is a hodgepodge of life in all its wondrous and repulsive variety, a world of 'ultimate pluralism.'"[4] Further, from God's perspective, Job shares "uncommon identity" with Leviathan, "a lumbering, fearless, playful creature of the wild. Job is no isolated creation and clearly not the apex of the created order. Rather, he is created with his monstrous twin, who receives the credit of being born 'first' or 'best.'"[5] In other words, this view of creation demonstrates kinship between human and other-than-human animals, a view consistent with the findings of current science.

Similarly, Brown heralds Psalm 104 as a portrait of creation in concentric terms: "The earth is created to accommodate myriad creatures great and small, people included. The earth is host and home to all living kind, and as such it is [to be] a source of joy," including for God.[6] In turn, faithful life for humans consists in a response of equally joyous coexistence with the rest of creation.

By shining new light on these and other creational texts in the Bible in addition to those in Genesis 1 and 2, Brown builds a case for a biblical portrait more in keeping with contemporary science: Human beings are created with a degree of freedom and agency not shared by other creatures, but they are not perched above them hierarchically. Nor is creation humanity's apple of the picking; instead, God's creative provision is for all creatures. In addition, by juxtaposing Job to Leviathan, the scriptures hint at a kind of animal kinship between them: after his encounter with God, "Job is to take home ... a recognition of his connection to the wild."[7] Finally, in these chapters from Job and the Book of Psalms, in place of God's understated acknowledgment that creation is "good," we find fervent divine passion for and delight in the details and diversity of creation. For Brown, God is the original "biophile," a posture of reverence and awe for nonhuman species combined with awareness that their well-being is interwoven with human well-being.[8] Biblical scholar Richard Bauckham acknowledges that most attention to the significance of creation is found in the Old Testament. Nevertheless, he maintains that in the Bible "the whole of creation is the world as also Jesus' story; he is its chief actor. The Bible characterizes Jesus as the world's 'origin and goal,' its 'Alpha and Omega.'" Bauckham adds that Jesus's culminating action—the fulfillment of a kingdom—isn't depicted as human escape from the natural world. Instead of human "emancipation from nature," the task is "keeping our mutuality with other-than-human creation."[9]

Bauckham locates support for his account in the hymn contained in Colossians 1:15-20. It depicts emphatically the cosmic Christ, whom Paul calls Jesus Christ (v. 15). Further, this Christ is the one in whom "all things still cohere." Bauckham describes how this holding together signals the crucial importance of Jesus's Crucifixion and Resurrection in the biblical metanarrative of God's salvation (v. 18). That things fall apart reveals the sinful distortion of persons, communities, and systems—all of which combine to cause creation's "groaning" (Romans 8:28). Yet Colossians also reveals how

Jesus's passion accomplishes the reconciliation of these things to God, while his Resurrection secures their renewal as new creation.

In addition to attending to the cosmic Christ, Bauckham offers a greener spin to the earthly ministry of Jesus. There biblical readers discover a messiah acquainted with the folkways of his country cousins. Jesus teaches in the cultural vernacular of people familiar with farming and animal husbandry; there we find an awareness of their dependence upon the land for life.

Bauckham also reinterprets Jesus's stilling of the storm in Mark 4. He first reminds the readers of the story's ancient cosmic overtones: In the beginning, God creates in part by pushing back the waters of chaos (Genesis 1; Psalm 104:7; Job 26:12). Jesus emulates that mighty act by stilling the storm. In addition, Bauckham perceives in this story Jesus's work of reconciliation and new creation. Jesus is depicted as one who renders peace over the watery chaos; in and through Jesus, God will "finally establish the harmony of his creation." And there is this cautionary note: "The Story of Jesus's pacification of the storm reminds us that control of nature is God-like, and humans may rightly participate in it only as creatures, dependent on God, not making themselves gods."[10]

Greening Theology

Similar to biblical scholars, theologians of various stripes also are addressing challenges posed by ecological crisis. In this section, I identify representative perspectives on pertinent theological themes, including creation, sin, Christology, and the Spirit.

Creation

Readers may well be familiar with the basic tenets of the doctrine of creation. It declares that God creates everything out of nothing and deems creation good. God's singular eminence as creator conveys the status of creature upon all the rest including humans. Importantly, according to the doctrine of creation, human beings are not self-creating beings; human life is a gift that comes from beyond themselves. Ultimately, we are dependent upon God (and the rest of creation) for bread and even for breath. Ecotheologians contend that the doctrine of creation has been muted or distorted, especially in the global north. They frequently point to Enlightenment thinker (and churchgoing Anglican) Francis Bacon (1561–1626) as emblematic of the move to sever all links between human creatures and other creation. According to ecotheologians Daniel L. Brunner, Jennifer L. Butler, and A. J. Swoboda, "Bacon stripped the creation of its aliveness and turned it into mere inert, dead matter, which humanity could then manipulate through science and technology." They claim that Bacon's views led to human objectification, devaluation, and detachment from creation, which encouraged their overexploitation of it. They also contend that an Enlightenment worldview was the source of theological distortion: "Within much of the evangelical Christian community the doctrine of redemption has taken priority over the doctrine of creation, and spirituality has been aliened above earthiness."[11]

Feminist theologian Sallie McFague goes further than shoring up doctrinal claims for creation to propose new ways of speaking about God and creation. Specifically, she suggests the need for new metaphors. Whereas traditional images ("father," "king," or "lord") imply God's hierarchical separation from the world, McFague proposes to imagine "the world as God's body." She suggests that this metaphor encourages Christians "to think of God's transcendence as radical immanence; that is, God's love is totally, though not exhaustively, incarnated in the world."[12]

More recently, Roman Catholic Pope Francis has been credited with successfully injecting theology into the global public conversation on climate change. In the encyclical *Laudato si'*, Francis strongly reiterates God as creator and affirms creation as good while decrying political and economic systems that inflict damage upon the world, including upon its poorest human inhabitants. Francis also declares caring for creation an essential matter of discipleship.[13] While some suggest that the document overemphasizes a generic view of God as creator and mutes the particularities of Christian faith in order to be palatable for non-Christian readers, others see it as reinforcement of "strong and traditional Catholic concepts such as the dignity of all human beings, faith in God as creator, hope in Christ who renews all things, and special devotion to Mary, who becomes not just mother of us all, but mother of the earth as well."[14]

Christology

Ecotheologians of all stripes have criticized depictions of Jesus that limit him to rescuing individual souls from their personal sins and to promising deliverance from this world for ethereal existence in the heavens. Ecotheological revisions to Christology cover a number of points; they include more nuanced descriptions of sin, appreciation for Christ's saving work of "New Creation," expansive characterizations of Incarnation (Jesus as fully human and fully God), and efforts to revive attention to Christ as creative Word. This section addresses each of these in turn.

Sin is sometimes described as less a list of bad things that we rebellious people do. While affirming this view, the apostle Paul, in his letter to the Romans, also seems to hold a vision of sin as an impersonal power or force that corrupts creaturely relationships. A relational view of sin displays its power to taint entire communities, institutions, and even systems. The other-than-human creation also gets caught up in sin-tainted relationships. In addition to being personal, sin can be systemic: this means that sin both disturbs individual members of creation and destroys the harmony between them.

In response, ecotheologians offer a vision of salvation in which Jesus saves not by promising private escape from the bodily baggage of worldly concern but by renewing the relational web of Shalom: Salvation looks like lions lying down beside lambs, human enemies reconciled, and economic systems built upon racism and poverty being overcome through justice, and the whole of the created order restored to balance. Orthodox theologian Elizabeth Theokritoff, says, "The saving work of Christ is the matrix within which we understand the meaning and purpose of all creation . . . We are thus looking for a concept of Salvation that connects us with the rest of creation. Such a concept sees Salvation as involving the whole created world and our relationship with it, which in turn entails an eschatological vision of Salvation with the world, not from it."[15]

John Wesley, 18th century Anglican priest and leader of the Methodist movement, was among the first of the modern theologians to redraw the essential link between God's delight in the goodness of creation, human and extra-human alike, and the Son's saving work. Although the young Wesley enthusiastically testified to an overly anthropocentric, spiritualized version of salvation popular in his day, the mature Wesley preached and wrote toward a more holistic redemption. For example, Wesley argued for animals possessing souls which necessarily implied divine concern for them in life and in death.[16] In addition, Randy Maddox demonstrates how Wesley disputed the views of Francis Bacon and others who "who championed the mandate to reclaim the mastery over creation that was lost in the fall," and "pleaded for resuming the loving stewardship of creation that [humans] abandoned in the fall."[17] To this end, he also recovered "new creation" theology where, in his view, the entire creation groaned for redemption (Romans 8) and waited in hope for the healing balm of Christ's saving grace. Finally, Wesley came to espouse an eschatological vision where, by grace, Christians could live actively into God's kingdom in the present. In addition to bedrock kingdom-invoking practices of worship, scripture study, mercy, and mutual accountability, Wesley also commended simplicity, frugality, care for domestic animals, modest diet, and vigorous outdoor exercise—what we might describe today as a more sustainable way of life. In other words, Wesley in his later years, "encouraged Methodists to 'anticipate their heaven below' by participating in God's salvific concern for the flourishing of all creation."[18]

Incarnation—the doctrinal affirmation of the fullness of God dwelling in the human being Jesus of Nazareth—is another theme of great importance to ecotheology. For the early church, the doctrine of Incarnation served to head off heresies depicting Jesus as either exclusively human or exclusively divine. It also supported the logic of Jesus's saving work. According to Gregory of Nazianzus (AD 329–390), "that [humanity] which [Jesus] has not assumed he has not healed."[19]

Presently, ecotheologians speak of "deep Incarnation." Their intent is to show how God's habitation of human flesh in Jesus means, on a deeper level, that God in Jesus enters the "whole malleable matrix of materiality." According to systematic theologian Niels Gregersen, deep incarnation is "the view that God's own Logos (Wisdom and Word) was made flesh in Jesus the Christ in such a comprehensive manner that God, by assuming that particular life story of Jesus the Jew from Nazareth, also conjoined the material conditions of creaturely existence (all flesh)," shared and ennobled the fate of all biological life-forms ("grass" and "lilies"), and experienced the pains of sensitive creatures ("sparrows" and "foxes").[20] Through this expansion of the meaning of Incarnation, Gregersen and others seek to both enlarge the realm of God's presence and include all creation within the realm of God's saving work.

I previously invoked the "cosmic Christ" when considering the first chapter of Colossians. Like their ecologically minded biblical colleagues, ecotheologians call attention to that passage and also to the Word Christology found in the first chapter of John's Gospel. Here as before, the purpose of this renewed attention to Jesus's cosmic status and role in the inauguration of creation is to correct a near-exclusive (and, for them, reductive) focus upon his role as savior of humanity. Their intent is not to dismiss Jesus's saving work on behalf of human beings, much less the human need for salvation! Instead, they portray Jesus as much more than a savior-come-lately—a repairman showing up on short notice to fix unexpected bugs in the system. Ecotheologians remind us that creation exploded into life through an overwhelming burst of triune love: In the beginning, the Christly Word of God, animated by the power of the Spirit, spoke all creation into being! Therefore, Jesus's saving work finds its proper meaning and context as the culmination of the Christly Word's grand creative project.

Pneumatology

The traditional doctrine of the Holy Spirit is associated with stirring up the original creation (Genesis 1) and with empowering the new creation begun in Jesus (Matthew 3). The Spirit is envisioned as the animating breath of life, the one who weaves human beings in the grace of God's love while prompting and propelling them into new relationships with fellow creatures and new possibilities for realizing abundant life. In prophetic traditions, the Holy Spirit often is imaged as a mischief-maker, kindred to stirring up "good trouble."[21] In prosaic terms, the Holy Spirit is credited with rousing Christians to imagine and act toward new practices of justice consistent with God's Kingdom.

Critics suggest that popular appraisals of the Spirit have reduced her role to occasional pastoral-care duty—delivering comfort to troubled hearts or assuring the church that God is present. Ecotheologians work to spark faithful imagination in relation to the Spirit's animating power toward new creation.

Theologian Dennis Edwards has seized upon the Spirit's dynamism to provide a theological means to underwrite evolution. For Edwards, the Spirit is a "flame of love," "an active, inviting, reconciling presence within the whole created order, bringing all creatures together."[22]

In addition, "life in the Spirit" is often connected to Christian discipleship. We've noted that Pope Francis commends practices of Earth care to followers of Jesus. Sallie McFague addresses the White middle class of North America along the same lines, exhorting them to Spirit life as "cruciform living," an alternative notion of the abundant life that will involve a philosophy of sacrifice and "enoughness." She champions the virtue (and Spirit gift?) of "frugality," calling it a "subversive" practice for resisting consumerism and finding solidarity with poor human communities and the other-than-human creation.[23]

Ecotheologies of Liberation

Theologians increasingly begin their work with attention to suffering and hope of people and planet. Put differently, many contemporary theologians are less concerned about shoring up elegant theological systems—God as triune, Jesus as fully human and fully divine, and so on—and proceed instead directly to the pressure points of real life. In particular, liberation theologians often work and live in solidarity with oppressed peoples. They accept as axiomatic the claim that God exercises a "preferential option for the poor." They argue that poor people the world over possess little access to political or economic capital, making them uniquely vulnerable to exploitation by the rich and powerful. Indeed, liberation theologians say the systems the powerful of the world have fashioned in order to maintain their positions of domination; even the writing of history "goes to the winners." Unsurprisingly, one essential task of liberation theology is unmasking these imbalances of social power and the systems that prop them up in the effort to transform them toward justice.

In this effort, liberation theology finds support from the tradition of Old Testament prophecy and especially from Jesus. In a liberative rendition of the Gospel story, Jesus is born among the poor, and he ministers in solidarity with the poor, seeking to restore dignity to a place of God's table. Jesus's teachings on God's kingdom envision a community of full inclusion, where the most vulnerable of God's children taste justice, equality, and dignity. Instead of gentle repose in the sweet by-and-by, liberation theology interprets Jesus's redemptive work as occurring in the social and historical zones of life here and now.

Since its inception in the late-twentieth century, the work of liberation theology has grown to minister to all the poor ones—human and other-than-humans—beloved by God. South American theologian Leonardo Boff chronicles crimes against ecosystems in the Amazon rainforest (torching rainforests with napalm) in conjunction with Indigenous people suffering the same attacks.[24] Less dramatic but no less telling, health-care workers have long recognized higher incidences of diseases like asthma and lead poisoning in poor communities in the United States due to lower air and water quality in their neighborhoods. In these cases, oppression is literally pressed into the flesh of poor people and their children. Hence ecological liberation theologians have come to view ecological restoration as essential and integral to human liberation.

Feminist Ecotheologies

Feminist theologians begin at a slightly different place from liberation theology but share many of the same ends. Their point of departure is the historic subjugation of women to men and to male (patriarchal) power systems. Ethicist and educator Nel Noddings suggests that because women historically have been tasked with child-rearing, they have had more practice with a maternal ethics of cooperation and nurture than men.[25] She thinks this historical burden can be turned to practical advantage by teaching caring and sharing to schoolchildren. Her position resonates with environmental educators' work to reintroduce children to the created world by taking them outside in order to rekindle creaturely kinship.

Womanist theologians—whose point of departure is their experience of dual oppression as women and people of color—inject a degree of complexity into ecotheology and the current environmental movement. Ethicist Melanie Harris describes the "beauty to burden paradox" African American women face in their responses to ecological crisis. On the one hand, Harris describes her African ancestors as blessed with intimate relations with their land and as bearing deep wisdom about how to live on it sustainably. These ancestors believed that living in relation to the land connected them spiritually with other life forms and with their ancestors. The land grounded their identity and sense of worth. Alternately, she expresses outrage at how land was taken as an instrument of African enslavement in the colonial West. Africans were first bound to it in chains and later, denied ownership of it even as "free" people.

Harris critiques the contemporary environmental movement, what she calls "colonial ecology," for its insufficient attention to "landless, voiceless, white privilege," the historical impact of white supremacy in the United States and globally, and [the] environmentally exploitative capitalist paradigm.[26] She argues that romanticized ecological visions for wide open spaces unspoiled by human imprint could only be conjured by Whites already possessing an abundance of property. Harris makes plain that this is not an ecological vision capable of addressing the hopes of Black, Indigenous, and Brown people who historically have been dispossessed of their lands by those same Whites. Worse, women of color—burdened with gendered associations between mothering and Mother Earth—experienced even more profound bondage to earthly toil than men but remained powerless to do anything about their double-bind oppression.

Harris maintains that the ecological movement must, by definition, include commitments to restore the dignity and status of oppressed peoples, especially women, as integral to efforts to restore the Earth. Such a movement may include returning land to oppressed peoples, though Harris, ever mindful of dual oppression, refrains from insisting upon a too-specific vision for renewed land ownership for women of color.

Practical Ecotheology

Practical theologians seek to describe and promote living faith embodied in persons and communities. They focus on practices, things Christians do in response to God's grace and to participate in the life and mission of God. The field has exploded with ecological implications recently, including by way of attention to food and food systems and also to the significance of place—the web of geological, biological, historical, and cultural relations that promote or prohibit flourishing. True to their descriptor, practical theologians have championed any number of practices for living sustainably on a fragile planet.

One case in point is agrarian theologian-philosopher Norman Wirzba, who theologizes the most basic of human practices: eating. "Food," writes Wirzba, "is a gift of God given to all creatures for the purpose of life's nurture, sharing, and celebration. When it is done in the name of God, eating is the earthly realization of God's eternal communion-building love."[27] Calling food "God's love made delectable," Wirzba reminds us how eating involves us in God's loving mission. Sharing food at table enjoins hospitable community, enacts shared abundance, and anticipates the heavenly banquet. When Christians eat together, they perform the embodied equivalent of saying grace.

Wirzba's friend, Christian agrarian farmer, writer, and poet Wendell Berry, makes plain the ethical significance of eating: "To live, we must daily break the body and shed the blood of creation. When we do this knowingly, lovingly, skillfully, reverently, it is a sacrament. When we do it ignorantly, greedily, clumsily, destructively, it is a desecration. In such desecration we condemn ourselves to spiritual and moral loneliness, and others to want."[28]

Christian religious educator Jennifer Ayres explores entire food systems, the web of policies and processes stretching from farm to table. As with all human systems, Ayres shows this one to be extremely complex and rife with sin. She documents the exploitative policies and practices of huge agricultural conglomerates (their efforts to declare seeds corporate property, for example), the economic pressure for farmers to go big or go broke and therefore risk crushing indebtedness, short-cut farming practices that strip the land of nutrients and cause erosion, cruelty to animals, government subsidies of food crops like corn in order to cheaply transform them into unhealthy junk foods, the unjust compensation for farm workers, the absence of fresh and affordable foods in poor neighborhoods—and this is a partial list.[29]

Ayres proceeds to cite examples of church-related efforts to engender just food policies and practices. In this she depicts more than churches planting gardens; she gives witness to faith communities engaging with food systems through outward-facing public ministry in pursuit of social justice. Christian communities are confronting impediments to food justice by helping to craft government food-access policies, using their community kitchens to distribute lunches to children during summer breaks, and fostering direct farmer-to-consumer relationships that help alleviate fresh food scarcity in poor urban neighborhoods.

Practical theologians have also called attention to the significance of place. Many North Americans have become accustomed to ignoring their place on the Earth and presuming that its only purpose is to supply the stage upon which they act out their personal dramas. Clueless about the natural and human systems they depend upon, they wouldn't know a watershed from a woodshed. Nor do they necessarily count their human neighbors as friends. One response from within practical theology is the effort to reweave communities by working to foster creative interdependence in local places. As Wendell Berry observes, "local economy rests upon only two principles: neighborhood and subsistence. In a viable neighborhood, neighbors ask themselves what they can do or provide for one another, and they find answers that their place can afford. This, and nothing else, is the practice of neighborhood."[30]

A small but growing number of Christians choose to "live in place" by joining intentional communities whose mission is to strengthen and support their neighbors. In Durham, North Carolina, a small urban ministry set out twenty-five years ago to support young adults with physical and developmental disabilities. Since its humble beginnings, the ministry has grown to encompass an entire square block of the city and become home to scores of disabled persons living intentionally with friends and family members. Remarkably, this unremarkable assemblage of 1950s duplexes has also become home to verdant flower and vegetable gardens, to beautiful yard art, to birds and butterflies, and to the happy chatter of friends meeting each other in the streets. Creating a place for people to truly belong has turned into a fine home for the rest of creation too.

Joy is palpable in that place. I can only imagine that it must be a gift of living faithfully to God's intentions for creation's flourishing. A friend says we are "created for delight," and, I would add, we are created for delight as well as for death. In the twenty-first century, joy will be the surprising gift of reinhabiting our own places as creatures who live dependent upon God and our fellow creatures and who seek to abide, sustainably, in the home God has provided us.

Notes

1. Ellen Davis, *Scripture, Culture, and Agriculture: An Agrarian Reading of the Bible* (Cambridge University Press, 2009), 3.
2. Davis, *Scripture, Culture, and Agriculture*, 30–31, emphasis mine.
3. William Brown, *The Seven Pillars of Creation: The Bible, Science, and the Ecology of Wonder* (Oxford University Press, 2010), 17.
4. Brown, *Seven Pillars of Creation*, 130.
5. Brown, *Seven Pillars*, 130.
6. Brown, *Seven Pillars*, 131.
7. Brown, *Seven Pillars*, 130–31.
8. Brown, *Seven Pillars*, 131, 159.
9. Richard Bauckham, *Bible and Ecology: Rediscovering the Community of Creation* (Darton, Longman and Todd, 2010), 144, 150.
10. Bauckham, *Bible and Ecology*, 169, 170.
11. Daniel L. Brunner, Jennifer L. Butler, and A. J. Swoboda, *Introducing Evangelical Ecotheology: Foundations in Scripture, Theology, History, and Praxis* (Baker Academic), 90–91 including n. 18.
12. Sallie McFague, *Life Abundant: Rethinking Theology and Economy for a Planet in Peril* (Augsburg Fortress, 2001), 140.
13. Francis I, Laudato si', "On Care for Our Common Home," encyclical letter, May 24, 2015, https://www.vatican.va/content/francesco/en/encyclicals/documents/papa-francesco_20150524_enciclica-laudato-si.html.
14. Celia Deane-Drummond, *A Primer in Ecotheology: Theology for a Fragile Earth* (Wipf and Stock, 2017), 62.
15. Elizabeth Theokritoff, "The Salvation of the World and Saving the Earth: An Orthodox Christian Approach," *Worldviews* 14 (2010): 141–56, at 142.
16. John Wesley, "The General Deliverance," I.4 (*Wesley Works* 2:440).
17. Randy Maddox, "Anticipating the New Creation: Wesleyan Foundations for Holistic Mission," *Asbury Journal* 62 (2007): 49–66, at 58.
18. Randy Maddox, "Salvation as Flourishing for the Whole Creation: A Wesleyan Trajectory" in *Wesleyan Perspectives on Human Flourishing*, ed. Dean G. Smith and Rob A. Fringer (Pickwick, 2021), 20.
19. Philip Schaff and Harry Wace, eds., *Nicene and Post-Nicene Fathers of the Christian Church*, 2nd series, vol. 7, *S. Cyril of Jerusalem and S. Gregory Nazianzen* (Peabody, MA: Hendrickson, 1994), 440.

Section 3

20 Niels Henrik Gregersen, ed., *Incarnation: On the Scope and Depth of Christology* (Minneapolis: Fortress Press, 2014), as quoted in Deane-Drummond, *A Primer in Ecotheology*, 76, parentheticals original.
21 "Good trouble" is a phrase favored by civil rights pastor and longtime member of US Congress John Lewis.
22 Dennis Edwards, *Breath of Life: A Theology of the Creator Spirit* (Orbis, 2004), 47–48.
23 McFague, *Life Abundant*, 14, 116.
24 Leonardo Boff, *Cry of the Earth, Cry of the Poor* (Orbis, 1997), 74.
25 See chapter 3 of Nel Noddings, *Women and Evil* (University of California Press, 1989).
26 Melanie Harris, *Ecowomanism: African American Women and Earth-Honoring Faiths* (Orbis, 2017), 17.
27 Norman Wirzba, *Food and Faith: A Theology of Eating*, 2nd ed. (Cambridge University Press, 2018), xiv.
28 Wendell Berry, "The Gift of Good Land," in *The Art of the Commonplace: The Agrarian Essays of Wendell Berry*, ed. Norman Wirzba (Counterpoint, 2002), 304.
29 Jennifer Ayres, *Good Food: Grounded Practical Theology* (, TX: Baylor University Press, 2013), part 1.
30 Berry, "Gift of Good Land," 260.

The Face of Christ in the Face of Conflict

Preaching the Nicene Creed in a Storm-filled Season

Jerusha M. Neal

> For it is the God who said, "Light will shine out of darkness," who has shone in our hearts to give the light of the knowledge of the glory of God in the face of Christ. But we have this treasure in clay jars, so that it may be made clear that this extraordinary power belongs to God and does not come from us. We are afflicted in every way but not crushed, perplexed but not driven to despair, persecuted but not forsaken, struck down but not destroyed, always carrying around in the body the death of Jesus, so that the life of Jesus may also be made visible in our bodies.
>
> (2 Corinthians 4:6-10 NRSVue)

No preacher worth his or her salt has ever suggested that the path of Christian discipleship is trouble free. Our Shepherd's rod and staff may offer comfort, but the valleys we traverse are real—an expected part of the journey of faith and an even more expected part of the work of ministry.

Section 3

There is a reason that so many United Methodist conferences sing the Charles Wesley hymn "And Are We Yet Alive" at the start of their clergy sessions![1] Preachers have stepped into pulpits to proclaim the good news of God in seasons of war and want, political division and pandemic, throughout the Church's history. Trouble is nothing new. And yet, as one ordained to help train and encourage the next generation of ministers and as a United Methodist clergy spouse, I am sobered by this season of denominational division and loss. Even as I acknowledge the ways that our faithful God has seeded new harvests of justice and peace in a rocky field, I see preachers struggle to speak to the challenges of the contemporary moment. A host of storms have battered the sanctuaries of God's people—some of them, quite literal. Climate catastrophes are no far-off phenomena. In recent years, storms amplified by rapid climatic change have displaced entire communities and the congregations that serve them.[2] Political rancor adds its own instability to the Church's foundations, and a rising tide of Christian nationalism erodes its witness.[3] The thunder of war fills the nation's media screens, and the lightning of gun violence strikes school yard and church pew alike. In the midst of these griefs, many congregations have failed to find solace and clarity from fellow believers.[4] Betrayals and slanders within the ecclesial body have left lasting scars. These storms do more than batter stained-glass windows. They batter preachers' hearts. Discouragement can sediment into the holiest reaches of the pulpit's witness.

I will make the rather audacious claim that a 1700-year-old creed is a bulwark against such storms, but not because it was written in a purer, more sanctified age. It wasn't. Trouble, as noted, is nothing new, and neither is church division, political collusion, or a distrust of God's good creation. The Council of Nicaea in AD 325 and the Council of Constantinople in AD 381 were marked by these storms—and others. The resulting Nicene Creed, tucked into the worship supplements of hymnals and rarely recited in United Methodist worship, is notable as evidence that fruit can be born in seasons of storm. But my assertion of the Creed's contemporary relevance is not grounded in these contextual similarities either. The Nicene Creed's power lies in its sustained, sacrificial meditation on the face of Christ. I will argue that this Nicene attentiveness is particularly timely for preaching that proclaims God's covenantal solidarity in the wake of the climate crisis, preaching that dismantles dangerous deifications of the body politic, and preaching that places its hope in the subversive potency of Jesus's salvific work to transform the witness of the Church.

The Creed is not alone, of course, in its meditation on what the face of Christ reveals about God and about God's people. Paul calls the glory illumined in Christ's face the "treasure" of the faithful (2 Corinthians 4:7), witnessing to the glory of God and witnessed to in the strangely-warmed hearts of those who reveal the death and life of Jesus in their bodies. This chapter will bring Paul's reflections in 2 Corinthians 4:6-10 into conversation with three core affirmations of the Nicene Creed. My hope is that this scripture—written centuries before Nicaea by a church leader who appears to have known his own discouragements—might help bridge biblical text and creedal affirmation, assisting preachers in addressing three of the Church's most urgent conversations.

"Of One Being": The Face of Christ as a Revelation of the Creator

Christopher Morse grounds his illumining theology of the Word of God in Paul's reference to Genesis in 2 Corinthians 4:6.[5] "For it is the God who said, 'Light will shine out of darkness,'" Paul writes, thereby uniting the Creator's speech at the start of the world with the embodied revelation of the Incarnate Word. This relationship between Creator and creation was a central debate at Nicaea and one of the reasons behind Arianism's protest of the Creed's affirmation of Christ's "consubstantiality"[6] with God.

Arianism is often misunderstood as depicting Christ as a creature, defined in a way similar to ourselves—depicting, in other words, a Christ like us. Rowan Williams corrects this misinterpretation, noting that "the Arius who wrote to Alexander that the Son was a 'perfect creature, yet not as one among the creatures . . . is eager to avoid any suggestion that the Son is simply 'like all others.'"[7] In fact, later Arians would shy away from the word "created" to describe the Son, preferring the term "only begotten" as a way to emphasize the Son's incomparability with any created thing.[8] Arians had no problem emphasizing Christ's supremacy over creation.

What Arians did object to was the suggestion that first-person of the Trinity—the Father—would have an intimate relationship with the created world. The role of the Incarnate Word was to act as a buffer between an invisible, impassable, unchanging God and messy materiality. Indeed, for Arians like Ulfilas, bishop of the Goths, the Son was "Our Lord and God, artificer (craftsman) and maker of the whole creation."[9] Arians readily accepted a Christ higher than humanity, but they could not conceive that God the Father might condescend to create a fragile world. Indeed, many believed such condescension was not possible. Asterius describes God's needing the Son to enact the work of creation, since "nature could not endure [God's] direct hand."[10] In such a theological framing, the Son replaces the Creator, protecting the world from being consumed by God's presence. What is missing from this view is the God of the Old Testament, hovering over chaos (Gen. 1:2) and breathing into soil (Gen. 2:7). What is missing is a God in covenantal solidarity with life.

When Paul argues that it is the same creator God who spoke light into existence that is revealed in the flesh of Jesus's face, Paul intends more than the glorification of Christ. Paul is also reframing God's glory as moving toward situations of crisis and bearing creation's suffering. Biblical scholars now argue that those who compiled the oral and written traditions that make up Genesis 1 were facing the catastrophe of exile.[11] From that devastated ground, scripture's testimony to God's solidarity with God's creation, human and non-human alike, bears a striking resemblance to the solidarity revealed on Golgotha.[12] Both testify to God's commitment to turn devastation into a seedbed for life.

September 29, 2024 was Founders' Day at Duke University Chapel. It was a day of particular celebration, as the University was celebrating its centennial year. But sitting under those stone buttresses, my heart was heavy. Pictures had begun to emerge from the communities swamped by the swirling waters of Hurricane Helene. The death toll from the storm was rising, and that morning, as we sat in the stone security of the Chapel, many Western North Carolina sanctuaries were under water. It was hard to hold these two realities together. An Arian understanding of God might even name their delineation as appropriate, worrying that a muddling of sweat-stained service with stained-glass serenity would mar God's glory. But a more complex, relational theology was worn on the haggard face of the Western North Carolina bishop present in the sanctuary that morning. When I thanked the bishop for his leadership in this season of crisis, he told me that he had driven across the state to be present and was leaving directly after the service to return to his flock. "But I had to come," he said, "because this place trained those pastors who are now without power and water. And to support them is to support the school that equipped them for this challenge."[13] His stalwart presence—and his hasty return to the submerged communities he served—gave embodied witness to the covenantal connections between communities in want and communities with plenty. More than this, it gave embodied witness to God's grief over devastated ground and God's fierce commitment to a groaning creation.

My preaching students regularly wrestle with the question: "Where is God in the face of climate change?" It is a deep and difficult question. But the good news of the Nicene Creed is the same good news that Paul proclaimed. The Creator God is one substance with the Word made flesh, which means that this God is not distant and removed, sequestered in the safe vastness of eternity. The God who created the world works alongside search and rescue teams in flooded valleys, weeps over washed-out hillsides, and speaks a crucified protest over a world numb to creation's suffering. Our God is no stranger to devastated ground. Indeed, our God is waiting for us there.

"Became truly human": The Face of Christ as a Face of Flesh

Cyril Hovorun is a Ukrainian-born, war-time dissident who used to serve as a theological advisor to the Russian Orthodox Church. In the decade prior to Russia's invasion of Ukraine, Hovorun watched with growing alarm as Vladimir Putin leveraged a self-serving version of Orthodox Christian Nationalism to consolidate his political power and justify the violent expansion of Russia's borders. In 2022, having left the country, Hovorun spoke with direct simplicity as he described a theological symptom of such violent conflations between ethnonationalism and faith. Those who wield faith as a cultural defense of nationalist aggression "don't speak about Christ. They speak about other things in the faith."[14]

The Nicene Creed speaks about Christ—particularly Christ's relationship to God the Father and his relationship to his fellow creatures. While more robust sections would be added in AD 381 concerning the nature and work of the Holy Spirit and the marks of the church, in AD 325 the mediatory vocation of Christ's life, death, and resurrection was front and center. For theologians like T. F. Torrance, Jesus's humanity is central to this mediating work. In the words of the Creed, Jesus "became truly human." His face did not only reveal the Creator; it was a face of flesh. For Torrance, God gives Godself to the world in Christ "*as God*, to be the Object of our love and worship . . . and at the same time [God] comes *as Man* to provide for us the life of human love, obedience, and worship for which we were made, and so constitute himself our savior."[15] This "double-movement"[16] has profound implications for Christian worship. Christ "is at once God whom we worship and to whom we pray . . . and at the same time the One who himself, for us, lived a life in the power of prayer that we might be restored to communion with the God for which we were created."[17]

For Torrance, there are political consequences to such theology. He suggests that when the church has been one-sided in its emphasis of the divine Christ as the object of prayer, thereby diminishing the human Christ who restores communion with the Father on our behalf, "the tendency is for the ecclesia to replace the priesthood of Christ."[18] More broadly there is a tendency for human institutions, human political systems, or human cultural identities to take upon themselves Christ's mediatory, salvific role by assuming that the *who* of Christ is not an essential element to the *how* of God's redemptive plan. In contrast, to insist that participation in Christ's humanity is critical to human redemption restrains these inclinations by stripping the nation-state and religious nationalism of their claims to salvific power. The body politic cannot substitute for the righteousness of Christ. Because Jesus "became truly human," he is not only a revelation of God; Jesus offers himself as the locus of humankind's restoration.

Dietrich Bonhoeffer takes the point further. While Torrance's credal interpretation of Christ's "vicarious humanity"[19] turns a bracing iconoclasm on any body (i.e., political, cultural, or ecclesial) that promises salvific righteousness apart from Christ, Bonhoeffer underscores what such participation in Christ requires of God's people. Living in union with Christ means living in union with those whom Christ embraces. It means standing in solidarity with the suffering. Stephen Estes notes that many in the Confessing Church of Bonhoeffer's day shared a healthy distrust of Nazi hubris. But few appreciated the importance of opposing the persecution of the Jews.[20] Bonhoeffer's understanding of Christ "for us" (*pro nobis*)[21] compels the church to stand in sacrificial solidarity with the afflicted. "It is with this humiliated one that the Church goes its own way of humiliation," Bonhoeffer writes.[22] This is not, he continues, for the purpose of "visible proof . . . that Christ is present in it . . . There is no law here . . . The humiliation of Christ is not a principle for the church to follow, but rather a fact."[23]

It is a fact to which Father Ioann Budin, a Russian priest who preached a sermon against the Ukrainian war, can attest.[24] He said, "Russian soldiers are killing their brothers and sisters in Christ. We Christians cannot stand on the sidelines . . . [and be] silent."[25] It is a starkly different message than the one preached over Russian military troops by Patriarch Kirill of Moscow: "Remember that if you die for your country, you will . . . have eternal life."[26] Because of Father Budin's sermon against the war, he was interrogated, fined, and removed from his parish. In June 2023, after refusing to renounce his preaching, he was banned from conducting religious services by a Russian Orthodox Church court that convicted him of "heretical" pacifism.[27]

Conflations of national identity, Christian loyalty, and racialized hierarchy are by no means confined to the Russian state. They are alive and well in the United States.[28] Amanda Tyler, of the Baptist Joint Committee for Religious Liberty, notes that resurgent Christian nationalisms in the U.S. not only present a danger to American democracy. They threaten Christianity itself. "Christian nationalism, which merges political and religious authority, can quickly lead to idolatry and a confusion of allegiance."[29] But the Nicene's Creed's assertion that Christ "became truly human" calls God's people to a different way. In Paul's language, it is a way that refuses to conflate the "treasure" (2 Cor. 4:7) of Christ's faithful, human righteousness with our own. The clay jars of human institutions and human hearts may carry Christ's light, participating in his glow through the Spirit's power, but Paul insists "that this extraordinary power belongs to God and does not come from us" (v. 7). The result is a dependence on an Other that no human political system can replace. Such a dependence means that we cannot go our own way; we must follow our Savior into the wilderness, drinking of his humanity to quench our deepest need.

Carlos Cardoza-Orlandi tells the story of an ecumenical, rehabilitation center named CRREDA in Agua Prieta, Sonora, Mexico. The organization is comprised of recovering addicts who leave gallons of water and first aid supplies across the desert as a way to keep migrants from dying.[30] It is a practice that emphasizes the interdependence of human lives, human suffering, and human hope. CRREDA's director, a recovering addict himself, describes the mystery: "What better way to be liberated from our vices than to be servants to the migrants who are in need and to see in them ourselves?"[31] Participation in Christ's enfleshed mission of reconciliation with God, neighbor, and creation makes such clarity of vision possible. It disrupts rigid definitions of self-sufficiency and belonging, creating a new vision of God and a new vision of ourselves. Crossing borders of space and time, it disarms histories of exclusion and reclaims the participatory identity of God's people. It creates the "we" that Paul references in 2 Corinthians 4:8-9 when he says, "we are afflicted in every way but not crushed, perplexed but not driven to despair, persecuted but not forsaken, struck down but not destroyed." In that honest recognition of participation's cost, held in the flesh of the God made "truly human," there is a holy dependence and re-membering of the world God loves.

"For Us and for Our Salvation": The Face of Christ as Reconciling Life

This re-membering changes us. It marks us with the grief of collectively-borne burdens, but also with the musculature of resilience and a hope that does not fail. For all of Paul's insistence on the cruciformity of Christian discipleship, he also asserts that the light of Christ does more than illumine. It transforms.[32] To carry the death of Jesus in one's body is to open oneself to Jesus's life—also "made visible in our bodies" (2 Corinthians 4:10).

The Face of Christ in the Face of Conflict

The content of Christian "salvation" is not easily defined. In Constantinople, additions were made to the Nicene Creed in an attempt to flesh out the difference Christ makes for God's people. Our contemporary version references the church's witness, the forgiveness of sin, the resurrection of the dead, and the life of a restored creation.[33] But even before these additions, the Creed orients "salvation" in significant ways, insisting that Christ's being and Christ's work are related. Indeed, it suggests that the former frames and contextualizes the latter. Bonhoeffer stresses this point, noting that Christ cannot be reduced to his effects in the world. Just as the Nicene Creed describes Christ's person before it describes Christ's action, Bonhoeffer prioritizes the question of *who* in his Christology (as opposed to *what* and *how*), underscoring that the person interprets the work and not vice versa.[34] This prioritization is precisely why Torrance understands Christ's "vicarious humanity"—Christ's righteous response to God on our behalf—as foundational to his saving work.

There is pastoral significance to this doctrine of "vicarious humanity," particularly in a season when the Church's divisions and inadequacies seem stark. Pastors have intimate knowledge of these shortcomings. To stake the Church's salvation on Christ's righteousness is to claim that Christ's faithful humanity is sufficient to our need. But Christ's Incarnation presses the content of salvation further. Christ's Person *marks* those who participate in his body, through the Spirit's power.[35] He holds them in his flesh, brokenness and all. And in the holding, change occurs. In Paul's words, the "life of Jesus," becomes "visible" in our human flesh (2 Corinthians 4:10), for flesh is no objectified, insulated category. It exists in relationship and in time. And through relationship and time, it responds. In becoming flesh himself, Christ offers the world more than his "vicarious humanity." He offers the world his reconciling life. For those who would be held in him alongside the brokenness he bears on our behalf, he offers a humanity that impacts our own. More than this, he offers a humanity that knits together the world.

Elizabeth Johnson takes that word "world" seriously. If Christ is flesh, then the "atoms comprising his body were once part of other creatures. The genetic structure of the cells of his body were kin to . . . flowers, fishes, frogs

[and] finches."³⁶ We cannot be carried in his body and stand over and against the creation reconciled there. Rebecca Copeland maps the significance of this insight. In Christ, God elects to be "being *for* another"—human and non-human alike. To participate in Christ's being, through the Spirit, is to be marked by the multiplicity and interdependence of Christ's embrace.³⁷ "Being *for* another" becomes central to salvation's content.

When the Church's communion has been broken, "being *for*" frogs and fishes might actually seem easier than "being *for*" one's Christian siblings! Ecclesial division is a painful road. Contemporary pastors are certainly not alone in wrestling with this grief. The Nicene Creed itself was forged in controversy, and Paul writes 2 Corinthians to a church threatening to devour each other and dismantle his ministry.³⁸ It is no accident that the language of "reconciliation" becomes significant for Paul in 2 Corinthians 5:11-21. Such reconciliation is not a matter of pretense or avoidance. It grows from the transforming revelation of Christ's face. The face of Christ, crucified and yet alive, holds the world in its gaze, making his life visible in the faces of those who suffer and mourn with him.³⁹ We are reconciled by the Face that choses to be *pro nobis* (for us). More than this, we are reconciled by that Face's reflected glory, marking us as those given to the world for Christ's sake.

By prioritizing Christ's being as an interpretive key to his saving work, the Nicene Creed centers Christ's reconciling life and his embrace of difference in its framing of God's transformative action. It is a different vision of salvation than has been centered at other moments in the Christian tradition, but it may be an especially timely vision in this season. It challenges the Church to be marked by a love that risks relationship and multiplicity, embracing the excluded. Such salvation would embrace even those parts of ourselves that have experienced the sting of rejection and failure. In that reckoning, Christ's salvation offers forgiveness through vicarious exchange—yes. But it offers something more. It marks the body of a bruised Church and the bodies of Christ's faithful with a life greater than our own.

From Doctrine to Doxology

The Nicene Creed's witness to a Triune God, incarnate for our salvation, is more than a systematized set of doctrines. It is a pastoral affirmation of God's character, Christ's sufficiency, and salvation's enfleshed relevance. It is an affirmation that even in the valley of the shadow, Christ's reconciling, resurrecting life is made visible in those who bind their lives with his.

At the end of Duke Chapel's 2024 Centennial service, musician, preacher, and recent Duke Divinity alumna, Dr. Patrice E. Turner, settles at the piano. Her selection focuses on the person and presence of Jesus. She has arranged a version of the Negro spiritual, *I Want Jesus to Walk With Me*,[40] a choice that might seem strange for the close of a celebratory service—even given the Dean of the Chapel's long interest in the genre.[41] Enormous histories of grief and oppression are embedded in such a song. To choose it is to name the ways these histories intersect the history of the Chapel and, indeed, the University. But even as the pain of the song's "pilgrim journey" echoes through the sanctuary, Dr. Turner's arrangement does not let it confine God's future. Its syncopated longing arcs toward promise, and her performance is marked by a fierce and defiant joy. "Be our shelter," she sings, as her yearning turns to prayer. Her voice rises, and her hands press with force into the piano's keys. "Be our guide," she continues, pounding out her insistent intercession. The boundary between praise and protest thins as her cadence intensifies, and her rhythm does not slow or stop.[42] We find ourselves before God's throne of grace, holding tight to nail-scarred hands. Or perhaps, we find that they are holding us. *Be our shelter*, we pray. *In the wake of a deadly storm, in a fraying and fearful nation, be the God You claim to be: a God who is* pro nobis *(for us) in the face of a future we cannot see. Let Your reconciling life be made visible in us.*

It is my prayer for all who stand in valleys of shadow, and particularly for those who minister in these narrow places. May you know, not only the comfort of your Shepherd's rod and staff, but the light of Christ's face. Let Nicaea point you there. The face it proclaims reveals your Creator's heart, and before that face, no idol can stand. It is a face that will change your own. Let doctrine turn to prayer, and prayer to testimony.

Section 3

And finally, let testimony give way to praise. For the God who called forth light from darkness shines in the face of your risen Savior, and that light shines in you.

Notes

1. Charles Wesley, "And Are We Yet Alive," *The United Methodist Hymnal* (The United Methodist Publishing House, 1989), 553.
2. Jim Patterson, "United Methodists Offer Relief After Helene," *UM News*, October 2, 2024, https://www.umnews.org/en/news/united-methodists-offer-relief-after-helene.
3. Public Religion Research Institute, "Support for Christian Nationalism in All 50 States: Findings from PRRI's 2023 American Values Atlas," *PRRI*, February 28, 2024, https://prri.org/research/support-for-christian-nationalism-in-all-50-states/.
4. Heather Hahn, "Bishop urges end to falsehoods, pivot to future," *UM News*, August 23, 2022, https://www.umnews.org/en/news/bishop-urges-end-to-falsehoods-pivot-to-future.
5. Christopher Morse, *Not Every Spirit: A Dogmatics of Christian Disbelief* (Trinity Press International, 1994), 87.
6. "Consubstantial" is a common English translation of *homoousios*, a Greek term meaning *of the same substance* or *same in essence*. In the Nicene Creed, the term describes the relationship between Jesus Christ and God the Father. The version of the Nicene Creed used in this chapter is from *The United Methodist Hymnal* which translates the term, "of one Being" (*The United Methodist Hymnal*, 880).
7. Rowan Williams, *Arius: Heresy and Tradition*, rev. ed. (Eerdmans, 2001), 104.
8. Robert P. C. Hanson, *The Search for the Doctrine of God: The Arian Controversy*, 318–81 (T&T Clark, 1988), 102.
9. Hanson, *Arian Controversy*, 105.
10. Hanson, *Arian Controversy*, 100.
11. The Hebrew scriptures were the result of centuries of narrative streams, both oral and written, but the impact of the exilic experience on the Hebrew Bible's current form is clear. See David Carr's discussion of exilic trauma in *Holy Resilience: The Bible's Traumatic Origins* (Yale University Press, 2014); J. Richard Middleton describes the importance of the Babylonian exile for understanding the creation account of Genesis 1 in particular: *The Liberating Image: The Imago Dei in Genesis 1* (Brazos Press, 2005).
12. My thanks to Rev. Wesley Neal for this insight. See, "Seeds of Hope," a sermon preached on the Festival of God's Creation, responding to the devastation of Hurricane Helene, Asbury United Methodist Church, Durham, NC, September 29, 2024, https://www.asburyunitedmethodist.com/.

13 My thanks to Ken Carter, Resident Bishop, Western North Carolina Conference of The United Methodist Church, for his willingness to share this conversation.
14 Tim Alberta, *The Kingdom, the Power, and the Glory: American Evangelicals in an Age of Extremism* (Harper Collins Publishers, 2023), 242.
15 T. F. Torrance, "The Vicarious Humanity of Christ," in *The Incarnation: Ecumenical Studies in the Nicene-Constantinopolitan Creed*, ed. T. F. Torrance, (Wipf and Stock, 1998), 149–69, at 158.
16 Torrance, "Vicarious Humanity of Christ," 158; Torrance draws here on the language of Athanasius and the Cappadocians.
17 Torrance, "Vicarious Humanity of Christ," 158.
18 Torrance, "Vicarious Humanity of Christ," 159.
19 Torrance, "Vicarious Humanity of Christ," 160.
20 Stephen Estes, "Christ For Us: An Analysis of Bonhoeffer's Christology and its Implications for his Ethic," *themelios* 48.1 (2023), https://www.thegospelcoalition.org/themelios/article/christ-for-us-bonhoeffers-christology-and-ethic/.
21 Dietrich Bonhoeffer, *Lectures on Christology*, trans. Edwin Robertson (Collins, 1978), 110.
22 Bonhoeffer, *Lectures on Christology*, 113.
23 Bonhoeffer, *Lectures on Christology*, 113.
24 Kirk Semple, Alexander Stockton, and Jonah M. Kessel, "Putin vs. the Priest," *New York Times*, December 7, 2022, https://www.nytimes.com/2022/12/07/opinion/putin-russia-ukraine-church-sermon.html.
25 Semple, Stockton, and Kessel, "Putin vs. the Priest."
26 Semple, Stockton, and Kessel, "Putin vs. the Priest."
27 Felix Light, "Banned Russian priest stands by condemnation of 'brother killing brother' in Ukraine," *The Reuters Daily Briefing*, September 24, 2024, https://www.reuters.com/world/europe/banned-russian-priest-stands-by-condemnation-brother-killing-brother-ukraine-2024-09-24/.
28 Joseph Wiinikka-Lydon, "New Dominionism Tries to Rule," *Southern Poverty Law Center*, June 4, 2024, https://www.splcenter.org/year-hate-extremism-2023/new-dominionism-tries-rule.
29 Guthrie Graves-Fitzsimmons, "Christian Nationalism Is 'Single Biggest Threat' to America's Religious Freedom: An Interview with Amanda Tyler of the Baptist Joint Committee," *CAP 20*, April 13, 2022, https://www.americanprogress.org/article/christian-nationalism-is-single-biggest-threat-to-americas-religious-freedom/.
30 Carlos Cardoza-Orlandi, "What does it take to learn leadership across cultural and religious boundaries? Perspectives, observations, and suggestions from a cross-cultural location," *Journal of Religious Leadership*, 10 (2011): 5–25.
31 Cardoza-Orlandi, "What does it take," 18.
32 For more on the transformative power of vision in Paul, see Janet Heath, *Paul's Visual Piety: The Metamorphosis of the Beholder* (Oxford: Oxford University Press, 2013).

Section 3

33 "We believe in the one holy catholic and apostolic church. We acknowledge one baptism for the forgiveness of sins. We look for the resurrection of the dead and the life of the world to come," translation from *The United Methodist Hymnal*, 880.

34 Bonhoeffer, 36-38.

35 Torrance recognizes this as well. His description of Christian worship and discipleship pairs Christ's "vicarious humanity" with our "participation" in Christ by the power of the Spirit. What that participation requires of us, however, and how we are changed by it, is underexplored.

36 Elizabeth Johnson, *Creation and the Cross: The Mercy of God for a Planet in Peril* (Orbis Books, 2018), 185–86.

37 Rebecca L. Copeland, *Created Being: Expanding Creedal Christology* (Baylor University Press, 2020), 71–72.

38 Douglas Campbell gives a concise overview of the challenges facing the Corinthian church in *Paul: An Apostles Journey* (Eerdmans, 2018), 74–79.

39 See Susan Eastman's reflection on the relationship between Christ's glory-bearing and crucified face in, "Unveiling Death in 2 Corinthians: Revelation, Mystery, and Death," in *Oneself in Another: Participation and Personhood in Pauline Theology*, Cascade Library of Pauline Studies (Cascade, 2023), 73–95.

40 For a concise historical and theological reflection on this hymn, see, Victoria Schwarz and Wilson Pruitt, "History of Hymns: 'I Want Jesus to Walk with Me,'" *Discipleship Ministries of The United Methodist Church*, April 7, 2019, https://www.umcdiscipleship.org/resources/history-of-hymns-i-want-jesus-to-walk-with-me.

41 Luke Powery engages African American spirituals for homiletic practice in *'Dem Dry Bones: Preaching, Hope, and Death* (Fortress Press, 2012).

42 Patrice E. Turner, "I Want Jesus to Walk with Me," performed at the Centennial Founder's Day Sunday Service, Duke Chapel, Durham, NC, September 29, 2024, https://www.youtube.com/watch?v=bU-RyA9O21U&t=3s. Dr. Turner's performance begins at 1:13:40.

Into God's Own Life

Reclaiming Nicene Faith for Church Renewal and Mission

Laceye C. Warner & Cameron Merrill

The 1700th anniversary of the Council of Nicaea arrives at a critical moment for Christian ministry. As churches navigate institutional decline, cultural upheaval, and internal division, the temptation is strong to seek solutions in better programming, updated worship styles, or enhanced organizational efficiency. While such practical adaptations have their place, they cannot address the deeper theological amnesia that afflicts much contemporary church life. The essays in this volume demonstrate that recovery of robust Trinitarian faith—not as abstract doctrine but as living reality—is essential for authentic church renewal and faithful mission in our time.

The Council of Nicaea's articulation of Trinitarian faith was forged amid controversy and challenge. As the preceding essays have shown, the Council's participants wrestled with fundamental questions about divine identity, Christ's relationship to God and humanity, and the shape of faithful witness in a changing world. Their context was not unlike our own. Then as now, competing visions of Christian faith vied for allegiance. Then as now, the church faced pressure to accommodate its message to cultural preferences. Then as now, theological confusion threatened to undermine the integrity of Christian ministry.

Section 3

Yet the Council's enduring gift to the church was not merely a set of doctrinal formulations. Rather, in wrestling with how to speak truthfully about the Triune God, the Council provided patterns for understanding the church's identity and mission that remain vitally relevant. As several contributors to this volume have argued, Nicene faith offers resources for addressing contemporary challenges from environmental crisis to political polarization. More fundamentally, it provides a theological foundation for reimagining church life and ministry beyond both rigid traditionalism and rootless innovation.

The contemporary context lends particular urgency to this task of theological renewal. Mainline Protestant denominations continue to experience dramatic membership decline while evangelical churches increasingly fragment over political and cultural differences. The rise of the "spiritual but not religious" demographic signals growing disaffection with institutional Christianity. Meanwhile, Christian nationalism threatens to co-opt religious language and symbols for political purposes while climate change and systemic injustice demand prophetic response. These challenges cannot be adequately addressed through better techniques or programs. These challenges require renewed theological vision.

Yet precisely in this moment of institutional uncertainty and cultural change lies an opportunity for rediscovering the transformative power of Trinitarian faith. When familiar patterns of church life are disrupted, space opens for asking fundamental questions about identity and purpose. When pragmatic solutions prove inadequate, theological resources gain fresh relevance. When external pressures mount, the need for robust spiritual foundations becomes clear.

This conclusion argues that authentic church renewal requires moving beyond both rigid repetition of traditional formulas and pragmatic abandonment of theological roots. Instead, it calls for rediscovering how Trinitarian faith necessarily shapes all aspects of ministry—from worship and education to mission and public witness. Drawing on insights from previous essays while pushing toward new applications, it demonstrates how core doctrinal affirmations translate into transformed practice.

The argument unfolds in four movements. First, it examines how key elements of Trinitarian doctrine, properly understood, reshape understanding of church identity and purpose. Second, it explores how Trinitarian theology reframes mission from institutional maintenance to participation in divine life and purpose. Third, it demonstrates how Trinitarian patterns inform reimagining of core church practices, public witness, and spiritual formation. Finally, it points toward future opportunities and challenges in pursuing church renewal through recovered Trinitarian vision.

Throughout, the focus remains practical even as it engages substantive theology. The goal is not abstract speculation but renewed ministry grounded in the reality of the Triune God. For ultimately, hope for church renewal lies not in human strategies or programs but in the church's participation in divine life. As the Council of Nicaea understood, faithful witness flows from right understanding of who God is and how God works in the world.

The essays in this volume have demonstrated the continuing relevance of Nicene faith for contemporary ministry. This conclusion builds on their insights while pushing toward concrete application. It invites church leaders to rediscover how robust Trinitarian theology enables faithful ministry amid today's challenges. For in the end, authentic renewal requires not just updated methods but recovered theological vision.

Trinitarian Faith as Foundation for Church Renewal

The renewal of church life and mission must be grounded in substantive theological vision. While practical strategies and organizational changes have their place, lasting transformation requires recovering the church's fundamental identity as a community shaped by and participating in the life of the Triune God. This section examines how core Trinitarian doctrinal affirmations necessarily reshape understanding of church life and ministry practice.

Essential Trinitarian Affirmations

Four key doctrinal elements deserve particular attention for their implications for ministry renewal. First is the affirmation of divine distinction (hypostasis)—the recognition that Father, Son, and Spirit are genuinely distinct persons within the unity of divine life. This is not merely abstract speculation but speaks to the character of God as inherently relational, existing eternally as a communion of distinct persons united in love. As earlier essays have shown, this understanding emerged through careful reflection on biblical witness, particularly Jesus's relationship with the Father and the Spirit's distinct role in the divine economy.

The practical implications are significant. If God's own being is characterized by distinction-in-unity, then authentic Christian community will likewise honor both particularity and communion. Unity does not require uniformity; indeed, genuine unity depends upon maintaining real difference. This offers theological ground for navigating contemporary conflicts over diversity in church life while resisting both fragmentation and false uniformity.

Second is the affirmation of Christ's divine-human nature (*homoousios*)—that Jesus is "of one substance" with both God and humanity. This doctrine, central to the Nicene controversy, maintains that in Christ, divinity and humanity are perfectly united without confusion or division. As previous contributors have demonstrated, this was no mere philosophical construct but arose from wrestling with the biblical witness to Jesus as both fully divine and fully human.

For contemporary ministry, this speaks powerfully to questions of incarnational presence and cultural engagement. It suggests that faithful witness requires both maintaining distinctive Christian identity and entering fully into human experience and struggle. It provides theological foundation for ministry that is both firmly grounded in divine revelation and genuinely responsive to human need and context.

Third is the affirmation of the Spirit's divine life (again, *homoousios*)—that the Holy Spirit is fully God, not a lesser divine power or created force. This understanding developed as the church recognized that the Spirit who gives life, guides into truth, and enables communion with God must share fully in divine nature. The Spirit's work is not subordinate to but coordinates with the work of Father and Son in bringing about God's purposes.

This shapes understanding of church life as fundamentally dependent upon and empowered by divine initiative rather than human effort. It suggests that authentic renewal comes through openness to the Spirit's transforming work rather than through enhanced programming or technique. At the same time, it maintains that the Spirit's work is always consistent with and directed toward the purposes of Father and Son revealed in scripture.

Fourth is the affirmation of unity in Trinity—that these distinct divine persons exist in perfect communion characterized by mutual indwelling (perichoresis) and shared purpose. This unity is not abstract but is expressed in the coordinated work of Father, Son, and Spirit in creation, redemption, and the bringing of all things to fulfillment. Each person participates fully while maintaining distinctive role and identity.

For ministry, this provides pattern for understanding how diverse gifts and callings work together in shared mission. It suggests that genuine unity comes not through imposed uniformity but through participation in God's life and purposes. It offers theological foundation for collaborative leadership and mutual ministry while maintaining proper order and distinction of roles.

Beyond Abstract Doctrine: Trinity as Living Reality

These doctrinal affirmations are not merely theoretical constructs but describe the living reality in which the church participates through Christ in the Spirit. They necessarily shape understanding of congregational life and ministry practice in several key ways.

First, divine communion patterns human community. If God exists as a communion of distinct persons united in love, then authentic Christian community will reflect this pattern. This means maintaining both real diversity and genuine unity, resisting both fragmentation into isolated individuals and absorption into undifferentiated mass. It suggests that conflict need not threaten unity when handled within the context of lasting communion.

Second, trinitarian relations inform church practices. Worship, for instance, is properly understood as participation through the Spirit in Christ's perfect response to the Father rather than merely human activity directed toward God. Similarly, ministry is participation in Christ's ongoing work through the Spirit rather than purely human effort to accomplish divine purposes. This reframes understanding of both success and failure in ministry.

Third, participation in divine life transforms ministry priorities. Rather than focusing primarily on institutional maintenance or numerical growth, ministry seeks to foster genuine participation in God's life and purposes. This may mean letting go of practices that, while practically effective, do not serve this deeper purpose. It also suggests different metrics for evaluating ministry effectiveness.

Reclaiming Trinitarian Vision

Contemporary church life often displays various reductions of trinitarian faith that diminish ministry vitality. Three common distortions deserve particular attention.

First is functional monotheism—operating as if God were a single divine person rather than Trinity. This appears in worship focused exclusively on praise to a generic deity, prayer that ignores Christ's mediatorial role, and ministry that relies on human effort rather than the Spirit's power. It reduces divine-human relationship to simple vertical connection rather than participation in the rich communion of trinitarian life.

Second are neo-Arian tendencies—subtle ways of subordinating Son and Spirit to the Father or treating them as lesser divine agents. This appears in theology that separates Jesus's teaching from his divine identity, mission that ignores Christ's ongoing lordship, and ministry that treats the Spirit as mere divine power rather than fully divine person. It undermines the church's participation in divine life through Christ in the Spirit.

Third are new forms of modalism—treating Father, Son, and Spirit as merely different expressions or functions of a single divine person. This appears in worship that blurs distinction between divine persons, theology that reduces trinitarian language to different aspects of divine activity, and ministry that ignores the distinct roles of divine persons in salvation. It flattens the richness of divine life and the church's participation in it.

Recovering robust trinitarian vision requires moving beyond these reductions to embrace the full reality of God's triune life. This means:

- Maintaining real distinction between divine persons while affirming their essential unity

- Recognizing both Christ's unique mediatorial role and the Spirit's distinctive work
- Understanding salvation as participation in divine life rather than merely individual relationship with God
- Grounding ministry in trinitarian patterns rather than purely pragmatic concerns
- Such recovery enables ministry that is both more faithful and more fruitful because it aligns with divine reality rather than human preference or cultural pressure.

In conclusion, trinitarian doctrine provides essential foundation for church renewal by revealing the divine life in which the church is called to participate. When properly understood, these affirmations necessarily reshape understanding of church identity and purpose while informing concrete ministry practice. Moving beyond both rigid traditionalism and pragmatic reduction requires recovering robust trinitarian vision as pattern for authentic church life and mission.

Mission in Trinitarian Perspective

Recovery of robust trinitarian theology necessarily transforms our understanding of Christian mission. Rather than seeing mission primarily as church activity directed toward the world, trinitarian perspective reveals mission as participation in the ongoing work of the Triune God. This reframing has profound implications for both congregational identity and ministry practice.

From Church-Centered to God-Centered Mission

The redevelopment of theological reflection on the *missio Dei* in the twentieth century marked a crucial shift in missiological understanding. Rather than viewing mission as something the church does to extend its influence or increase its membership, *missio Dei* theology recognizes that mission originates in God's own being and action. As several contributors to this volume have noted, the eternal communion of Father, Son, and Spirit naturally overflows in creative and redemptive action toward the world. Mission thus begins not with church strategy but with divine initiative.

This theological shift carries several important implications for contemporary ministry. First, it relativizes institutional concerns about church growth or survival. While such concerns are not irrelevant, they cannot be primary when mission is understood as participation in God's work rather than institutional expansion. Second, it places mission at the center rather than periphery of church identity. If God is inherently missionary, then the church as people of God must be likewise. Third, it suggests different criteria for evaluating mission effectiveness—focusing on faithfulness to divine purposes rather than merely numerical results.

The trinitarian ground of mission also reshapes understanding of its scope and character. As previous essays have demonstrated, God's mission encompasses the whole creation—human and non-human alike. This means mission necessarily includes care for creation and work for ecological justice, not as optional add-ons but as integral to participation in God's purposes. Similarly, because God's mission aims at reconciliation of all things in Christ, mission must address systemic injustice and structural evil, not merely individual conversion.

Trinitarian Patterns of Ministry

Understanding mission as participation in divine life provides patterns for ministry practice in several key areas:

Unity and Diversity

The unity-in-distinction that characterizes trinitarian life offers a model for mission that honors both particularity and communion. This appears in:

- Cross-cultural ministry that respects cultural distinctiveness while seeking genuine fellowship
- Ecumenical collaboration that maintains denominational identity while working toward visible unity
- Local ministry that celebrates diverse gifts while pursuing common mission
- Interfaith engagement that maintains Christian distinctiveness while seeking genuine dialogue

Mutual Indwelling

The mutual indwelling (perichoresis) of divine persons suggests patterns of reciprocal relationship in mission:

- Partnership rather than paternalism in global missions
- Mutual learning between sending and receiving communities
- Recognition that those being served often minister to those serving
- Understanding that giving and receiving are reciprocal rather than one-directional

Participation in Divine Life

Mission as participation in God's life shapes understanding of both means and ends:

- Focus on formation in Christ rather than merely behavioral change
- Emphasis on communal transformation rather than purely individual conversion
- Recognition that mission happens through sharing in divine life rather than merely human effort
- Understanding that the goal is incorporation into divine communion rather than merely church membership

Contemporary Challenges and Opportunities

Trinitarian perspective on mission provides resources for addressing three pressing contemporary challenges:

Cultural Fragmentation

In a world of increasing polarization and division, trinitarian patterns of unity-in-diversity offer:

- Theological ground for maintaining fellowship amid difference
- Resources for bridge-building across cultural and ideological divides

- Models for handling conflict without sacrificing either truth or love
- Vision for genuine unity that does not require uniformity

Environmental Crisis

Understanding mission as participation in the work of the Creator, Redeemer, and Sustainer enables:

- Recognition of creation care as integral to mission rather than optional addition
- Resources for addressing climate change as theological rather than merely political issue
- Connection between ecological and social justice as related aspects of God's mission
- Hope grounded in God's faithful commitment to creation's renewal

Justice and Reconciliation

Trinitarian theology provides foundation for work of justice and reconciliation through:

- Understanding justice as participation in divine righteousness rather than merely human construct
- Recognition that reconciliation flows from God's prior work of restoration
- Resources for addressing both personal and structural dimensions of injustice
- Vision of beloved community grounded in divine communion

These applications demonstrate how trinitarian theology provides not only theoretical framework but also practical wisdom for mission in contemporary context. Several key principles emerge:

1. Mission must be understood as participation in divine activity rather than merely human enterprise
2. The character of mission should reflect the character of the Triune God

3. Mission encompasses both creation care and human flourishing
4. Unity in mission does not require uniformity of method or expression
5. Mission effectiveness must be evaluated by faithfulness to divine purposes rather than merely numerical results

The challenge for contemporary churches is moving from theoretical acceptance of these principles to genuine transformation of mission practice. This requires:

- Ongoing theological formation of church leaders and members
- Careful examination of current mission practices in light of trinitarian patterns
- Willingness to change strategies that do not align with divine purposes
- Patient development of new approaches grounded in trinitarian understanding

Such transformation will not happen quickly or easily. But trinitarian perspective offers both foundation and direction for reimagining mission in ways that are both more faithful and more fruitful.

In conclusion, understanding mission through a trinitarian lens necessarily reshapes both theory and practice. It moves focus from church activity to divine initiative, from institutional maintenance to participation in God's purposes, and from human strategy to faithful witness. Most importantly, it grounds mission in the very nature of God rather than merely church preference or cultural pressure. Such grounding provides both stability amid change and flexibility in method while maintaining focus on the ultimate goal: drawing all creation into the life of the Triune God.

Reimagining Church in Light of Trinity

The recovery of robust trinitarian theology necessarily reshapes understanding of core church practices. Rather than viewing practices merely as traditional activities to be preserved or updated, trinitarian perspective reveals them as means of participation in divine life and witness to divine reality. This section examines how such understanding transforms three key areas of church life: ecclesial practices, public witness, and spiritual formation.

Ecclesial Practices

Three foundational practices particularly demonstrate how trinitarian theology reshapes church life:

Worship

Trinitarian theology transforms understanding of worship from human activity directed toward God to participation in Christ's perfect response to the Father through the Spirit. This has several practical implications:

- Prayer is understood as joining Christ's ongoing intercession rather than merely expressing human needs or praise.
- Sacraments are recognized as means of incorporation into divine life rather than merely commemorative rituals.
- Music and liturgy should reflect both the unity and distinction of divine persons rather than addressing an undifferentiated deity.
- Corporate worship expresses and enables participation in divine communion rather than merely individual devotion.

The challenge is moving beyond merely including trinitarian language to shaping whole worship services according to trinitarian patterns. This means:

- Careful attention to how different elements of worship relate to distinct divine persons while maintaining unity
- Recognition that worship forms worshippers—shaping theological understanding through regular practice
- Balance between maintaining historic forms that carry trinitarian wisdom and allowing fresh expressions
- Focus on formation in trinitarian faith rather than merely individual spiritual experience

Education

Christian education must be reframed from transmission of information to formation in trinitarian life. This affects:

- Curriculum design—moving beyond merely teaching about Trinity to fostering trinitarian imagination
- Teaching methods—using interactive and relational approaches that reflect divine communion
- Evaluation criteria—focusing on growth in trinitarian understanding and practice rather than merely knowledge retention
- Teacher formation—requiring deeper trinitarian formation for those who teach others

Specific practices might include:

- Using multiple learning styles to reflect divine diversity-in-unity
- Incorporating contemplative practices that foster awareness of divine presence
- Connecting biblical study to participation in divine life rather than mere information gathering
- Developing community practices that reflect trinitarian patterns of relationship

Governance

Even church administration and decision-making should reflect trinitarian patterns through:

- Leadership structures that balance unity of purpose with diversity of gifts
- Decision processes that seek consensus while respecting distinct voices
- Budget priorities that reflect participation in divine mission rather than mere institutional maintenance
- Conflict resolution approaches that maintain communion amid difference

Section 3

Public Witness

Trinitarian theology shapes church engagement with broader society in several key ways:

Cultural Engagement

Understanding church identity as grounded in trinitarian life enables:

- Confident engagement with culture without fear of losing distinctive identity
- Critical distance from both wholesale rejection and uncritical embrace of cultural trends
- Recognition that God is already at work in culture while maintaining prophetic edge
- Balance between particular Christian witness and pursuit of common good

Prophetic Voice

Trinitarian perspective provides foundation for prophetic witness through:

- Grounding critique in divine reality rather than merely human opinion
- Maintaining both truth and love rather than sacrificing either
- Addressing both personal and structural dimensions of injustice
- Offering hope grounded in God's faithful work rather than human effort

Bridge-Building

Trinitarian patterns of unity-in-diversity enable:

- Genuine dialogue across difference without compromising conviction
- Recognition of truth in other traditions while maintaining Christian distinctiveness
- Work for common good with those of different beliefs
- Ministry of reconciliation grounded in God's prior reconciling work

Spiritual Formation

Formation in trinitarian faith happens through intentional practices that:

Personal Practices

Individual spiritual disciplines should be reframed as means of participation in divine life through:

- Prayer that joins Christ's communion with the Father rather than merely expressing personal devotion
- Scripture reading that seeks encounter with divine persons rather than merely information or inspiration
- Contemplative practices that foster awareness of divine presence
- Service that expresses participation in divine mission rather than merely doing good

Communal Formation

Corporate practices should reflect and enable participation in divine communion through:

- Small groups that foster genuine relationship rather than merely study or support
- Mentoring relationships that reflect trinitarian patterns of giving and receiving
- Intergenerational ministry that values both unity and distinction
- Regular practices of confession and reconciliation that maintain communion

Leadership Development

Formation of church leaders must include:

- Deep grounding in trinitarian theology and its practical implications
- Development of trinitarian imagination that shapes ministry vision
- Skills for leading practices that form others in trinitarian faith

- Personal spiritual practices that sustain leadership from trinitarian center

Several key principles emerge for implementing these transformed practices:

1. Start with theological formation of leaders who will guide practice.
2. Make explicit connections between theology and practice.
3. Maintain balance between historic wisdom and contemporary expression.
4. Focus on long-term formation rather than quick fixes.
5. Evaluate practices by how well they enable participation in divine life.

The challenge is maintaining focus on theological substance while developing accessible practices. This requires:

- Regular teaching about theological foundations of practices
- Patient development of new practices rather than hasty implementation
- Willingness to evaluate and modify practices that don't serve formative purposes
- Ongoing attention to how practices shape theological understanding

In conclusion, trinitarian theology provides both foundation and direction for reimagining church practices. Such reimagining requires more than surface changes to language or form. It demands fundamental reorientation of how we understand and approach core activities of church life. The goal is not mere preservation or updating of practices but their transformation into genuine means of participation in divine life and witness to divine reality.

Looking Forward: Church Mission in Trinitarian Key

As the church approaches the 1700th anniversary of the Council of Nicaea, opportunities for theological renewal coincide with pressing challenges to faithful ministry. The path forward requires neither rigid preservation of past forms nor wholesale abandonment of theological heritage, but creative recovery of trinitarian faith for contemporary mission.

Opportunities for Renewal

Several promising developments suggest possibilities for trinitarian renewal of church life and mission:

First is growing recognition that pragmatic solutions alone cannot address the church's deepest challenges. As previous strategies focused on programming or technique show their limitations, space opens for substantive theological reflection. The very pressure of contemporary challenges creates opportunity for recovering theological foundations.

Second is renewed interest in spiritual formation beyond individual devotion. Many Christians hunger for deeper grounding in faith that encompasses both personal and communal dimensions. Trinitarian theology provides resources for formation that is both personally transformative and communally enriching.

Third is increasing awareness of the need for theological responses to contemporary issues. From environmental crisis to political polarization, church leaders seek wisdom that goes beyond surface solutions. Trinitarian theology offers frameworks for addressing such challenges while maintaining distinctive Christian witness.

Fourth is emerging appreciation for unity that does not require uniformity. As simplistic approaches to church unity prove inadequate, trinitarian patterns of communion-in-distinction provide fresh possibilities for genuine fellowship amid difference.

Challenges To Address

Significant obstacles to trinitarian renewal must also be acknowledged:

Institutional inertia often works against substantive theological reflection. Pressure for quick fixes can override patient work of formation in trinitarian faith and practice. Leaders need both courage and wisdom to maintain focus on theological renewal amid practical demands.

Section 3

Theological formation of church leaders remains thin in many contexts. Seminary education sometimes treats doctrine as merely historical artifact rather than living reality. Ongoing formation in trinitarian theology must become priority for leadership development.

Cultural pressures push toward both radical individualism and false uniformity. Maintaining genuine unity-in-distinction requires swimming against powerful cultural currents. Churches need both clarity of conviction and grace in disagreement.

Resource constraints limit capacity for careful theological work. Many churches struggle simply to maintain basic operations. Yet precisely such pressure reveals the need for deeper grounding in divine reality rather than human effort.

Hope in Divine Life

Ultimate hope for church renewal lies not in human strategies but in the faithful presence of the Triune God. Several theological convictions sustain such hope:

First, mission belongs ultimately to God rather than church. While human faithfulness matters, final responsibility for mission rests with divine rather than human agency. This frees churches from anxiety about results while maintaining call to faithful witness.

Second, the Spirit continues to work in and through church despite human weakness. Evidence of divine activity appears even amid institutional decline. Hearts continue to be transformed, communities renewed, and witnesses raised up through the Spirit's power.

Third, Christ's lordship is not dependent on church success. The reign of God advances even when church seems to falter. This enables realistic assessment of challenges without despair.

Fourth, the Father's faithfulness sustains hope for creation's renewal. Divine commitment to creation provides foundation for patient, persistent ministry amid what seems like failure.

While not eliminating the necessity of human action, such hope places human action in proper perspective. Churches must continue patient work of formation in trinitarian faith while trusting divine faithfulness. Leaders must maintain focus on theological substance while developing fresh expressions of ancient truth.

The essays in this volume demonstrate the continuing relevance of trinitarian theology for contemporary ministry. May their insights inspire fresh appreciation for this theological heritage while encouraging creative application in today's context. For ultimately, church renewal depends not on human wisdom but on participation in the life of the Triune God who creates, redeems, and sustains all things.

Acknowledgments

Permission to reprint the essays in this book is gratefully acknowledged to the following publishers, journals, and editors:

Chapter 3 originally appeared as Christopher Kavin Rowe. "Biblical Pressure and Trinitarian Hermeneutics," *Pro Ecclesia* 11.3 (Sum 2002), 295–312. It is reprinted with thanks to the editors of *Pro Ecclesia*.

Chapter 4 originally appeared as Janet Martin Soskice. "Creation and Monotheism," in *T&T Clark Handbook of the Doctrine of Creation*, ed. Jason Goroncy (London: T&T Clark, 2024), 244–49. It is reprinted with thanks to the editors at T&T Clark, all rights reserved.

Chapter 6 originally appeared as Luke A. Powery. "Variety Anxiety," Sermon, Duke University Chapel, June 4, 2017. It is reprinted with thanks to Duke University Chapel.

Chapter 7 originally appeared as Brent A. Strawn. "My Favorite Part of the Creed," in *Journal for Preachers* 38.3 (Easter 2015), 20–25. It is reprinted with thanks to the *Journal for Preachers* editors.

Chapter 11 originally appeared as Edgardo Colón-Emeric. "Into the Trinity," Sermon, Duke University Chapel, May 26, 2013. It is reprinted with thanks to Duke University Chapel.

Chapter 12 originally appeared in William H. Willimon. "Preaching: God's Speaking," *Preachers Dare: Speaking for God* (Nashville, TN: Abingdon Press, 2020), 91–95. All rights reserved.

Acknowledgments

Chapter 13 originally appeared as Lester Ruth. "How Great Is Our God: The Trinity in Contemporary Christian Worship Music," in *The Message in the Music: Studying Contemporary Praise and Worship*, eds. Robert Woods and Brian Walrath (Nashville, TN: Abingdon, 2007), 29–42. All rights reserved.

Chapter 14 originally appeared as M. Jan Holton. "Theological Touchstone: Wayfinding through Times of Uncertainty," in *Reflective Practice: Formation and Supervision in Ministry* 41 (2022), 234–49. It is reprinted with thanks to the editors of *Reflective Practice: Formation and Supervision in Ministry*.

Chapter 15 originally appeared as Fred P. Edie. "Ecotheology and Contemporary Christianity," in *Handbook of Contemporary Christianity in the United States*, ed. Mark Lamport (Lanham, MD: Rowman and Littlefield, 2022), 421–32. It is reprinted with thanks to the editors at Rowman and Littlefield, all rights reserved.

Contributors

Kenneth H. Carter Jr. is Bishop-in-Residence and Bishop, Charlotte Area, The United Methodist Church.

Daniel Castelo is Associate Dean for Academic Formation and William Kellon Quick Professor of Theology and Methodist Studies.

Jung H. Choi is Associate Dean for Global and Intercultural Formation and Director of the Asian House of Studies, and Administrative Faculty.

Edgardo Colón-Emeric is Dean of Duke Divinity School and Ruth and A. Morris Williams, Jr. Professor of Theology and Christian Ministry.

Fred P. Edie is Associate Professor of the Practice of Christian Education.

M. Jan Holton is Associate Professor of the Practice of Pastoral Theology and Care.

Cameron Merrill is Editor, MinistryMatters and Leadership Resources, United Methodist Publishing House and Pastor, Hillsborough United Methodist Church.

Jerusha M. Neal is Associate Professor of Homiletics.

Luke A. Powery is Dean of Duke University Chapel and Professor of Homiletics and African and African American Studies.

C. Kavin Rowe is Vice Dean for Faculty and George Washington Ivey Distinguished Professor of New Testament.

Contributors

Alma Tinoco Ruiz is Royce and Jane Reynolds Assistant Professor of the Practice of Homiletics and Evangelism, Director of the Hispanic House of Studies, and Foundation For Evangelism Fellow.

Lester Ruth is Research Professor of Christian Worship.

Connie Mitchell Shelton is Bishop, Raleigh Area, The United Methodist Church.

Janet Martin Soskice is William K. Warren Distinguished Research Professor of Catholic Theology.

J. Warren Smith is Professor of Historical Theology and director of the Th.D. program.

Brent A. Strawn is D. Moody Smith Distinguished Professor of Old Testament and Professor of Law.

Laceye C. Warner is Associate Dean for Wesleyan Engagement and Professor of the Practice of Church Ministry and Methodist Studies.

William H. Willimon is Professor of the Practice of Christian Ministry and Bishop, retired, The United Methodist Church.

www.ingramcontent.com/pod-product-compliance
Lightning Source LLC
Chambersburg PA
CBHW010015070326
40759CB00017B/503